THE REVOLUTION
HAS BEEN
POSTPONED.

dot.bomb

Rory Cellan-Jones
is the BBC's Internet and
Business Correspondent.
He lives in London with his
wife and two children.

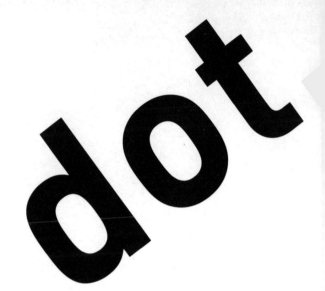

THE RISE & FALL OF
DOT.COM BRITAIN

Rory Cellan-Jones

AURUM

First published in Great Britain
2001 by Aurum Press Ltd
25 Bedford Avenue, London WC1B 3AT

Design by Roger Hammond

A catalogue record for this book is
available from the British Library.

Books quoted:
A Brief History of The Future by John
Naughton, Weidenfeld & Nicolson,
1999.
The Devil Take The Hindmost by
Edward Chancellor, Macmillan, 1999.

ISBN 1 85410 790 9

10 9 8 7 6 5 4 3 2 1
2005 2004 2003 2002 2001

Typeset by M Rules
Printed in Great Britain by
MPG Books Ltd, Bodmin

Contents

TO DIANE

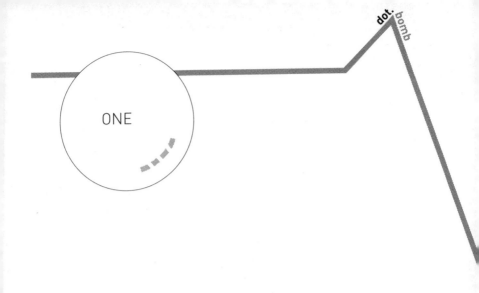

ONE

The day the bubble burst

EARLY ONE MARCH MORNING in 2000, a 27-year-old woman arrived at her office to find that the world wanted to see her. A row of TV satellite trucks and a gaggle of reporters were waiting in Park Street in London's West End. They were there to cover the stock market debut of a company that had never made a profit and had not even existed just two years earlier.

Looking back, Martha Lane Fox remembers her instant reaction to this welcoming party. 'I just looked at them and thought, "Bloody hell, why didn't I wash my hair?"' While a blizzard of interviews and photographs had turned her into the poster girl of Britain's dot.com boom over the previous six months, even she was startled by what she found camped on the doorstep of lastminute.com's offices. She had been eager – some said too eager – to promote her company in the papers and on television. But she had been out of the country when the interest in her and her business was building to a crescendo.

She had arrived back in London the night before, after selling her company's merits to investors in a month-long tour across the United States and Europe. Now, pale and exhausted, she had to carry on that pitch to journalists who were just beginning to wonder whether they had gone too far in painting this woman with little business experience as a combination of Michelle Pfeiffer and Sir John Harvey Jones.

She set to work, moving from camera to camera, talking down the line to one breakfast television show host after another in her familiar machine-gun delivery. Yes, the company would make a profit one day. No, becoming a multimillionaire overnight was not something she was concentrating on.

Upstairs in the cluttered, nondescript offices that were home to last-minute.com she joined Brent Hoberman. It was he who had come up with the idea that the Internet was the perfect medium for selling perishable goods – flights leaving Heathrow tomorrow, seats for a West End show tonight. In the summer of 1998 he had recruited Martha, a former colleague, to join him in launching one of Britain's first attempts to prove that online retailing was the future.

Now it was floating on the London Stock Exchange on a wave of almost hysterical enthusiasm, not just from the big institutions that determine the fate of public companies, but from a new army of small investors bewitched by the possibility of instant fortunes which the Internet seemed to promise.

The night before, Hoberman and Lane Fox had gone straight to their merchant bank advisors Morgan Stanley on arriving back from Paris, the final leg of a roadshow that both remember as an endless series of airports, conference rooms and snatched cups of coffee. The price range that would determine the initial value of the company had already been increased by 67 per cent just days before. Now the bankers told their two twenty-something clients that the final price would be fixed at £3.80 a share, valuing the company at an extraordinary £570 million. Neither Hoberman nor Lane Fox was inclined to argue. 'That's why you hire people like Morgan Stanley to fix the price,' she says. 'They've done this kind of thing before, they've got the experience.'

At 8 a.m., as trading started on the London Stock Exchange, Brent and Martha posed in front of a large screen. On it was projected the live share price, instantly reflecting the orders from dealers across the City. When a new share issue is 47 times oversubscribed, as was the case with last-minute.com, it can only head in one direction. Soon the price had climbed to £5.55, making the company worth £832 million. This meant that the founders' stakes were now worth £150 million.

As excitement mounted in the crowded conference room, a pack of photographers looking for an image which would convey instant wealth tried to encourage the new multimillionaires to crack open a bottle of champagne. But Hoberman and Lane Fox were too canny to provide the lottery winners' shot that the pack was hunting. 'We normally have champagne in the mornings,' said Martha with a knowing smile, 'but today is the exception.'

The camera crews began to drift away as some of the 160 staff arrived at their desks in their dot.com uniform of T-shirt and combat trousers. As they set to work, updating the website, calling suppliers or chatting about last night's soaps, they ignored the crews struggling manfully to get some pictures to illustrate their correspondents' reports.

Visually, Britain's most exciting young company was deeply dull. The old economy offered broadcasters showers of sparks from a welding torch, black-faced miners, the mechanical ballet of a production line. The new economy, on which Britain's leaders said her future depended, offered a hand clicking on a mouse or, at best, the table football game which seemed to be a standard feature of every dot.com office.

As the press pack shuffled off, the two founders could begin to ponder the morning's awesome events. As the day wore on, the share price slipped back from the giddy levels it had achieved in the first half-hour. But by any measure the market's verdict on their company was extraordinarily optimistic. Lastminute.com had the turnover of a reasonably successful London pub and was expected to lose around £20 million that year. But it was now worth more than many long-established and very profitable companies. More than First Choice holidays, which employed 900 people and made nearly £50 million in profits. More than the store group Debenhams or the dairy company Unigate or the construction business Taylor Woodrow. But then, of course, they were desperately old-fashioned companies that had yet to embrace the Internet.

It should have been a moment for Hoberman and Lane Fox to savour. But, both were feeling weary and a little uneasy. Despite the extraordinary valuation that investors had put on lastminute, Hoberman was not satisfied: 'I thought it wasn't enough, the rise in the share price should have been steeper. The expectations were so huge . . . it needed to rise more.'

At 5 p.m., desperate to get out of the office, they went for a walk around the block in the pouring rain. 'We both knew just what the other was feeling,' Lane Fox remembers. They went into a newsagent to buy chocolate and were confronted with the *Evening Standard*'s front page, with a big picture of Martha. 'I was thinking, "Cor blimey, I hope I can deal with this."'

That night they took all the staff down to the Saint, a bar in Soho. But there was a sense of anti-climax and the party did not go with a swing. The next morning Martha had to be up at 5.30 to set off for a meeting in Frankfurt. As she sat on the plane, the sense of unease grew. She saw her picture on the front page of the *Daily Telegraph* and thought how much she would prefer to be at home under the bedcovers rather than on another business trip.

The following day something snapped: 'It was another very early morning – we hadn't had a break for a month. I came into the office, saw Brent and just burst into tears. I couldn't explain why I was so hysterical.' He took her up the road to Selfridges and bought her a silver bracelet. 'It worked. It was very nice to have someone else who knew what was going on in your head. He was the only other person in the world who knew about this mixture of elation, exhaustion and nerves.'

As the week wore on, she also had to face a storm of electronic abuse. Small investors had been so desperate to get a stake in the company that shares had been strictly rationed. However many they had wanted, each investor was given just 35 shares. Many went straight to their computers to tell Martha Lane Fox exactly what they thought. Over the next few days she received 2,500 e-mails. 'It started with "bitch" and got a lot worse,' she remembers.

By the weekend, as the share price began to sink back, many may have been grateful to receive fewer than they had originally wanted. Martha was staying at a friend's house, not wanting to be by herself. She spent most of the weekend in bed. 'I lay there with a feeling I'd never had before. I just couldn't move – it was like being a depressive.' Within days the upbeat temperament of a woman still convinced that her firm was the future had reasserted itself. But the rest of Britain's dot.com economy was sinking into depression.

Looking back, 14 March 2000 was the day that Britain's dot.com bubble reached its maximum girth. Those who were listening carefully could hear the faint hiss of escaping air. Within weeks share prices were tumbling, investors were watching their profits melt away, and the paper fortunes of dozens of dot.com entrepreneurs had become just that – worthless paper.

By November Martha Lane Fox and Brent Hoberman had seen the value of lastminute.com's shares fall by more than 80 per cent. Their combined stakes, worth almost £150 million on 14 March, were now worth less than £20 million. Still a tidy sum – but they knew that if they sold a single share, the rush of investors for the exit would turn into a panic. Their company was still apparently doing everything it had promised but investors had woken from their dream of instant riches to the realization that the Internet would not completely rewrite the rules of business.

For those who had always warned that it was too good to last, these were happy months. They smirked as lastminute.com's share price sank, they chortled as boo.com collapsed amid revelations of extravagance and management incompetence.

But for a short period, roughly stretching from September 1999 to May 2000, Britain had been in the grip of an extraordinary wave of enthusiasm about the potential of the internet economy to create new wealth. It was a time of energy and optimism that promised to change the way the nation looked at itself.

A country that had struggled to shake off the disdain of its ruling classes for the business world and which had long regarded money as a far more vulgar topic of conversation than sex or religion seemed to have been transformed. Suddenly the expression 'dot.com' had entered the language and the people behind the new internet companies were being hailed as the pioneers who could lead Britain into the Information Age. At last the roll-call of business leaders familiar to the man and woman in the street did not start and finish with Richard Branson's name.

A stuffy business community, accustomed to making deals over lunch at the Savoy Grill or in a Pall Mall club, was suddenly finding that the real action was happening in cafés in Clerkenwell. The fifty-something pinstriped titans of the FTSE 100, with their fleets of secretaries and chauffeured Daimlers, were taken aback to discover that upstarts – even women – in their twenties, with little more than a desk and a laptop, were now making bigger waves than them.

But Britain was not just watching this revolution, it was actually taking part in it. For a few months everyone seemed to have an idea for a dot.com scribbled on the back of an envelope. People who had grown used to the numbing routine and the security of working for a large organization were leaving to join start-up companies with no history and uncertain prospects.

Students were telling careers officers that they were binning the applications to the BBC and Goldman Sachs, and setting off to look for funding for a dot.com. In back bedrooms across Britain, teenagers had discovered that sitting up into the small hours hammering at a computer keyboard did not just make you a geek. If you had the right idea, you could end up being a multimillionaire before you even made it to college.

For decades, the bankers and financiers had been accused of short-termism. Their critics said they had starved entrepreneurs of capital, refused to back the ideas of our brightest scientists, so that Britain ended up with a clutch of Nobel prizes but few innovative companies. Suddenly it was easy to get money for the flimsiest of ideas, with little in the way of a business plan and no unique technology. Traditional manufacturers, now regarded as hopelessly old hat, watched from the sidelines in disbelief.

Celebrities, too, were co-opted into this movement. Joanna Lumley became the face of a health website, Clickmango.com, while Hugh Scully of *Antiques Roadshow* fame was used to promote the auction site QXL and was rewarded with shares which were worth £3 million at the time of the deal. Even the Queen got a look in. Her Majesty's investment in a company called getmapping.com added another seven-figure sum to her fortune.

It was also a time of excess. Excessive hours were worked by young managers and software engineers, convinced that if they stayed up all night they could iron out the glitches in the new site. Excessive amounts of drink and drugs were consumed in the struggle to compete in this contest where it seemed the winners would take all. Excessive amounts of sex were the talk of many a dot.com office – but in reality most people were just too tired.

And the whole movement was fuelled by the promise of extraordinary, outlandish sums of money. Five years earlier the British media had gone into a fit of the vapours at the news that Cedric Brown, the head of the privatised British Gas, was earning an annual salary of £450,000. But now seven-figure fortunes were being created in a matter of weeks, and the annual Rich List published by the *Sunday Times* was filling up with the digerati. Mr Brown no longer seemed quite so fat a cat.

Meanwhile a parallel revolution was taking place amongst investors. New online share-dealing services were attracting hundreds of thousands of new customers who were taking their first halting steps into the stock market. And where did these virgin investors want to put their money? Not into blue-chip companies with solid records, but into dot.coms which had just arrived on the market. The shareholding democracy was dreamt up under Margaret Thatcher but it became a reality during the dot.com boom.

This made some people very uncomfortable. The fund managers who controlled shares worth many billions of pounds and held sway over the fortunes of Britain's corporate giants suddenly found that the market was being moved by the actions of people logging on from laptops in Burnley and Berwick. The amateur traders crowding into internet chatrooms could start rumours which would send share prices on a sickening roller coaster ride.

So for a time this technological and financial earthquake appeared to have wider social implications. It had shifted power structures, swept away the remaining cobwebs from an economy that was once again aspiring to play a leading role in a new industrial revolution.

The traumatic loss of great swathes of manufacturing industry – shipbuilding, steel and coal – which had marked the 1970s and 1980s, was at last fading from the British consciousness as the 1990s drew to a close. The populace had been told that Britain's future lay not in those old industries, but in the new world of communications and services. Until the dot.com boom, however, most people had not quite believed it. Every time another factory closed, or an order was lost to a cheaper Far Eastern competitor, the event became an occasion for national soul-searching.

But the internet bubble began inflating at a time of optimism and growing self-confidence. London was reasserting itself as one of the world's great cities, culturally and economically. The first Labour administration in eighteen years had come to power with the economy gearing up for rapid growth. The new government was as keen to cloak itself in a shining high-tech mantle as Harold Wilson had been in the 1960s when he talked of the white heat of the new technology.

The new Prime Minister could barely pick his way around a keyboard, but he committed his government to making Britain the number one location for e-commerce. With an economy almost as deregulated as America's, but handily placed to storm the fast-growing European market, it did not seem too outlandish an aim.

The trouble was that this glorious new dawn was such a short-lived affair.

Britain's dot.com bubble lasted roughly from the late summer of 1999 to the spring of 2000. By the time Freeserve's shares arrived on the Stock Exchange in late July as Britain's first major internet flotation, the United States had been playing this game for at least three years. Indeed, Americans were already worrying about the inflated prices attached to any companies with '.com' on the end of their names. Before the wave of hot money had even crossed the Atlantic to start funding European internet start-ups, the sceptics were warning that an almighty crash was imminent.

And when that crash came many of the fledgling British dot.coms were too fragile to survive it. The wave of selling which began on New York's high tech Nasdaq market in March 2000 spread instantly across the Atlantic, and as investors began to fight shy of internet shares, the dot.coms suddenly found that nobody wanted to give them the money they needed to survive. Many went under, others were taken over by old economy companies. But by the end of the year there was only a handful of dot.coms of any size still in British ownership.

Even those who survived were lying low. Companies started quietly dropping the dot.com from their names and stressing that they were actually quite old-fashioned businesses with no objection to selling goods over the telephone – or even in one of those high street shops which online retailers were supposed to make obsolete.

There were still plenty of eager young entrepreneurs, desperate to pitch ideas for new internet companies – some convincing, others paper-thin. But both the good and the indifferent suddenly found that nobody wanted to hear their story. The venture capitalists, so keen a year earlier to woo anyone with half a dot.com idea and a sketchy business plan, were no longer returning calls.

I spent much of 1999 and 2000 covering the rise and fall of dot.com Britain for the BBC. After years of seeing the same old faces in British business there was suddenly a new cast list. What they had in common – whether they were running high profile companies like Freeserve and lastminute.com or operating a franchise to put small firms on the net – was a sense that they were participating in something that was bigger than just a business. Yes, the prospect of instant riches was a huge motivating factor. But many were inspired by the Internet's power to change the way the world worked. If a second industrial revolution was underway, they wanted to be manning the barricades. Twas bliss in that dawn to be alive, to be a young dot.com entrepreneur was very heaven.

I lost count of the number of dot.com people who said to me, as the bubble expanded and then burst, that they would be writing a book about this if they only had the time. So this is an attempt to piece together their stories and work out what it meant for Britain. It begins with the people who saw the revolution coming but found it hard to get anyone to listen.

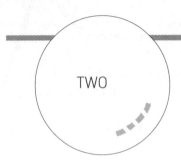

TWO

The pioneers

IN 1994 DARRYL MATTOCKS went into a bookshop in Oxford and picked up a book he had ordered a few days before. He paid for it, then walked a few doors down to the Post Office. There he put the book in a jiffy bag and stuck on a label bearing the rather smudgy logo of the Internet Bookshop. The parcel was then despatched to the customer who had e-mailed his order to Mr Mattocks the previous week. In retrospect, it sounds like a ludicrously inefficient piece of business – but this was among Britain's, indeed the world's, earliest e-commerce transactions.

The reason you have probably never heard of Darryl Mattocks is that his Internet Bookshop was soon eclipsed by Amazon.com. When the American company rapidly grew into a global force, other online book retailers became pointless exercises.

We think of the pioneers of e-commerce as being exclusively American, and, in truth, most of what happened in Britain was inspired by the example of companies like Amazon, Netscape and Yahoo. But a handful of brave souls on this side of the Atlantic were quick to spot the potential of the Internet to rewrite the rules of business.

Indeed, Darryl Mattocks was getting his company off the ground at a time when much of the world had not even heard of the World Wide Web and the term 'e-commerce' was yet to be invented. Dot.coms were soon to be dominated by an assortment of management consultants and recent graduates from top business schools, whose knowledge of computers was limited to manipulating the odd spreadsheet; but Mattocks was different.

When we met in a London café he was wearing the uniform of the new economy entrepreneur: a well-cut black suit and a black V-neck sweater. On his way to a board meeting of one of the many dot.coms in which he was now involved, and with several million in the bank, he had the confidence of a self-made man. But the geek in him was still clearly visible.

'I'm basically just a propellerhead,' he told me. As a teenager in the 1970s he spent hours with a soldering iron assembling computers in his bedroom. Then came the first personal computers, amazing pieces of technology like the Sinclair ZX that you could just lift out of a box and start using without having to resort to a screwdriver.

When the first mass-market computer, the Commodore VIC20, arrived in the UK, young Darryl swung into action. He and his then-girlfriend sat down for two weeks designing a computer game. It involved getting a frog across the road without it being crushed by passing trucks and it was called Hoppit. He sent it off to Commodore and it was soon being packaged with every computer they sold.

Suddenly Darryl was earning serious money. 'It gave me a huge taste for business – I went from getting 50p a week pocket money to earning thousands of pounds.' It also turned him into a temporary celebrity. Camera crews and reporters turned up on his doorstep: 'They wanted to paint me as this teenage whizzkid and I felt under quite a lot of pressure.'

Then he disappeared back into obscurity. After a degree in software engineering at York University, he became an IT consultant. He advised major companies like the National Westminster Bank and Marconi Electronics. These were the days when much of Britain's business world still thought of the IT people as a different, even lesser, breed. The kind of people you yell at when the system crashes but not candidates for the board.

But in his own mind Darryl Mattocks had always been more than a 'propellerhead'. He set up several businesses without any great success but in 1993 he was losing heart. 'I'd had a company that just ran out of steam – just ground to a halt basically.' He told his wife that he would never start another company.

But just as his imagination had been fired by the arrival of the

Commodore in the 1970s, so the buzz surrounding the Internet nagged away at him now. 'The power of e-mail really got to me. I'd been using it since I was at university, but it was now starting to become pervasive.' He realized that e-mail allowed you two-way communication with customers in a way that had not been possible before. He reasoned that what was needed was a big database of products, connected to another database of customers, and then combined with a third database of those customers' past activity. 'I thought if you start spitting out customized e-mails to those people, there's a powerful business there.'

Now this may sound simple stuff, but back in 1993 it was radical, even heretical. The Internet, which was created as the by-product of an American defence project, had developed as a network of academics. Gradually more people, mostly devoted computer users, had discovered its charms. But the internet community was fiercely anti-commercial. Early attempts to use the net to advertise or sell things were often greeted by a concerted barrage of flaming – a blizzard of outraged e-mails.

Regardless, Mattocks was determined – all he had to do now was work out just what he wanted to sell online. He had vague visions of some kind of internet shopping mall, but then, on a weekend stay in a country cottage, inspiration came. The cottage belonged to a friend of his wife who was in publishing. As he sat in front of the fire describing his vision of online shopping, the friend suggested that books were the obvious starting-point. And Darryl was off. He decided that an internet bookshop was just the best idea anyone had ever had, and over the next year he flung himself at the project with energy and determination. None of it, however, would have been possible without the work of another Englishman.

In 1991 Tim Berners-Lee, a computer scientist working at the CERN nuclear research laboratories in Geneva, had posted on the Internet the software which gave birth to the World Wide Web. It was this advance which made it possible for ordinary mortals, as well as computer obsessives, to start using the Internet.

The Net had been waiting for what the computer industry calls a 'Killer App', the application which reaches out to everyone. In 1993 an American student, Marc Andreesen, took the work of Berners-Lee further by launching Mosaic, a web browser which could run on the kind of computer that people had at home. As John Naughton puts it in his gripping account of the Internet's growth, *A Brief History of the Future*, 'Mosaic turned the internet into the Killer App of all time.' Mosaic later became Netscape and turned Andreesen into a billionaire – for a while at least.

So, in late 1993 when Darryl Mattocks heard of this program that allowed you to click your way simply around the Net, he decided that this was the technology which would make his internet business sing. 'I had friends who said, "You've got to use Gopher" – a program which involved the user typing in a series of commands before anything came back. I said, "No, I'm going with Mosaic."'

He spent the next seven months tangling with the technology and the finances of setting up the business. 'I spent every penny I could squeeze out of the bank. Then I borrowed loads on my credit cards. In the end I even took out a new credit card just to borrow more.'

The Internet Bookshop was created on a laptop. It was then launched from that laptop in June 1994. And for three months absolutely nothing happened. Not surprising, perhaps, at a time when there were still only a few hundred thousand people connected to the Internet in Britain. And at first, buying a book from Mattocks was not exactly point and click – the earliest version of the site required you to print out a form and fill it in.

But, after that triumphant visit to the bookshop to buy and despatch his first order, things did begin to stir. The Internet Bookshop had a database of 16,000 books, puny by today's standards, but it was growing fast. Of course, the list was just a virtual warehouse. Mattocks still had to pop down to a bookshop to pick up the orders – but after a while he was emerging with handfuls of books rather than just one. Still, it was a tiny operation with no substantial investment behind it. Darryl Mattocks knew he had to find someone to put up some cash.

Then a friend introduced him to James Blackwell. As a member of the family behind the venerable Oxford booksellers, he was an unlikely backer of an industry that would soon come to be seen as the nemesis of the traditional book trade. But, in what was Britain's first dot.com investment, he put up £50,000 for a 50 per cent stake in the Mattocks vision. He was buying into what was one of the very few e-commerce ventures then in existence, and it was to prove a lucrative move.

With that cash the Internet Bookshop could begin to behave like a proper company. It hired a couple of staff; it even got an office. That itself was a challenge. When he went to talk to the people at the Magdalen Science Park, designed to turn ideas originated at Oxford University into businesses, he was greeted with some puzzlement: 'We had to convince them that we were a science business. They said, "you're a bookshop", we said "no, it's all about the Internet", they said, "what's that?"' Even getting a line installed by BT was a problem. Mattocks again found himself patiently explaining to staff at the sleepy telecommunications giant just what the Internet was.

The Internet Bookshop continued to grow, building its database of books up to 1 million titles. But visitors to the company still found a ramshackle operation. Robert Norton, later to found the hugely hyped but short-lived Clickmango.com, was then in charge of researching e-commerce opportunities for America Online's UK operation. 'I remember visiting Darryl in Oxford,' he says. 'There were just piles of books everywhere. Even the guy who picked us up from the station had to move books off the seats so we could get in.'

The company was also stumbling across the hard fact that was later to derail many a dot.com. The Internet might promise to change everything by giving you a direct relationship with each customer, but if your business involved physical goods, it still faced a lot of old-fashioned problems. Like waiting while an order for different books from different wholesalers trickled in. It was not exactly just-in-time delivery. What the Internet Bookshop needed now was a substantial injection of cash to improve its systems and to tell the world about itself.

But suddenly there was competition out there. The distant rumble from Seattle on America's West Coast was the sound of Amazon.com gearing up to take on the world. Amazon went live in July 1995. Its founder Jeff Bezos, a former investment banker, quickly raised seven-figure sums from Silicon Valley venture capitalists who were well placed to see where the technology was heading. This at a time when Darryl Mattocks was struggling to raise tiny amounts for a company that had a head start on Amazon. He took out a £200,000 bank overdraft in 1995 and set out on a determined drive to get some serious funding from venture capitalists and business angels.

It is the venture capital industry that is supposed to spot the new trends and risk its money backing them. It works on the basis that the return on the investment in the few companies that make it big will pay for the many duds that don't. In the late 1990s the big Silicon Valley venture capital funds made extraordinary sums by funding companies like Amazon and Yahoo.

But in Britain Darryl Mattocks found closed doors and closed minds. 'At one stage we spent a couple of months conducting maybe three or four meetings a day with venture capitalists and business angels. We did road-shows and slick presentations about what I thought was a sound business plan. But they were suspicious of the whole idea.'

Mattocks felt more like an evangelist trying to convert a bunch of heathens to the gospel of the Internet than a businessman with a saleable idea. Just about everyone who tried to be an internet pioneer in the UK faced a similar reception. While the internet boom was taking off in the US, Britain slumbered. Yet there were those who were determined to make a difference.

Eva Pascoe, a combative woman who arrived in Britain from Poland in the mid-1980s, was among them. She had studied computer psychology at London University, a course that examined the interface between computers and people. It was groundbreaking stuff, and many of those who took the course ended up playing a role in the development of the Internet in the UK.

In 1994 Pascoe was involved in setting up what she believes was the world's first internet café, Cyberia in Whitcomb Street in London's West End. She had wanted it to be part of London University but the authorities there were not keen. 'The Internet was obviously something that was going to be commercially successful, but the university was still perceiving it as a scientific tool,' she remembers, with a large dollop of exasperation in her voice. 'They were not able to embrace it as something that was going to change practically everybody's life.'

So she put in £10,000 she had made from a software company she ran in Poland and got together with the Internet provider Easynet to start Cyberia. The idea took off immediately. 'The second we opened the word got out. We had a small launch party for friends and family but 400 people turned up.' Pascoe had a mission to get more women interested in the Net, and tried to create an environment which would feel more like somewhere you dropped into for a coffee and a little light e-mail rather than the school computer lab. But she soon saw that it was an uphill task. 'We completely misread the market – we looked at the bloody queue on the first day and it was all men!'

That changed over time, and within three years the gender split was 50:50. Cyberia provided a focus for media interest in the Internet in the UK. Desperate for something to film, TV reporters would pitch up at Whitcomb Street to cover any Net story. Pascoe herself was part of the attraction. This forthright, attractive young Eastern European did not fit the nerdy stereotype. In February 1995 she and her fellow Cyberia director Gene Teare were pictured in *Vogue*. Elsewhere she was quoted as an authority on cyberfashion. 'Hi-tech plastics, fluorescent colours and functional shapes inspired by combat gear are all in tune with the desire to get online,' she pronounced.

Someone who fitted the nerdy stereotype to a 't' dropped into Cyberia in 1995. Microsoft's UK operation had provided some help to the café, and when Bill Gates came to London in 1995, his local manager brought him along. Pascoe even claims that Cyberia helped Microsoft's boss realize that it was time to get serious about the Internet. 'Microsoft was in big denial about the Internet at that time,' she says, 'I think it was soon after that trip that he realized that the Internet is everything.'

The café became the launchpad for some of Britain's early web business. The basement provided a home for Webmedia, London's first web design agency. The café was also a training ground for future dot.com entrepreneurs. 'People with two degrees got taken on as cyberhosts,' says Pascoe. 'They spent six months serving coffee and learning about the Web, then left to start their own company. At the last count there were eighteen firms originating from Cyberia.'

In 1995 it seemed that Britain might be only a few months behind the USA in adopting the Internet and turning it into a tool for revolutionizing business. *Wired*, the magazine that had chronicled the development of cyberspace in the United States, decided to set up a UK edition. Its editor was John Browning, an American who had made his home in London and had covered technology for *The Economist* for some years. Browning was full of missionary zeal: 'We expected that what was happening in San Francisco would start happening immediately in the UK. The digital revolutionaries would come out of the woods and they would understand entrepreneurship.'

It didn't happen. Instead, Browning found himself and his magazine under attack for promoting the commercialization of the web. The critics loved *Wired*'s day-glo graphics, but hated the content. The UK internet community was more interested in the Net as a cultural phenomenon than as an opportunity to create new businesses. The magazine folded early in 1997. Like other pioneers, Browning had found that it did not pay to be ahead of the times.

And despite her handy position at the centre of the UK's web activity, Eva Pascoe never managed to spin Cyberia into something bigger. She did attract some funding – but from celebrities rather than venture capitalists. George Soros and Maurice Saatchi – high net worth individuals, as the jargon has it – both put money into the business. And another multimillionaire also saw the potential. 'Mick Jagger backed us – he just found us on the Net. We were one of a number of internet companies he invested in.' But as for the more standard routes for expanding companies: 'It was terrible – the banks said no way and venture capital just did not exist in this area until September 1999.'

In 1996 the *Daily Telegraph*, itself a pioneer in going online, interviewed half a dozen of what it described as Britain's internet millionaires and asked who was making money. 'Well I am,' Eva Pascoe told the paper, claiming that Cyberia's combination of a real life high street presence and an online business was a potent mix. Nowadays she concedes that Cyberia was never very lucrative. In 1997 she decided to get out. 'You needed £25 million to create the systems that were necessary if you were to do e-commerce properly.'

Back then nobody was going to give a start-up venture that kind of money. So Eva Pascoe teamed up with Arcadia, the store group behind high street names like Top Shop and Burton, to run its web shopping service. She was very early in spotting that the established players might have the last laugh.

Some people were making serious money from Britain's tiny internet population – around 400,000 homes were online in 1996. That same *Telegraph* article on net millionaires featured Cliff Stanford, the man behind Britain's biggest Internet service provider at that time, Demon. It also quoted Peter Dawe who had made £30 million from selling his Internet provider Pipex to an American firm. His advice to others seeking to make money from the Internet? 'Don't. I'm serious, it's too late. The window's shut. All the players are already there. I don't think anyone else can add any value.' In 1996, three years before the dot.com explosion hit Britain, this seems to have been a little premature.

By this time others were deciding it was time to take the plunge. Darryl Mattocks had set off a chain reaction. David Windsor Clive was an Old Harrovian who had decided to go into business rather than join his father, Lord Plymouth, in farming the family's 40,000 acres in Shropshire. He had met Mattocks in 1995 and had been bowled over. 'He was a fantastically enthusiastic character and I was captivated by what he was doing.' Windsor Clive, who had started his career as a broker in the London Potato Futures Exchange, knew a bit about excitable markets. After all, he had seen a potato shortage in the 1980s push the price up tenfold. Now he was hoping that the Internet might prove even more exciting than potatoes.

He suggested to Mattocks that what worked for books might also work for CDs and videos, but Mattocks said he just had too much on his plate. So Windsor Clive ended up licensing the Internet Bookshop's technology and putting some family money into starting the Internet Music and Video Service, or IMVS. 'This was the time when people were just beginning to wake up and smell the silicon,' is how he puts it. Knowing that relationships with the record industry would be crucial, IMVS set up shop in a tiny office in Fulham, near the headquarters of industry giants like Polydor and EMI. Later, it was the record business that would seem most vulnerable to attack from the new medium. But in its early months IMVS certainly posed no threat.

Just like Darryl Mattocks, Windsor Clive found that he was loitering in the doorway of his virtual shop smiling at passers-by rather than standing at the cash-till dealing with a queue of customers. The problem was that the site launched in May 1996 was just too clever for its own good. It was overloaded with graphics, and at a time when most internet connections were slow and clunky, nobody could be bothered to wait while the images crept their way onto the screen.

By September hardly a CD had been sold. Then the site was relaunched on a much simpler basis and sales started to kick in. By the following spring IMVS was offering a selection of 70,000 CDs and 24,000 videos – a typical record store might have 10,000 titles. It was taking in £16,000 a month –

nothing to impress that typical store – but the difference was that it was growing rapidly.

Old money had got the company this far. New money was not interested. Windsor Clive found the same blank stares from the venture capitalists that had greeted Darryl Mattocks. 'They were very polite but they just said, "I've never made an investment like this – it's not for me."'

Enter the man who would become the Godfather to many of Britain's dot.coms. Geoffrey Chamberlain ran a small out-of-favour stockbroking firm called Durlacher. But in the late 1990s he became captivated by the new economy, and put himself and his company's resources behind many a fledgling dot.com. For a time this turned Durlacher itself into one of the hottest internet firms, and put a lot of zeros onto the end of its value.

IMVS was one of Chamberlain's early successes. He guided the company through a flotation on the small Ofex market in 1997. 'Like all Ofex issues, speculative,' the *Daily Mail* advised its readers. The issue raised £670,000 for the company and valued it at £2 million. A lot for what was still a small business, but pocket money for some of the firms beginning to flex their muscles in the United States.

By 1999 Windsor Clive was coming to terms with the fact that he would need some serious money if the company was to become more than a corner shop. He had plans to expand across Europe. Then he realized that another online record shop was doing exactly that.

A Swedish company, Boxman, had four times as many customers and four times as much cash as IMVS. It might have a chance to take on the record companies, seriously undercutting the high street retailers in a way that Windsor Clive had never dared to do. He merged his company with Boxman in the autumn of 1999, accepting shares as payment in a deal which valued IMVS at £10 million, despite the fact that it had lost £500,000 in the previous year.

Soon the investment bank Morgan Stanley was grooming the merged company to float on the London Stock Exchange the following year. It seemed that the peer's son who had gone into trade was about to become an internet multimillionaire.

Selling up to someone with more muscle was becoming a habit for Britain's internet pioneers. By 1997 Darryl Mattocks had grown the Internet

Bookshop into a respectable business. There were no more trips to the high street for supplies – instead articulated lorries arrived with mountains of books.

Mattocks, too, had raised money on Ofex. But the £1 million this had put into the bank was pocket money compared to what Amazon was spending in the United States. In just the first three months of 1997 Jeff Bezos of Amazon had spent $4 million on marketing while Darryl Mattocks was only starting to think about advertising.

That year *The Economist*, in an acute if typically lofty article, had pointed out the difference in ambitions between Britain's and America's two biggest online bookshops. One had sold nearly $16 million worth of books the previous year, the other had turnover of under $1 million. One had taken on the traditional book trade with big discounts; the other was tiptoeing cautiously for fear of upsetting the trade. Mattocks now says that what he describes as a clique in British publishing threatened to cut off his supplies if he did not play by the rules. 'Jeff did not have those problems,' he says, 'he could simply set out his stall.'

By 1998 Mattocks had realized that he needed to get out. He sold the business, in which he still owned 30 per cent of the shares, to the high street book retailer and newsagents W.H. Smith for £9.8 million. At that time the £3 million he was able to bank seemed like a very good return for what was still a small business. A year later Darryl Mattocks looked like a man who had given away a stake in a goldmine in return for a drink at the saloon. And another year on he looked like one of the few who had made real money from a dot.com.

Another of the pioneers made a bigger fortune by giving Amazon its foothold in Britain. Simon Murdoch had launched his internet bookshop Bookpages two years after Mattocks. He had faced the same problems in getting funding – only worse because he was second in the queue.

However, Murdoch had some advantages. Like Mattocks, he was a computer scientist by training but he had more solid managerial experience, having run his own software company for some years. What's more, his company specialized in stock control and ordering systems for booksellers. When Bookpages launched, Murdoch had the benefit of good contacts in the book trade and software that could be adapted for the Internet.

By 1998 the business was challenging the Internet Bookshop for leadership of the UK market but Murdoch was realistic enough to know that he did not have the means to compete on a bigger scale. When Jeff Bezos came to Britain that year to run his slide-rule over the online booksellers which might provide a platform for his expansion into Europe, it was Murdoch's operation which caught his eye.

Bookpages ended up selling out to Amazon for around $20 million, with Murdoch staying on to head up Amazon.co.uk through its birth and rapid expansion. He took his payment in Amazon shares and says he did very well out of it. 'The share price went up six or sevenfold soon afterwards – and I was able to sell. If you're running your own business, first the rules lock you in to the shares for months, then you can't sell for fear of setting off a panic amongst the other investors.'

Eventually Murdoch left Amazon to cross the fence and become a venture capitalist himself. He will play a role later in this book as the man who helped decide the fate of First Tuesday, the networking organization.

So far then the pioneers' story is one of determination to cross a barren landscape against insuperable odds – followed by a sale to someone with a bigger wagon just as the promised land hoves into view. But some companies did manage to complete the journey.

Some businesses are made for the Net – others are always going to struggle. The Internet is not best suited to selling physical goods, particularly those where the look and feel are vital, as boo.com was later to discover to its cost. If you get the logistics right though, as Amazon did, it will be difficult for others to replicate your service. But where the Internet is brilliant is in delivering intangible products – music, software, betting, financial services. The problem with this second category is that it is all too easy for someone else to enter the market and take your business away by offering lower prices.

To Tim Jackson, founder of QXL, the auction business seemed to offer the best of both worlds. Jackson was a very different character from Darryl Mattocks or Simon Murdoch. He is not a computer scientist but a journalist by training. After a degree in politics, philosophy and economics at Oxford, his career in newspapers took him from the *Independent* to *The Economist* and then the *Financial Times*. He also found time to write books about Richard Branson and Intel. By the summer of 1997 he had spent two years writing a weekly column for the *FT* on internet businesses.

Like many a journalist, he had tired of being a bystander and was desperate to jump in and prove that he could do it himself. Unlike most, he jumped – and with great success. Jackson had spotted the rise of two online auction companies in the United States, Ebay and Onsale, and had decided that this was the business where he could prove himself as an internet entrepreneur.

The Internet provided a place where buyers and sellers could meet with ease, ensuring that prices were set with greater efficiency than hitherto. But – or so Jackson's theory went – auctions were also a localised business. A European firm could prosper, bringing local buyers and sellers together without fear of being trampled by an American giant.

Tim Jackson called his firm Quixell.com – pronounced Quick Sell. It started by acquiring products cheaply to auction on its site. That meant holding goods and facing all of the problems that any traditional retailer faces. Later it followed Ebay's lead by switching the emphasis to providing a marketplace where individuals could auction goods.

Like all the other pioneers, he faced the twin challenges of wooing investors while struggling to make the technology work. On New Year's Day 1998 he came in to his office to find out that Quixell had managed to send all its customers the same e-mail 50 times. He set about trying to repair the damage with a personal e-mail apologizing to each customer.

Later that year Jackson used the column he was still writing in the *Financial Times* to outline the differences between commenting on businesses and actually running one. He was finding that perspiration mattered even more than inspiration. 'Ideas are ten a penny,' he wrote, 'the hard part is making them happen.' His contact book may have contained the names of just about everybody who was anybody in the internet world, but he had struggled to convince venture capitalists to fund him. In just a few months he had burned up £100,000 of his own money and put countless hours into the business.

He also wrote bitterly of hiring someone he describes as, 'a smoothie marketing man of 28' at a salary of £52,000, which he had insisted was his current income. The man, not named by Jackson, refused offers to become a partner in the business while losses were mounting. Then he demanded one-eighth of the company when the corner had been turned and walked out when he failed to get it. The smoothie marketing man was Brent

Hoberman, who left to found lastminute.com. Friends of Hoberman paint a very different picture of what happened. They say Hoberman had played a big role in building the company and then found he was only being offered a 1.5 per cent stake for his pains. Whatever the truth, the result was lasting animosity between two of the most effective young internet pioneers in Britain.

Jackson – who refused all requests to talk to this author – is described by all who know him as a prickly individual. He would probably not disagree with that assessment. Asked by an online magazine how he would describe himself in a listing on his own auction site, this was his answer: 'Scruffy, cynical dad of four. Hates people, lousy manager.'

But the lousy manager was making a success of Quixell.com. The company was getting underway at a time when growth in the Internet was accelerating – it was a better climate than that which faced the Internet Bookshop or IMVS. By November 1998 its Ladbroke Grove offices in West London housed 23 people and its customer base had doubled in three months. It was, of course, still a long way from making a profit – black ink would not arrive until 2001 according to Jackson.

However, he had managed to raise some money. Much of the early funding of around £2 million came from the United States. Among the backers was Johnathan Bulkeley, an American who had run the bookseller Barnes and Noble's online operation and had headed up AOL's UK branch. But he told Tim Jackson that if he was going put money into his company, he wanted to keep a close eye on its progress, so he joined the board as chairman.

Then early in 1999 came the big breakthrough. One of the most solid and influential venture capital groups, Apax Partners, put £12 million into the company. It was the biggest single investment so far in any European dot.com and it valued Jackson's company, which by now had changed its name to QXL, at £40 million.

As part of the deal, Apax wanted new management brought in. Tim Jackson agreed to step aside in favour of a new chief executive. Jim Rose was an American who had worked in Britain for five years and was a senior executive at United News and Media. At that time he was being offered jobs in Silicon Valley but he decided to take the post at QXL: 'I decided I could be a big fish in a small pool. The American market was beginning to mature – Europe was taking off.'

Many growing companies hit problems when the founders can't let go. Tim Jackson was different. 'Tim was as good as his word – he said he'd let me get on with it,' Rose remembers, 'and within two weeks he was gone. He's a very bright guy with twenty ideas a day, nineteen of them pretty good – but an organization can't handle nineteen new ideas. He knew he wasn't the guy to move the company forward.' Eighteen months after he had decided to be a doer rather than a viewer, Jackson left QXL to pursue other internet opportunities. But he still had a 15 per cent stake in a company whose value was appreciating by the day. Within a year his company would be on the fringes of the FTSE 100 and he would be one of the richest people in Britain – on paper at least.

Apax's investment in QXL marked the end of the beginning for Britain's dot.com sector. New internet companies were at last attracting serious funding and luring experienced managers away from established companies. But Britain still lacked an internet blockbuster, a company like Amazon or Netscape that could catch the imagination of the investing public. The American giants were still losing money hand over fist but their shares were soaring and they had valuations bigger than the likes of Boeing.

The first British company to generate that kind of excitement was born out of a dull old high street retailer and its big idea was to give away something that people had just got used to paying for.

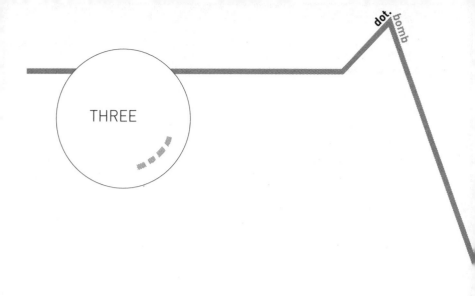

Free for all

THE PAPER NAPKIN HAS always played a major role in business mythology, along with the odd tablecloth and cigarette packet. Countless ideas that have spawned major corporations are supposed to have been scribbled down on the nearest thing that came to hand in a bar or on a plane. Often these stories do not quite stand up to closer scrutiny.

But Peter Wilkinson insists that somewhere in his home near Harrogate, tucked into an old diary, is a red paper napkin bearing the logo of Great North Eastern Railways and a series of scrawled calculations which gave birth to Freeserve. Those sums were to turn the Internet into a mass medium in Britain and trigger the dot.com boom across Europe.

Wilkinson, a Yorkshire businessman, is one of the most colourful multi-millionaires created by the internet boom, but also one of the least well known. He likes it that way. He has always shunned publicity and tries to avoid being photographed. For the record, he is in his mid-forties, has shoulder length hair and peppers his conversation with some fruity Yorkshire expressions. But the one thing he does want the world to know is that it was he who gave the idea for Freeserve to Dixons, the high street electrical retailer.

By the late 1990s Peter Wilkinson had built his second major business, Planet Online, which had become the biggest Internet service provider for small companies. His partner for some years had been another forthright

Yorkshireman, Paul Sykes, a man who had put millions behind his Eurosceptic beliefs, although they were now going their separate ways. But as Wilkinson explained to me in his smart London office just round the corner from the Bank of England, his career had started many years earlier with a chip business. I assumed he was talking about microprocessors, but what he meant was the deep-fried variety. 'When I was at boarding school in York the food was so horrible that I started cooking chips.' He turned it into a major operation, getting the other boys to man the deep fryers and to despatch orders around the school. 'I made a fortune but eventually one of the teachers complained about the smell and closed us down.'

So this was someone who had always been able to spot a gap in the market. When he came to do business with Dixons in 1998 he was the man who could provide the spark of inspiration to a project which had been making slow progress. Dixons had been thinking about starting its own Internet service provider since 1996. The idea was to help Britain's biggest computer retailer shift more hardware.

Computer use had been growing in the UK but research for Dixons had shown that many customers were unclear about why they were spending money on their machine. They claimed they would use it to sort out the family finances or write letters but in fact 70 per cent of them spent most of their time playing games. One day they might wake up and realize that they were buying a £1000 machine to do something better suited to a much cheaper Nintendo or Sony games console.

'What we needed to drive sales forward was a killer application,' says Dixons' Chief Executive, John Clare. The company decided that the 'Killer app' was the Internet and started to build promotional areas about the Internet in its chain of PC World stores. The problem was that the major Internet service providers at that time were American companies like CompuServe. When PC World sales staff showed the customers round the Internet they found news about Congress and baseball scores. 'They just walked away,' says Clare, 'and went over to the games section.'

So Dixons thought long and hard about starting its own ISP. There were great doubts about the idea. 'It just wasn't our kind of business,' John Clare admits. But gradually a team was assembled to consider the feasibility of the project. It was to bring together some of Dixons' brightest and best young executives who would later form the backbone of Freeserve.

Among them was Ajaz Ahmed, another Yorkshireman who can claim to have been one of Freeserve's founding fathers. Ahmed had been born in Pakistan and had moved with his family to Huddersfield when he was three years old. He had joined Dixons straight from school and by 1994, at the age of 32, he had worked his way up to a position as a PC World store manager in Leeds. 'I immediately bought myself a computer,' he says, 'and the first thing I wanted to do was go on the Internet. But none of the staff in my store could tell me how to do it.' Ahmed began a crusade to get Dixons to launch an ISP. He insists that his original idea was exactly what eventually emerged four years later. Not just a way of roaming the Web, but a portal which would give Dixons' customers all kinds of services, and earn money through e-commerce and advertising.

He took the idea to some senior executives but got a short answer: 'They said no. They just weren't interested.' The internet idea became a crusade for Ahmed. So frustrated was he by the lack of response from his seniors that he decided to leave Dixons. In 1996 he joined the company's main computer supplier Packard Bell for what he now describes as his 'eighteen months in the wilderness'.

But he kept in close touch with Dixons who were still thinking in a haphazard way about some kind of internet business. Packard Bell was brought into the project and Ajaz Ahmed became the driving force keeping it alive. The computer company was the sponsor of Leeds United Football Club, where Peter Wilkinson was a frequent visitor. It was through this connection that Wilkinson's Planet Online came on board

The idea at this stage was to create a service that would undercut existing players like AOL and Virgin.net, offering to connect people for around £9 a month. But, according to Peter Wilkinson, getting Planet, Dixons and Packard Bell to agree to a common approach proved impossible. The plan drawn up by Ahmed saw the new internet business winning 50,000 customers in its first year and Dixons thought that was too few to be worth bothering about.

Then onto the scene came the man who would make all the difference at Dixons. John Pluthero was a 34-year-old executive on the fast track to the top. The son of an Essex publican, he had been educated at Colchester Grammar School and then got a First Class degree in economics at the London School of Economics. Jobs in management consulting, and then at

P&O and Bass, had led him to Dixons, where he had swiftly risen to a position as Director of Corporate Development. Tall, sporty, shaven-headed and with a ferocious smoking habit, Pluthero had a nervy determination to get things done.

Corporate Development was a hothouse for new ideas to keep Dixons ahead of the game. It was staffed by young thrusters, many of them business school graduates, who were paid £60,000 a year and expected to deliver. When Pluthero took over he quickly decided that the Internet project was worth pursuing – but found that none of his half-dozen staff was keen to take it on.

Then in April 1998 Mark Danby arrived back in the office. A recent recruit from a management consulting firm, Danby had been away in Scotland setting up a new computer sales business for Dixons. As Pluthero walked across the office to Danby's desk, his colleagues shouted to him to watch out because the boss was about to land him with his pet project. But Danby was more computer literate than his colleagues and agreed to take it on.

Danby, Pluthero and Ahmed then set about some serious research. Their object was to work out just how low a subscription fee they could charge. Internet service providers had been finding it very expensive to win new customers. For every person America Online put on the Internet, the company had spent £100 in marketing and other costs. But Dixons had a huge advantage in the form of the millions of customers who trooped through its stores every year. This captive audience could be wooed without a massive marketing campaign.

Then there was content. The team was convinced by what it saw of the American internet industry that it was vital not just to connect people to the Internet but to keep them for as long as possible in your territory, using services and being subjected to advertising. That meant buying in services like news and sports coverage, and, up until now, they had been expensive. But suddenly the big media companies were becoming aware that they needed a bigger presence on the Internet. They were now prepared to give away content in return for a share of advertising revenues.

They looked again at the sums and realized that a big factor was the cost of actually collecting people's subscriptions and chasing up those who failed to pay. For the first time they began to wonder if they could drop the subscription charge altogether. The numbers still did not quite add up. Until, that is, Peter Wilkinson had his brainwave.

The Yorkshireman had been taking a close look at the way that telephone calls were priced and who actually got the resulting revenue. Every time someone dialled up the Internet from his or her home computer, the call started its journey on a BT line but then often headed off on a network controlled by another company. BT collected all of the charge for the local call – but then paid a portion of that money on to the firms that carried the call to its final destination at the Internet service provider.

Wilkinson wondered whether the new phone companies, eager to draw more business away from BT, would be willing to share some of that revenue. He was already talking to one of those firms, Energis, about whether they might buy Planet Online. Now he saw the possibility of the perfect deal. The fact that he could bring the Dixons internet plan to Energis made his business more attractive to the phone company. And if he could bring Energis on board, Dixons might at long last agree to push the button.

Energis agreed that it would share the revenue from the internet phone calls. This was when Wilkinson had to do some detailed mathematics. 'It was all about tiny fractions of the 1p per minute cost of a local off-peak call. I worked out that we could just about sustain the business, but it was very marginal.'

In late July 1998 Wilkinson got on a train from York to travel to London for a meeting with Dixons and Packard Bell about the internet project. With him were a couple of his senior staff, and he asked them to check the vital calculations which he scribbled on the famous red napkin. 'When it comes to maths, I'm not the sharpest tool in the box,' says Wilkinson. 'I wanted to make sure the sums added up – and they did.'

But as he travelled down to London, Wilkinson was making another calculation. He decided that, with three parties in this deal, it would be too crowded. Packard Bell would have to be eased out. So, when the parties assembled in a conference room in Planet's City offices, Wilkinson dropped a bombshell. 'In business I try never to tell a lie – but I had to be just a little untruthful. I told them Planet was losing interest in the whole ISP plan, it wasn't going to work.' John Pluthero and Ajaz Ahmed both reacted with anger and dismay.

Then Wilkinson said he had to pay a visit to the gents. A couple of minutes later, he put his head around the door to say that Pluthero was wanted on the phone. 'I kept saying to tell them I'd call back later, but he was very insistent,' Pluthero remembers. Outside, Wilkinson told him briefly of the plan and of the need to get rid of Packard Bell. Once the meeting had broken up, the two men stood outside smoking in the car park. 'When I told him about my calculations and about the deal with Energis, Pluthero started literally shaking with excitement,' says Wilkinson.

The young executive drove back to Dixons' headquarters in Hemel Hempstead, working out how he could now sell the plan to his boss. He phoned the chief executive John Clare that evening. 'His initial reaction was why would we want to give it away for nothing. I insisted that going free would be a fantastic way to enter the market.'

But Clare was won over once he realized that Dixons' investment would be tiny. It was to be a 'virtual' company. Planet Online would host the site, Energis would supply the telecommunications network, and the content would come from organizations like the Press Association and Lycos, which would supply a search engine.

The only real money from the Dixons purse would be spent on printing the 250,000 CD-ROM disks that would be given away in its stores. The bill for that would be £75,000. John Clare agreed to the plan and took it to the Dixons board. The final hurdle was to get approval from the grand old man of British retailing, Sir Stanley Kalms, who had built Dixons into one of the most powerful brands on the high street.

According to Clare, 'Stanley Kalms did not understand it – he is a great retailer and that was his world. But he went along with it because I wanted to do it.' John Pluthero sees it slightly differently. 'Neither John nor Stanley knew anything about the Internet,' says Pluthero. 'They just saw it as a marketing tool.' But he says it is to the company's credit that it allowed keen young executives to pursue pet projects like this.

With approval granted at the end of July, and a launch date set for 22 September, the team had set themselves a very tight deadline. The first thing John Pluthero did was to make sure that a key person was back in the fold. 'Ajaz Ahmed had been destroyed when we told Packard Bell that we were pulling out. I rang him and just told him not to worry – I would come and get him.' Ahmed told his bosses at Packard Bell there was nothing left for him to do now that the internet project had been shelved. He left and rejoined Dixons.

With him, he brought an idea for a name. Ahmed wanted to call the service Channel 6, a name he had already registered. It would convey that this was more than an internet provider. Channel 5 had recently got underway and here was Dixons bringing you Channel 6, a whole new entertainment medium.

Pluthero liked the idea but John Clare was not convinced. He believed that there was a choice between something wacky like Egg or Orange, or a straightforward name which conveyed the service's main selling point. Dixons was not going to hand over a large marketing budget to establish a wacky name in the public's mind, so it would have to be something simple which told people they were getting a free service.

Even in 1998 finding an internet domain name was a tricky business. Speculators had already begun buying up likely names and then trading them at increasingly outlandish prices. The team tried Freeinternet, freeforyou, and dozens of others, but all the names had already been snapped up. Then someone suggested Freeserve. When the searches were carried out, freeserve.com, freeserve.co.uk and freeserve.org were all available. Nobody thought it was a brilliant name but they decided to go with it.

It would be up to the sales staff at Dixon's stores to make sure customers picked up the Freeserve disks. John Pluthero held a meeting with the marketing directors of the group's different chains, Dixons, Curry's and PC World. He thought they would be enthused by this exciting new development. He was wrong. 'They hated it. They said the stores would be full of kids getting in the way of the regular customers.'

It took two or three more meetings before they reluctantly agreed to co-operate. By now the team was deep in the launch frenzy that became familiar to many a dot.com. 'We worked ridiculous hours to make it happen,' says Mark Danby. Pluthero remembers sitting bolt upright at 2 a.m. one Saturday and realizing that some vital piece of work had not been done. 'I rang Mark's mobile, intending to leave a message. He answered and said he was still at work. Neither of us made anything of the fact that it was the small hours of the morning.' They did not realize it then, but this was the way it was to be for a long time. 'I had absolutely no personal life for eighteen months,' says Danby, 'but it was worth it because we felt we were creating something.'

Pluthero refuses to talk about his personal life, but he was under particular strain. His marriage was breaking up around the time that Freeserve launched.

Even then, working in a team of four on a tiny project in which Dixons had invested a paltry sum, Danby says they felt they were doing something hugely important. 'There was a sense that this was a momentous time. Back then rumours were flying around that AOL was about to be taken over for $34 billion. That made us see there was potential for creating something of huge value.'

They worked right up to the wire. Rob Wilmot, a 26-year-old from Planet Online, had joined the team to oversee the technical side. Later he was to become Freeserve's chief technology officer. He stayed up all night before the launch to make sure that the site would be ready. The idea was that customers would be able to sign up immediately after the existence of Freeserve had been announced to the media. In the event, the work was only completed fifteen minutes before the announcement.

So on 22 September John Pluthero and John Clare took to a stage at the *Financial Times* conference centre in London and unveiled Freeserve. The Dixons PR machine had briefed journalists to expect something big, and the room was packed. The story made an instant impact. Journalists had woken up by now to the fact that the Internet was important, but had found it difficult to pinpoint events to sell to their editors. Here was a household name doing something extraordinary. Many questioned how Dixons could possibly sustain a free service, but they found no difficulty in getting their copy into the papers. In fact there were a couple of small companies which had already been offering free internet access for a few weeks. But they did not offer a full service – and in any case nobody but dedicated netheads had heard of them.

That afternoon Mark Danby remembers taking calls from the *Sun* and realizing that they were at the centre of a big news story. In the evening John Pluthero went on *Channel Four News*. The presenter Jon Snow conducted a debate between Freeserve's boss and the manager of one of the existing players, Virgin.net. The man from Virgin said Freeserve would never work. 'He kept trying to draw a distinction that wasn't there,' says Pluthero. 'He'd say with us you get e-mail, you get webspace and so on. I came right back and said we offer that too.' Within nine days Freeserve had overtaken Virgin and Pluthero's luckless opponent soon left the company.

Success has many fathers, and as Freeserve took off spectacularly, a lot of people were quick to claim paternity. But Peter Wilkinson has a key document. The day after the launch a letter arrived on the fax machine in his Yorkshire headquarters. 'Dear Peter,' the letter began. 'Yesterday, going through what seemed like a hundred interviews, radio and TV slots, it hit me like a brick. You changed the industry. You, Peter, you. I know you are not a man for the limelight (and I don't blame you) but I want you to know that the people that matter will always remember it as your idea, your vision.'

The letter was signed by John Pluthero.

Having launched Freeserve, Pluthero was immediately swept away to a new post running Mastercare, Dixons aftersales and distribution operation. Mastercare's extended warranty business had at times produced more profit for the company than that made from selling televisions and computers. It was seen as a very big job, far more important than running the internet start-up.

But within weeks the tiny creature hatched by Dixons was growing so quickly that it threatened to squash its parent. In the run-up to the launch, someone at Planet Online had suggested a sweepstake on just how many customers would sign up by the end of October. The guesses were written on a whiteboard. Someone started off with 6,000, but the most optimistic was Rob Wilmot – he went for a massive 100,000. But when Ajaz Ahmed travelled back to Leeds on the day of the launch, he arrived at Planet Online late in the afternoon to find that hundreds of people had already been in to Dixons, picked up a disk and were now online, filling in the subscription form.

In the first week 50,000 signed up and by the end of October even Rob Wilmot's optimistic guess had been left far behind. A quarter of a million people were now Freeserve customers. New disks had to be printed in a big hurry. The frosty attitudes of the stores towards Freeserve had melted away. Managers were finding that customers who were using the Internet for the first time were often keen to upgrade to a better computer.

Three people were now running the whole operation – Mark Danby, Ajaz Ahmed and Rob Wilmot. Danby was in overall charge, looking after the corporate, legal and financial matters. Ahmed was out signing deals as the business development manager and Rob Wilmot was running the technical operation. 'It worked,' says Ahmed, 'because we each had complementary skills and we all got on well. It was the most amazing journey. Every day was a new adventure – we didn't mind if we slept in the office.' For Mark Danby it was almost impossible to keep up. 'It was like that plate-spinning game on the *Generation Game*. We wrote the copy for adverts, negotiated commercial deals, ordered new modems from the States so we could cope with the extra traffic.'

In October they set off from Hemel Hempstead to New York for the Internet World conference. But instead of schmoozing with the American dot.com aristocracy, they spent much of the time at their hotel, logging on and answering customer e-mails. Freeserve quickly passed AOL as the UK's leading Internet service provider and it was generating a phenomenal amount of traffic across the telephone network. Soon it had the most frequently dialled number in Britain.

By Christmas half a million customers had joined. Freeserve was transforming public attitudes to the Internet by convincing a whole swathe of the population that they could afford to go online. It was also doing extraordinary things to Dixons' shares. Over the years the retailer had enjoyed an uneven relationship with investors, and in the winter of 1998 there was a chill wind blowing down the high street as consumers reined in their spending. That meant retailing shares were right out of fashion, but Dixons was bucking the trend. The company was back in the FTSE 100, from which it had been relegated the previous March. There was wild talk of dull old Dixons turning into an internet stock.

Dixons' chief executive, who had expected to get on with the important business of running a retail chain, was beginning to realize that this tiny internet offshoot was quite a big deal. John Clare called John Pluthero at Mastercare and told him that he would have to come back and take over Freeserve again. Pluthero, who had maintained a close interest in his baby, was delighted.

But first he had an important duty to perform. Every year Sir Stanley Kalms was in the habit of making a tour of the Far East to glad-hand Dixons' major suppliers and get a peek at the hot new products that might appear on the stores' shelves in a few years time. With him went some of his key aides and this year John Pluthero was to sit at the right hand of the great man. The tour took in Malaysia and Hong Kong and culminated in

Tokyo at the headquarters of the powerhouse of Japanese consumer electronics.

In Sony's top-secret research and development facility the Dixons team was given a glimpse of things to come. Products designed to exploit the digital future – like the Memory Stick Walkman – were shown off. Then the visitors were shown into the inner sanctum, the office of Sony's Chairman Nobuyuki Idei. 'There was a great deal of bowing and formality,' Pluthero remembers. 'Then there was about five minutes of polite chit-chat with Mr Idei asking Stanley how business was going.' Then, the Sony Chairman turned to Pluthero. 'He said, "Tell me about Freeserve." And we spent 35 minutes out of the remaining 45-minute meeting just talking about the internet business.' That the leader of one of the world's most powerful companies should be so interested in a part of his business which he had waved through with barely a look certainly made an impact on Sir Stanley. Pluthero says there was even a discussion about whether Sony might take a 20 per cent stake in Freeserve. 'After that, Stanley realized how important it was.'

By February Freeserve had a million subscribers and the Dixons share price, which had been under £6 at the time of the September launch, had climbed above £10. From now on Dixons shares were to move in line with the frenzied rhythm of New York's Nasdaq index of high-tech shares rather than coast along at the sedate pace of a British retailer.

For Sir Stanley Kalms and John Clare the huge boost to their company's value might have seemed like an unexpected Christmas present. Nevertheless, it made them uneasy. 'We just could not work out what percentage of our share price was represented by Freeserve,' says Clare. 'It became seen as a problem.'

So a great debate began within Dixons about the upbringing of this unruly child which was outgrowing the family home. John Pluthero had strong views. Now back in charge, he was ambitious to see continued rapid growth. That would mean buying in more content and employing more staff, perhaps acquiring other internet businesses. However, Dixons had conceived Freeserve principally as a marketing initiative to sell computers rather than as a business in its own right. It was not expected to contribute a profit but it was intended to break even within a year.

Pluthero felt that this approach lacked ambition. He had his eyes on what the dot.coms had achieved across the Atlantic. They had enjoyed spectacular growth in their revenues but had spent all their money and more in the quest to grab the new market before anyone else. Their tactic was to float on the stock market and then use their shares as a currency. Investors had pushed the Amazons and Yahoos to prices greater than the likes of Boeing, simply on the hope that, one day, extraordinary growth would turn into extraordinary profits. Then the dot.coms used their high priced shares to go out and buy other businesses.

So Pluthero wanted his own currency, and that meant a stock market flotation. Dixons' merchant bank advisors did not see it like that. Goldman Sachs said Europe was not ready for a big internet flotation and counselled a less ambitious approach. The bankers thought Dixons should sell a stake in Freeserve to someone like AOL. 'I was furious,' Pluthero remembers. 'They were just so Goldman Sachs about the whole thing.'

But then another of the giants of the investment banking scene came knocking at Dixons' Hemel Hempstead offices. Credit Suisse First Boston had already shown in the United States that it would fight tooth and nail to stake a claim to internet flotations and the lucrative fees which came with them. The bank had snatched away a star team of technology specialists from its rival Deutsche Bank by offering them mouth-watering salaries. That team had put CSFB at the top of the league for internet flotations.

But it was a 35-year-old British banker, Andrew Cornthwaite, who masterminded the bid to win Dixons' business. He told Sir Stanley Kalms and John Clare that they had built a business that married what had become known in the US as the three Cs – connectivity, content and commerce. Only AOL had managed to do that. 'We came in aggressively and said, "You don't have to wait – you can go public in six months, you can be a European pioneer",' Cornthwaite states. 'It was a message which Stanley and John were happy to hear.'

So in February Dixons agreed to float 20 per cent of Freeserve on the London Stock Exchange and on New York's Nasdaq. For CSFB, which would steer the flotation, this was a notable coup. The Initial Public Offering, to use an American term which was now becoming commonplace in the City of London, was a notable coup for CSFB. If Freeserve's IPO succeeded, dozens of dot.coms would be eager to stage their own. 'This was the first dot.com deal in Europe,' says Andrew Cornthwaite. 'It was prestigious, but if we screwed it up then the whole internet scene across Europe would be set back.'

It was four years since Netscape had made its stock market debut in New York and turned the rules of investment upside down by proving that you did not need to make profits to be worth many billions of dollars. Netscape had doubled the price of its shares from $14 to $28 on the day before its IPO in August 1995. After the first day of trading the shares closed at $58.25. The huge excitement surrounding this flotation had inspired others to follow Netscape's lead. Since then, the dot.com investment boom had taken off with a vengeance in the United States – but in Europe nothing had happened.

One reason was that such flotations were simply not allowed on the main exchanges. To be listed on the London Stock Exchange a company had to have a trading track record of at least three years. There were exceptions for biotech and mining firms, but certainly not for a start-up internet business. On top of that little problem there was almost total ignorance about internet companies amongst the pension funds that would be the main customers for the shares. What's more, nobody really knew how to value a company unlike any that had been floated before in Europe.

This is how Andrew Cornthwaite summed up the task facing the Freeserve IPO team: 'Nobody understood it, we could not measure it – and the London Stock Exchange would not allow us to do it anyway.' CSFB had promised that Freeserve shares would hit the market by the end of July. There was a vast amount of work to be done to hit the deadline. First of all, the rules had to be changed.

The London Stock Exchange has been left flat-footed in recent years as other more nimble operators have taken chunks of its business. The Exchange was smart enough to have seen what had happened to American internet stocks and was desperate not to lose out to its European rivals when the whole game moved across the Atlantic. Nevertheless, it was also petrified of being blamed if a dot.com flotation went wrong and small investors lost money.

'We took on the Freeserve IPO assuming that the LSE would change the rules,' says Andrew Cornthwaite. 'But it took until the final weekend before the prospectus was issued for them to say yes. They were afraid that it would be seen as Dixons cashing in at the top of the market – but that was really none of their business.' On two occasions when a deadlock had been reached, CSFB threatened to take the issue to the Listings Committee, a gathering of the City's great and good, which acted as a final arbiter. Both times the Stock Exchange backed down. In the end, the two sides painstakingly worked out new rules that would allow a company just nine months old and with no profits on the horizon to join the corporate big league. The price exacted was that the prospectus had to be packed with bloodcurdling warnings to emphasize just how speculative a venture this was.

The team that had built Freeserve and was now steering it towards the stock market was still very small. The almost obsessively meticulous Mark Danby was now Chief Operating Officer – or Chief Worrying Officer as the others called him. This is how he describes his colleagues: 'We weren't new media luvvies, we weren't software guys, we were hard-nosed business types. We were in it to create value.'

At the head of this collection of thirty-something hard-bitten former accountants and consultants was John Pluthero. As a Dixons' high-flyer, he would have been among the candidates jostling to step into John Clare's shoes in five or ten years' time. Now, at the age of 35, he was about to become the chief executive of a public limited company. Often in such circumstances the original inventors of ideas like Freeserve have to step aside when someone more experienced in a senior role is drafted in as chief executive. But Pluthero got to stay in charge.

He tried to educate himself by talking to various senior business figures who might be drafted in as non-executive directors. 'One of them told me something which stuck in my mind. He said to be a chief executive of a plc, you have to be able to do two things. You've got to know how to run the company – but you've also got to be able to sell shares.'

Some felt that Pluthero, a hugely energetic manager who described himself to one interviewer as 'a human dynamo', did not have the cool, strategic vision needed to guide a company in the world's fastest changing industry. Andrew Cornthwaite disagrees: 'He really grew into the role – nothing fazed him. He was not spooked by the process of IPO, which happens to a lot of people.' Cornthwaite became close friends with Pluthero and still sees him socially. For an investment banker in his mid-thirties, this was a deal unlike any other he had ever done. 'I'd been involved in maybe twenty IPOs, and with some of them it's just another deal. But this was the first time I had been working with people of my own age. It was exhausting but exhilarating.'

Freeserve now had to be transformed into something that could pass muster as a plc. By the spring of 1998 it was employing twelve people, but they were packed into an office in Hemel Hempstead, sitting next to staff ordering mobile phones for Dixons' new outlet, The Link. The next step was to acquire the infrastructure to survive as a separate company. Nick Backhouse, a banker with ING Barings, was recruited as Chief Financial Officer. 'The company had been set up on a shoestring,' says Andrew Cornthwaite. 'For a little division within Dixons, financial controls did not matter. For a billion-pound public company, they did.'

And yes, extraordinarily, Freeserve was about to acquire a price tag of more than £1 billion. There had been feverish speculation in the press about a valuation of over £2 billion, but that was purely based on how much Dixons' share price had increased since it launched the Internet service provider. Working out a credible price which could be sold to the market proved to be a mixture of rigorous financial modelling and sheer voodoo.

There are two techniques used by the finance community in valuing a new company coming to the market. First, the story painted by the numbers on its balance sheet – its turnover, profits, debts and the cash it is generating each year which will be available to shareholders. In its first eight months Freeserve had taken in £2.73 million but its losses amounted to just over £1 million. Pluthero and his colleagues painted a picture of rapid growth, where the revenue gained from call charges would soon be dwarfed by a torrent of cash from advertising and e-commerce. Even so, on the basis of the existing numbers, Freeserve was not worth a great deal.

But the other technique involves examining the value of similar companies. A garage in Knightsbridge may not look very attractive at first sight – but if the one next door has just gone for £100,000 you would be mad to sell for less. The garage chosen by CSFB as a comparison was America Online, AOL. Even in 1999, the year before it used its platinum-plated shares to seal the world's biggest merger with Time Warner, AOL's value seemed to defy all logic. In 1998 its share price had grown by 586 per cent, making it worth $71 billion dollars. A dull, old economy company might be valued at between ten and twenty times its annual earnings. But, in the jargon of the investment analysts, AOL's price/earnings ratio had now hit 275.

So CSFB did some sums. Unlike Freeserve, AOL made money from subscriptions, so that had to be subtracted. What was left was a business based on e-commerce and advertising which could be valued according to the number of customers who logged on each day. Obviously there would have to be a discount because Freeserve had a much shorter track record. But eventually the CSFB number crunchers came up with a price range of between £1.30 and £1.50 a share. That meant a value of between £1.3 and £1.5 billion on the company as a whole; more than tired old firms like the newsagents WH Smith or the glass firm Pilkington.

As part of the deal John Pluthero would receive £1 million worth of shares and Mark Danby and Nick Backhouse would each receive £700,000 worth. They would also stand to gain much more in the form of options, although these could not be cashed in for another two years. In comparison to the United States, where companies like Yahoo and Netscape had created billionaires, these were small sums. But only nine months earlier Pluthero and Danby had been faceless Dixons executives. They had not needed to risk their own money to start this business.

Before the price range was published, the bankers had spent months on a discreet campaign. They had held lunches for journalists and fund managers with the aim, as Andrew Cornthwaite puts it, 'of educating them and trying to raise the level of debate'. The Freeserve IPO was already getting a lot of press coverage – to Cornthwaite's dismay. 'Generally, I just don't like media coverage; I would rather they ignored us. The tone of what was written was excitable but moralistic – "How can this be allowed to happen? Who are they trying to kid?"' But the customers, in the form of the institutions, were more receptive: 'Fund managers were saying with some trepidation "God, I'm going to have to buy this."'

The price attached to the shares might have looked outlandish, but most of the City analysts who looked at the sums did not demur. There was one dissenting voice. Miles Saltiel, an experienced technology analyst at the German owned bank WestLB Panmure, put out a note to his customers saying 'Avoid'. Saltiel disagreed fundamentally with the way the company was being valued on its fast growing turnover rather than on any profits. 'The underlying premise just stuck in my craw. It was being valued on the basis of revenue growth. But I believed you had to make profits.'

However, the crucial exercise that determines the success of an IPO is the roadshow, where company executives and their advisors present their case to the potential investors. Freeserve's began on 12 July when the price range was announced and ran for a fortnight. The final price the institutions and the small investors would pay would be determined on 26 July according to the orders that CSFB received during this process.

The new Chief Financial Officer, Nick Backhouse, joined the company just as the roadshow got underway. His first job was to take part in a London presentation on a Monday morning and then hop on to Concorde with John Pluthero and Mark Danby to give the same speech in New York that afternoon. 'They were all having a great time,' says Andrew Cornthwaite, 'doing things they'd never done before.' Pluthero says it was both glamorous and exhausting. 'It was a lunatic schedule. At one stage I flew from San Francisco to Frankfurt, went into the gents in a hotel to change my shirt, and stepped out to give a speech to 300 people.'

It quickly became clear that the share issue was going to be a roaring success. The hard-bitten American audience asked difficult questions but, having feasted on homegrown internet companies, the investment funds were keen for some fresh European meat. In London the institutions had rapidly gone from ignorance and suspicion to outright enthusiasm.

And for the first time Joe Public, or in City parlance the 'retail investor', was getting a taste for internet shares. CSFB had been cautious about marketing Freeserve to the general public, aware of the bad publicity which would result if widows and orphans ended up losing out. 'You have to be incredibly careful what you do about retail demand,' says Andrew Cornthwaite. 'It is never seen as quality and it attracts 90 per cent of the publicity for 10 per cent of the shares.'

But the share issue was also seen as a way of boosting traffic to the website. The shares were only available to Freeserve customers and the only way to get hold of a prospectus was by downloading it from the website. Over 100,000 people did just that, and at times the traffic threatened to bring the site to a halt. The level of excitement surrounding this flotation was beginning to rival the buzz that had accompanied the privatisations of the 1980s. But British Telecom, British Gas and British Airways were businesses with huge turnovers and virtually guaranteed profits. For small investors they were very safe bets. In comparison, Freeserve was a 100–1 outsider in the Grand National.

As the roadshow drew to a close, CSFB could see that there would be no problem in fixing the price at £1.50, the top end of the range. In any IPO, the trick is to pitch it so that most people don't get quite as many shares as they would like. That means that there will be plenty of demand when trading gets under way. The bank totted up the orders and found that the offer was 38 times oversubscribed.

Just 15 per cent of the shares, around £45 million-worth at the issue price, went to retail investors. Some 40,000 people received a maximum of 500 shares each. But the arrival of Freeserve on the market would be the cue for a massive surge in online investment. It would spark a thousand online discussion boards and be the subject of often intemperate debate by a new breed of investor.

On 22 July 1999 John Pluthero and his team came to the Credit Suisse First Boston dealing-room in Canary Wharf to watch as shares in Freeserve plc started trading. Throughout the privatisation years, this had become a familiar ritual, with ministers looking over traders' shoulders as shares which had been 'priced to go' moved inexorably upwards. This time it was a group indistinguishable from the traders – apart from their Freeserve baseball caps – who watched as the Freeserve share price moved swiftly above £2. It peaked at £2.37 before ending the day at £2.05.

It was almost a year to the day since Peter Wilkinson had climbed aboard that London-bound train and scrawled some sums on a napkin. Now a company had been created which the stock market thought was worth more than £2 billion. By selling just 20 per cent of it, Dixons had made £300 million – and as John Clare wryly puts it, 'after paying off CSFB and the other advisors, there was a little left for Freeserve and for Dixons' shareholders'.

The Freeserve team had transformed a traditional retailer into a hot technology company. It had changed the Internet in Britain from a nerdish hobby into a national pastime. And it had fired the starting gun for a dot.com boom. All that the Freeserve story lacked was a couple of people with star quality. Another company was about to fill that gap.

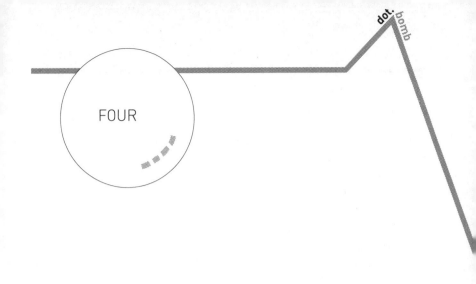

FOUR

When Brent met Martha

WHEN BRENT HOBERMAN FIRST outlined his plan for an internet company to Martha Lane Fox she told him it would never work. The woman who was to become the most familiar face in Britain's dot.com boom might never have joined Hoberman at lastminute.com. He called her at Carlton Communications in the spring of 1998 and told her of his idea for a website that would offer last minute deals for people in a hurry, the cash rich, time poor generation so beloved of the marketing gurus.

Her reaction was tepid. 'She just wasn't that in love with the Internet and she wasn't convinced by my idea,' Hoberman remembers. He approached another friend who worked in investment banking – but he was about to get married and did not have the spare time to start a dot.com. So back he went to Lane Fox and she agreed to work on the business plan for the company in the evenings while staying on at Carlton.

If a PR firm or a marketing consultant had been asked to pick two people who could go out and sell a new company to everyone from City institutions to the *Sun*, they could hardly have done better than Brent Hoberman and Martha Lane Fox. In 1998 when lastminute was born Hoberman was 29. He was dark and handsome in a preppy sort of way – ironed jeans, open necked shirt, sometimes a blazer. Lane Fox was 25, blonde with green eyes, hugely enthusiastic and slightly scatty. Anyone joining her in conversation found themselves pinned in her gaze as words tumbled out at breakneck speed.

Both came from prosperous backgrounds and neither is likely to choose 'My Struggle' as the title for an autobiography. Hoberman was born in South Africa and moved with his family to Boston, New York and then London. He was educated at Eton and Oxford. He is no computer scientist but is a self-confessed gadget freak. On every visit to his office I have found him playing with some new toy, from the latest electronic organizer, to a next generation mobile phone.

As a teenager he played with his father's computer and discovered the Internet. The Web had not been invented, but he worked out how to dial into an online service in New York called The Source. He even did a little programming at prep school, helped by a friend who turned out to be much smarter with computers.

Hoberman's entrepreneurial flair surfaced at Oxford, where he studied languages. He took over the running of the French club and quickly boosted its membership from 80 to 500. He persuaded the cosmetics firm L'Oreal and the French bank Société Générale to sponsor the club, and by the end of the year it had even turned a small profit. He then entered a competition to find the Oxford Entrepreneur of the Year and came second with a plan to free magazines into cinemas. When he graduated he was clear that he wanted to run his own company.

Like many a bright Oxbridge graduate with an interest in business but a reluctance to start off in some outpost of British industry, Hoberman began his career as a management consultant. What the companies who employ firms like McKinsey and Bain at eye-watering expense actually gain is a moot point, but the waves of young consultants sent in to recommend mass sackings or a new computer system win invaluable experience. Hoberman could not get into McKinsey and ended up at Mars and Co., another long established consulting firm. He hated every minute of it: 'There was a rule of fear – I ended up being fired after twenty months.'

He then found work at a new consultancy, Spectrum, which had just been set up to advise on telecommunications and new media. Its relaxed atmosphere was far more to his liking and he was soon advising clients like BT, Cable and Wireless and the BBC. He also learnt a tremendous amount about the fast growing internet industry. More importantly, it was at Spectrum that he met Martha Lane Fox.

She was a far more unlikely candidate for a major role in British business. Her father Robin Lane Fox was an Oxford archaeology don who also wrote a gardening column in the *Financial Times*. But while her mother ran a small business arranging lectures and her grandfather had founded an upmarket estate agent, Martha was definitely not an *FT* reader. Business was not something the Lane Fox family talked about. Childhood holidays were spent in some far-flung country where their father was pursuing research. He would get them to sleep on the airport floor for the first night and that would be the most comfortable berth of the holiday.

Later she backpacked her way around Asia, then spent a miserable three years at university in Oxford, which she found a stifling, unfriendly place. She had emerged from Oxford with a poor degree in Ancient History and the vaguest of ambitions. 'I wanted to join the prison service or be an actress – or perhaps work in the media, but behind the scenes.' She was offered a job at Pearson, the media company which owns the *Financial Times* and *The Economist*, but turned it down.

Then an uncle introduced her to the man who had founded Spectrum and he asked her to come for an interview. She arrived, somehow convinced that Spectrum was a television production company, and found that she was to be interviewed by someone called Brent Hoberman. 'He liked me – but thought I wouldn't be very good at financial modelling,' she remembers. 'He was right – and I still can't do it.' But somehow she got the job and her life changed completely.

After an upbringing in an academic family that had been rather sniffy about big business, she suddenly found herself immersed in the world of new technology and high finance. She loved it: 'My eyes were opened up to the fact that it was OK to be in business, that technology was fascinating.' At 21 she was working on major projects and travelling the world.

She also got on hugely well with Brent, although she could not help noticing just how much time he spent on the phone to a string of different women. Meanwhile, he tried to set her up with some of his old friends. He also got her to do lots of his work while he sat and thought about starting his own business.

Hoberman was convinced that the Internet was a wonderful medium to sell products in new, inventive ways but as he clicked from site to site he could find nothing that appealed to him. 'So I thought, "What do I want?" I realized that I was always trying to book things at the last minute – a hotel, a table at a restaurant – and was getting skilled at knocking down prices.' However, what he really wanted was some service that meant he did not have to spend time ringing round to get the best deal.

He realized that travel goods had a 'sell by' date – flights leaving Heathrow tomorrow morning or vacant hotel rooms in London at the weekend – and there was a huge incentive for the suppliers to fill the seats or rooms at a bargain price rather than leave them empty. Surely there was money to be made by using the power of the Internet to match up last minute customers with suppliers desperate to do a deal?

Still worrying away at this idea, he left Spectrum to work for LineOne, the Internet provider part owned by BT. He was supposed to be researching e-commerce ideas for the company but found the pace slow, and after trying and failing to sell them his own 'last minute' idea he left.

In October 1997 he joined the new online auction company Quixell, later to become QXL.com. Hoberman was the third person recruited by Tim Jackson but by the following spring he was gone. Later he told a journalist, 'I never felt anything for QXL, I never empathized with it.' The truth is that the affable but ambitious Hoberman and the cerebral, introverted Jackson proved an explosive mix. After what friends describe as a spectacular row, Hoberman left. He immediately set to work on the business plan for lastminute.com.

By now Lane Fox had moved to Carlton to work in its digital division. She too found life in a big company a little slow. 'I'm the kind of person who gets bored if they're not busy every millisecond.' So despite her initial doubts about Hoberman's internet venture, the idea of doing something that would occupy her every waking minute eventually proved irresistible.

In April 1998 they incorporated lastminute.com, registered the domain name and then set to work on refining the business plan. They spent the whole Easter weekend in Hoberman's Notting Hill flat, hammering away at something that could be presented to the venture capitalists who would decide their fate.

From the flat they moved to a desk in the office where Martha Lane Fox's mother ran her lunchtime lecture business. Even before they got any funding, they set about wooing the suppliers who would provide the last minute offers. Executives from airlines and hotel chains trooped up the narrow staircase to the cramped office to meet the two young people who were promising to change the way their industries worked. 'They took us seriously because they loved the idea,' says Lane Fox.

The birth of any new business may entail a clever concept, but it also involves an awful lot of mind-numbing drudgery. Lane Fox and Hoberman wrote to all of the best hotels in Britain and then sat ringing them hour after hour, day after day, trying to get them to come on board. They felt compelled to put in extraordinary hours because of the fear that their idea might just have occurred to someone else. 'We were paranoid that someone else might do it,' says Lane Fox. 'We thought, "If someone like Virgin gets hold of this, we'll be stuffed."'

But compared to many start-up ventures, getting funding was accomplished with some speed. They called ten venture capital funds. Half of them agreed to see them. Among their appointments was one with Tom Teichman, an investment banker who had made his fortune in the City and started putting money into technology firms in the mid-1980s. By 1996 Teichman had spotted that the Internet was going to provide big opportunities and he started a firm called New Media Investors with the aim of hunting down promising new Web ventures.

The problem was that he just could not find any. One investment in an auction firm planning to put art and antiques on the Net went disastrously wrong. The galleries and antique shops that were supposed to be the customers did not have the scanning equipment needed to put images of their stock on the Net. It was a good idea – but too early in the Internet's development, and Teichman ended up losing £100,000.

However, when Brent Hoberman rang him in the spring of 1998 the venture capitalist was immediately impressed. Hoberman had actually got through by mistake – he had been looking for a number for a publication called New Media Investment and had got Teichman's firm instead. Once he realized that he was speaking to a venture capitalist, Hoberman stayed on the phone for as long as he could. Eventually he was invited to send in his business plan and then to come and pitch at New Media Investors.

For any hopeful entrepreneur the pitch is a daunting experience, much like an audition for an actor. Tom Teichman has seen dozens of the young and hopeful troop into his offices and put on a show. He knows what he is looking for; 'Are they bright? Are they consistent? Do they know the details of their business plan? Will they react well under stress?' He insists that what he values most is the people not the product. 'Brilliant people with a good business plan have a better chance than good people with a brilliant business plan.'

If Hoberman and Lane Fox are good at anything it is putting on a sparky presentation, and just ten minutes into the Brent and Martha show, Teichman had decided to back them. 'I thought they were a fantastic combination. The business plan was very crisp, they presented it very clearly, they bounced off each other very well.' There were formalities to be observed, but the deal was quickly done. New Media Investors put together a consortium that included another venture capital business Arts Alliance, and France Telecom.

Together they put £600,000 into lastminute.com and Tom Teichman became a non-executive director. One of Teichman's employees, Julie Meyer, then spent a lot of time with Hoberman and Lane Fox helping them to recruit key personnel. Meyer, an American in her early thirties who had just arrived in Britain from the INSEAD business school near Paris, is described by Brent Hoberman as the best networker he has ever met. Later that year she was to be one of the founders of First Tuesday, the networking organization for dot.com people.

The money was enough to last until Christmas, but the founders knew the really hard work was ahead of them. When venture capitalists put money into a start-up company they set targets which have to be met by the time the next round of funding is needed. That will increase the valuation of the company. If the targets are not met and the value falls, the investors will not be too keen to put in more money. So by Christmas 1998 lastminute needed to have its site up and running and it had to prove there was a market out there.

Technology was what made dot.coms different but, bizarrely, it was a part of their business that many of the start-up companies seemed to neglect. Young entrepreneurs with a background in finance or marketing were more interested in discounted cash flow analysis and new forms of advertising than the intricacies of HTML. At first, this was the case with Hoberman and Lane Fox.

Dominic Cameron, later to join the company as chief technology officer, was invited to lunch with the founders at the Covent Garden restaurant Orso in the company's early months. He was a former BBC producer who had left the corporation to run his own graphics design business and had then moved into various internet ventures so he could give them some flavour of the challenge ahead. 'They were worried about relationships with suppliers, they were worried about marketing, but they did not see technology as the big challenge. I tried to persuade them otherwise. I told them they had done amazing work getting the airlines and hotels on board, but from now on technology should be a priority.'

Cameron put them in touch with one of their first employees, Phil Barrett, who had been working for beeb.com, the BBC's commercial online venture. Single-handed, and under great pressure, Barrett worked to prepare the site for launch. Other employees were joining – including Henry Lane Fox, Martha's brother. But, with just ten in the company at the end of the year, everyone had to do everything. At the office in Ladbroke Grove, where they were now based, the lights burned deep into the night.

Lastminute.com went live in October, the month after Freeserve had launched. And, as with most websites, the technology proved shaky. Lane Fox and Hoberman sat and watched the site obsessively as it repeatedly crashed and was put back up. They knew that it worked because a girlfriend of Lane Fox's bought some theatre tickets from the site. Then there was huge excitement as a genuine customer arrived. It was a woman and she bought a room at Nutfield Priory, an imposing Victorian hotel in Surrey. Martha Lane Fox rang the hotel several times to make sure that everything was all right.

Unlike Freeserve, lastminute.com was not an overnight success. In its first three months it had a turnover of just £2000. That revenue came from commissions paid by its suppliers on every flight booked, every hotel room sold – and while the site was attracting attention, few people were spending money. By Christmas Hoberman and Lane Fox had come to realize that they lived or died by the strength of their technology. They were in the middle of building a new version of the site but the money was close to running out.

There was a real danger that this was the end of the road. The founders and the team around them were exhausted. Almost everyone was on less money than they had been earning a year before. But after much agonizing they decided that it was worth another shot. After negotiations with Tom Teichman, they persuaded New Media Investors and their other backers to provide them with a bridging loan.

It was a decision that was to prove extremely lucrative for those backers. Early in 1999 it all started to happen. Traffic to the site was more like that on a busy dual carriageway than a quiet country road. By the beginning of 1999 just 236 customers had bought anything from the site; by the end of the year that figure had grown to over 28,000, and it was in the early months of 1999 that revenue started to build. But what really happened in 1999 was that one of the most successful PR offensives ever seen in Britain got underway.

Narda Shirley took on the contract to promote lastminute.com soon after it was launched. She had started her PR firm Gnash Communications early in 1997, aiming to recruit clients from the internet industries. With her ever-present pack of Marlboro Lights and her weakness for designer labels, Shirley looks at first glance like many of the identikit well-born women who flit their way from party to party across the PR world. But she has a lot more grit to her. After working at Gartner, a leading communications industry research firm, she could talk about everything from object-oriented programming to mezzanine finance. She also had a nose for a good story.

At first it was difficult to find customers to advise or journalists who had the slightest interest in writing about the Internet. They all thought it was a technical subject, best suited to the science correspondent. But eventually she was representing many of the best known names in the dot.com world and generating huge amounts of copy in national newspapers.

When lastminute.com came along she could see that she would have no trouble promoting the founders: 'They were confident, articulate, intelligent – and totally aware of what PR could do for them.' They discussed how Amazon had built the best known brand on the Internet through PR rather than advertising. If you could persuade journalists to write about you and broadcasters to put you on the television, then you could reach millions of potential customers without a big marketing budget. The only problem was that it was difficult to control the message.

The first article about lastminute appeared just weeks after its launch when the site was written up in the *Scotsman* in November 1998. Then the coverage gradually increased, although most of it was in the form of reviews of the clutch of travel websites now appearing on the Internet.

Meanwhile Hoberman and Lane Fox were accepting every invitation that came their way to speak at conferences about their experiences. This was the time when the captains of British industry were waking up and worrying that this new phenomenon called e-commerce might come and bite them very badly. So they wanted to hear what some of its protagonists were saying.

But the explosion in media interest really began in the summer of 1999. Suddenly the company was looking far more secure after raising over £6 million in new funding. The money came from the original backers and some new investors, including the computer chip giant Intel. By now Freeserve's imminent arrival on the London Stock Exchange had made everyone realize that you did not need to make profits to be a quoted company. Brent Hoberman started talking about his own stock market flotation. Journalists in publications including the *Guardian*, the *Wall Street Journal* and *Newsweek* started writing in glowing terms about Britain's hottest internet firm – a company, let's remember, which still had a smaller turnover than the average petrol station.

But from then on Hoberman's profile was to fade and it was Martha Lane Fox who became the face most people associated with lastminute.com. What turned her into a media star was that old combination of looks and money. As speculation mounted about a flotation, it suddenly dawned on journalists that somebody was going to make an awful lot of money. A valuation of £400 million was being bandied about. The Internet was being transformed from something spotty people did in their back bedrooms to a new kind of National Lottery, where complete unknowns could make millions.

And here was an attractive and lively 26-year-old blonde who was about to become a big winner. By September the personality pieces were appearing: 'Astonishing Success of High Flier Who Put Profits Before Romance', wrote the *Daily Express*, in an interview detailing a fourteen-hour day which left no room for a boyfriend. 'The Girl Aged 26 who could make £200m in a Year,' said the *Daily Mail*, making the inaccurate assumption that she still owned 50 per cent of the company. She firmly put that right in an interview with the *Evening Standard*, headlined 'They call her Fast Lane Foxy'. She told the paper it was boring to talk about money, but conceded that her paper wealth might amount to £50 million. Profiles appeared in just about every major newspaper over the coming months.

A business story had fought its way out of the City sections of the posh papers and into the front of the tabloids. Martha Lane Fox remembers coming home and finding a *Daily Mirror* journalist on her doorstep: 'I thought, "Gosh, this is very odd."' She insists that it was not a conscious marketing ploy: 'I was naïve about it. We tried just to talk to City editors about the serious side of the business, but even they were writing about how I was 26 and worth a fortune.' Whether naïve or not, the blanket coverage provided huge amounts of free advertising for a company which needed to win new customers as quickly as possible.

Even when the coverage was in the investment pages, it was perhaps a little less penetrating than it might have been. There is no doubt that middle-aged City editors, accustomed to lunching with grey corporate barons at the Savoy Grill, found it a refreshing change to be spending time with someone rather younger and a lot more fun.

The broadcasters also began to catch on. Many business figures sound good in print but freeze in front of a camera. Lane Fox was different. My first encounter with lastminute.com was in September 1999. By then the company was occupying two floors of a 1960s office block in the West End. The block was also home to a number of much bigger businesses, including a major oil company. But when I pitched up in the reception area with a cameraman in tow, one passer-by heading for the lift had no doubt about my destination. 'You must have come to see Martha,' a young woman said to me, her eyes shining. 'Martha's wonderful!' In my experience, few employees talk of their boss in such glowing terms. I wondered nervously whether this was a company or a cult.

But the object of this adoration was certainly impressive. Her desk was in the middle of a room heaving with young people and there was nothing to distinguish the boss from her juniors. When she stood up and came to be questioned on camera she delivered a series of perfect soundbites, albeit at such breakneck speed that it was difficult to keep up. The average company boss has to be asked the same question half a dozen times before something that makes sense in fifteen seconds emerges.

That month Martha Lane Fox faced the man most would acknowledge as the most daunting interrogator in British television. She was invited to appear on *Newsnight* to be interviewed by Jeremy Paxman. She travelled to the studio in White City with Dominic Cameron, lastminute's chief technology officer. In the 1980s Cameron had been a producer on *Newsnight*.

He knew how television worked and how it could be used to last-minute's advantage. The show's headlines included a shot of Martha over which Paxman asked why this woman was worth a 'virtual' £400 million. There was to be a report on the internet bubble, followed by a discussion in which she would be confronted with a sceptical commentator on investment matters who would pour cold water on this dot.com nonsense.

Meanwhile, in the Green Room where guests are entertained before and after the programme, Lane Fox and Cameron were making a beeline for this opponent. 'We nobbled him and buttered him up,' says Cameron. On air, lastminute's youthful founder put up a spirited defence of her company and its apparently fanciful valuation. Paxman, who was soon calling her Martha, was not at his most ruthless, and the financial commentator, after warning against the gold-rush mentality, conceded that lastminute.com had carved itself a niche in the market and might prosper more than most. On one of Britain's most influential television programmes Martha Lane Fox had made an immediate impression as a sparky performer. The rest of the London media took note.

Journalists and broadcasters are at one and the same time very busy and very lazy. If they are asked to come up with an article or a news report in a hurry, they turn for a quote to people who have already proved themselves quotable. Martha Lane Fox fitted the bill and within weeks it was almost impossible to find an article about the new economy which did not mention her name. It was the same at the BBC. When I suggested pieces about the new economy to editors, they would often say, 'See if you can get that Lane Fox woman.' But there is another side to such ubiquity. When the mood changes, applause can turn to catcalls with astounding speed – as lastminute was to find to its cost.

Throughout 1999, far from the spotlight, the technical team was in a constant battle to keep the site up and running. Dominic Cameron had been drafted in to head the team. After a year of almost solo effort, Phil Barrett was close to exhaustion. Brent Hoberman was a difficult taskmaster – not because he ranted and raved but because he was easily upset. 'Brent gets very stressed,' says one of the technical team. 'He doesn't shout, he just gets very sad, so sad you just want to help him.'

There were also repeated clashes with the company hosting their site, Planet Online. The Yorkshire-based firm, headed by Peter Wilkinson of Freeserve fame, appeared impatient with what it regarded as the rather hysterical demands of these affluent southern youngsters who did not understand the mucky world of internet hardware. From the other side, lastminute's staff believed they were getting a poor service from Planet Online. The site was very slow at times and that could have a critical impact on customers staring at a web page and waiting for something to happen. The two sides clashed over whose fault this was. Brent Hoberman was given the home phone numbers of Planet executives, and often spent the weekend calling them to ask why his site was down. Eventually lastminute severed the connection and moved to another provider.

Getting the site right became ever more important as the flotation moved closer. Suddenly all the company's attention was focused on getting to the stock market. With internet share fever moving from the United States to Britain, now was the time to move: 'We all knew there'd be a crash,' one of the management team remembers, 'the question was how soon and how deep. So there was a small window to get to IPO.' A stock market flotation became ever more vital to the company's future. It would provide the original investors with the opportunity to recoup their money many times over – the exit every venture capitalist is keen to find. It would also provide lastminute with the money it needed to continue expanding, indeed to survive.

But in many ways the hullabaloo of a stock market flotation was a dangerous distraction for a company that was barely out of nappies. In the closing months of 1999 lastminute had expanded across Europe, launching sites in France, Germany and Sweden. It was a period when its executives should have been at full stretch managing that expansion. Brent Hoberman admits that trying to run a growing business while handling the pressures of a high profile flotation was not ideal: 'It's always stressful. You're racing against time. You don't want to spend too much time away from the business but you want to hit the market when conditions are right.'

In December one visitor to the company was not convinced that this was a business that would stand the travel industry on its head. Jim Riley, head of strategy at Britain's biggest package holiday firm, Thomson, spent two days with lastminute as his firm pondered taking a stake in its online rival. 'When I met Brent and Martha I had two emotions,' says Riley. 'Yes, I was impressed by their huge drive and energy – but I felt antagonistic because they knew so little about the leisure travel market where it's fantastically difficult to make money.' Riley remembers that as she showed him to the lift, Martha Lane Fox said that what they really needed was someone who understood the travel business. Eventually, Thomson decided not to invest. Instead it did its utmost to put the upstart online challenger in its place. 'We told our staff that it would be a disciplinary offence for anyone to offer any content to lastminute.com,' says Riley. 'We called it "The Empire Strikes Back".'

But it was the prospect of an instant windfall that was preoccupying at least some members of the staff in Park Street. Nearly everyone had stock options, and even the most junior employee among a workforce which had grown to 200 by the end of 1999 stood to make several thousand pounds in profits. At one staff meeting a receptionist suddenly called out, 'We're all going to be millionaires.' Everyone laughed, but Martha Lane Fox, who was always rather puritanical about anything that smacked of a get-rich-quick mood, called for calm.

The big investment banks, hungry for fees, came knocking on the door, offering to shepherd the company to the market. Hoberman and Lane Fox conducted a beauty contest, interviewing the representatives of these emperors of finance about their qualifications to run this IPO. Just a year earlier they had been the supplicants, going cap in hand to the financiers. Now the tables were turned. 'The chairmen of these banks were calling up to chat,' says Hoberman.

After a close contest with Goldman Sachs, it was Morgan Stanley that won the prize. Morgan Stanley was the most prominent bank in American internet flotations and lastminute.com was to be its first UK dot.com offering. Having missed out on the flotations of Freeserve, QXL and Interactive Investor International, it was determined not to be beaten to the punch this time. Morgan Stanley was also appointed to float Boxman, the online music retailer which had been merged with IMVS. Boxman was told that it would come onto the runway immediately after lastminute.

Lastminute's founders were delighted to be in the hands of such a big player. 'Morgan Stanley is the only bank never to have had an internet flotation that has fallen below its issue price,' Martha Lane Fox told the *Guardian*. But she and Hoberman had played hardball to make sure they got the best out of the bank. They had insisted that, as part of the package, the goddess of American internet research would be an advisor. Mary Meeker of Morgan Stanley was Wall Street's most respected internet analyst and had helped steer Yahoo's and Amazon's flotations. She was rumoured to have made £9 million in 1999, the year in which *Fortune* magazine described her as the third most powerful woman in American business. 'Mary Meeker was a great selling point when it came to choosing Morgan Stanley,' says Brent Hoberman. 'She had an amazing following – she was an internet brand.'

Now, news that she was to be connected to this deal made many in the City revise their view of its value upwards. She had praised the business, pointing out that it had no equivalent in the United States. Meeker's name went on the Morgan Stanley research document about an IPO that was puny compared to those with which she had earlier been associated. The result was sour grapes from one of the bank's rivals. An unnamed investment banker at Goldman Sachs poured scorn on Morgan Stanley's excitement about this small UK deal, telling the online news service TheStreet.com, 'This deal is becoming MaryMeeker.com.' Morgan Stanley returned fire: 'We admit this deal and its success are very important to us,' a spokeswoman said. 'We expect our rivals to be hopping mad.'

It was not until February 2000 that the company confirmed that it would be floating the following month. But long before that there was a huge amount of work to be done. The bankers, the stockbrokers, the lawyers and the PR advisors were all spending many hours going through every aspect of the firm's operations. For that work they would earn fees many times greater than the company's annual turnover.

The technology came under especially close examination. It had to prove that it could be defended against hacker attack. It had to prove that it was robust enough to deal with huge surges in traffic. There was an expectation that the wave of publicity surrounding the flotation could generate four times as many visitors as normal.

To float this most modern of companies there was to be an ultra modern approach. The application process was even more rigorously 'online' than it had been for Freeserve nine months earlier. Any small investors wanting to get onboard had to be registered as lastminute.com subscribers. A link on the website would take them to Interactive Investor International, the online finance site which itself floated in mid-February. They would also have to register with Interactive Investor, after which they would be able to download the prospectus. Potential investors would only be able to obtain the application form online.

There were two benefits to this procedure. It saved money on posting out thousands of forms, and it drove a lot of traffic both to lastminute and to Interactive Investor. It also magnified the effect by which shares in dot.coms were most attractive to people who were already in love with the technology.

At this stage in the dot.com bubble British investors had become used to exchanging news and (often scurrilous) views about companies on internet bulletin boards. These online discussion areas had come a long way from the Internet's early years where they were the preserve of geeks swapping programming tips. Now they covered every imaginable topic, and share trading was one of the big growth areas.

By the time lastminute's prospectus was published on 1 March the bulletin boards were alive with frenzied debate about the hottest share issue of the year. This was a time when shares in other internet companies had climbed to extraordinary levels. Interactive Investor, floated at £1.50, had soared above £4. QXL, which had launched at £1, was flirting with the £10 barrier. There were already a lot of Cassandras on the discussion boards warning that a mighty crash was just around the corner. There were also many who had missed out on what they regarded as the free lunch at QXL and Interactive Investor and did not intend to make the same mistake again. But a careful examination of the prospectus should have given them pause for thought. It contained no fewer than ten pages of warnings about threats to the company's future. 'Rapid technological changes may render our technology obsolete,' it stressed on one page, 'we may not be profitable for the foreseeable future' on another.

While lastminute was stressing its phenomenal growth rate, it was still a tiny company. It was keen to trumpet the fact that it now had over a million subscribers. But the most recent results showed that in the three months to 31 December it had just under 21,000 customers. A lot of people were coming to have a look but few were buying. In those three months, turnover amounted to just £409,000. Just to make a comparison, the Federation of Small Businesses recently surveyed its members about their turnover. An independent high street chemist, a large health food shop and a small garage were amongst the companies making similar amounts to lastminute. None of them was talking to Morgan Stanley. But then none of them was an internet company able to use the Net to spread its name and grow its business at the speed of light. After all, lastminute's turnover had quadrupled in the last three months. If that growth rate continued, the company would end up bigger than Microsoft. If…

Just over a fifth of the shares in the company were going up for sale at a price of between £1.90 and £2.20, putting a value on the company of around £300 million. The final price to be paid would be announced on 14 March. But applicants were also told that the price could be revised upwards at the last moment if demand was particularly strong, and they would then get the option of withdrawing their applications. This was a new and controversial technique, introduced from the United States with the aim of making sure that the company squeezed the most out of a flotation. As part of the package, Lane Fox and Hoberman were turning some of their paper money into cash. They were selling some of their shares to the mobile phone company Orange, raising almost £1 million each.

As in any major share issue, it was not the general public that had to be convinced but the big institutions, the pension funds that manage billions of pounds worth of assets. The shares were being marketed in Europe and the US as well as the UK, so the founders and their advisors now had to set off on a promotional tour, or roadshow as the investment bankers like to call it. The trail blazed by Freeserve the previous summer would now be followed by lastminute.com. The Brits were coming.

Those who have taken part in IPO roadshows describe them in much the same way as rock stars relate their touring experiences – an endless series of airports, private jets, and meeters and greeters, with nothing to distinguish one venue from the next. Martha Lane Fox and Brent Hoberman insist that their roadshow involved no groupies and the only drug was an endless supply of caffeine. But taking lastminute on the road was probably as costly as an Oasis tour. At the very first roadshow presentation the chief technology officer Dominic Cameron got a laugh when he pointed out that the engineering for the original website had cost £100,000, less than the fees now being paid to the advisors for this one meeting. The tour began with three days in the UK, followed by six days in the United States and another four around Europe.

The reception they got from what were supposed to be hardheaded fund managers and stock analysts was warm. This despite mounting anxiety about the hysteria surrounding the flotation. Many senior City figures were warning that the price on the shares was ridiculously inflated. As the first day of trading neared, both the Chancellor of the Exchequer, Gordon Brown, and Sir Howard Davies, head of the main City watchdog, the Financial Services Authority, cautioned small investors not to get carried away with the promise of high-tech stocks. But even while they shook their heads over this frenzy, which many were comparing to the tulip mania in seventeenth-century Holland, big institutions were ordering tulips as fast as they could. There was a certain method to this madness. It was called 'momentum' investing. Those who invested in companies like lastminute.com were not necessarily convinced of their fundamental merits. But they were convinced that they would be able to get rid of the shares at a higher price to someone else. Until the merry-go-round stopped, it was an exhilarating and profitable ride.

As they crossed the United States in a private jet, Hoberman and Lane Fox found the pace exhausting. 'It was incredibly intense – from 8 a.m. to 8 p.m. we were doing presentations,' says Hoberman. 'We were in San Diego for three hours, then San Francisco, Houston, Denver, Boston, New York, all in three and a half days.' Repeating the same presentation time after time grew tedious, especially as the audiences did little to keep them on their toes: 'We used to long for a penetrating question to liven it up.'

Back in London the technical team was facing a real crisis. The biggest fear was that the site would crash at some stage during the roadshow. Suddenly one afternoon rumours began to spread that hackers had penetrated lastminute.com. If someone had managed to break through the different levels of security, perhaps even obtaining customer details, it would be hugely damaging to a business where customers had to be confident about using their credit cards to buy online. The company called in an organization called Ethical Hackers, which uses the expertise of experienced hackers to check for security breaches.

All over the UK guys in ponytails and Grateful Dead T-shirts spent a night trying to get through lastminute's defences. By the next morning there was good news for the technical managers when they got to their desks. The verdict from the Ethical Hackers was clear – your site is safe. They had not been able to get in and found no signs of forced entry by anyone else.

But with Lane Fox and Hoberman out of the country there were signs that the media tide was turning. In the month leading up to the IPO one database of newspaper coverage shows 400 articles mentioning the company. By now there were three different PR companies handling the story and they were fielding calls day and night from Britain and around the world. But the ever-brighter spotlight on the huge fortune about to be showered on lastminute's founders began to raise hackles. An article headlined 'Dot Com Envy' quoted 'friends' of Lane Fox expressing astonishment at just how far she had come. 'She's not so bright,' said one.

Then on 9 March, just five days before trading in the shares was due to get underway, Lane Fox and Hoberman's paper fortunes grew even larger. Lastminute and Morgan Stanley announced that the price range for the shares had been lifted to between £3.20 and £3.80, about a two-thirds increase from the original range of £1.90 to £2.30. As the roadshow neared its end, the bank had advised its clients that the share issue was already massively oversubscribed, with the institutions and small investors clamouring for a stake. At the top end of the new price range Brent Hoberman's stake would be worth £60 million, Martha Lane Fox's £39 million.

With hindsight, this was the moment when dot.com hysteria got completely out of hand. Morgan Stanley's move to upgrade the price so sharply alienated many of the institutions that bought the shares. A rival banker puts it like this: 'With the institutions it's a contract. Raising the price range was a pretty new tactic in Europe. People were pissed off that they did it at the last moment, giving people no time to react. That broke the unwritten rule.' Sources at lastminute say Brent Hoberman and Martha Lane Fox were themselves uneasy about the move, but bowed to the superior wisdom of the bankers.

Small investors had to confirm by e-mail that they still wanted the shares at the higher price. This was the time when everyone could have stopped, drawn breath and asked whether a start-up company with uncertain prospects was really worth more than half a billion pounds. But by now an unofficial verdict on the success of this gamble was available through the spread betting firms. They provided a means for people to take a punt on what would happen to shares in a company without actually going through the tedious process of applying for a stake. They were quoting prices for the lastminute shares at around £5.75. Convinced that they would make an instant profit, investors big and small closed their eyes and sent in their money.

On 10 March a picture of Martha Lane Fox was unveiled in an exhibition at the National Portrait Gallery entitled '21 Leaders For the Twenty First Century'. Then at the weekend the *Sunday Times* published its annual Rich List, and Lane Fox and Hoberman were amongst the dot.com millionaires smashing their way into the catalogue of British wealth. Two days later the shares would start trading. Just nine months after Freeserve had floated, the dot.com cult had reached its peak. Now was the time for it all to go up in flames.

FIVE

Fashion victims

IN SEPTEMBER 1999 A most unattractive image was spread across two pages of the fashion bible *Vogue*. On a path through what looks like a New York park, a jogger is bent over a waste bin. There is a big patch of sweat spreading from the armpit of his yellow T-shirt, and two strings of vomit are hanging down from his mouth into the bin. The jogger's companions are disappearing into the distance but a young boy stands by the bin looking on impassively while sucking on a carton of drink. A small caption at the top of the page reads, 'Earl Blewett 24, works: Software Developer, lives: Queens, likes: New Balance, Puma.' Another, bigger caption says, 'boo.com, the sports shop on the net'.

There are two ways of seeing this relic from the dot.com archive. Perhaps it is a piece of advertising as bold in its ambitions as the company it is trying to sell, an arresting image designed to subvert the way we see fashion and get us to visit the website of a company which is about to prove that the Internet can transform the way our lives work. Or perhaps the guy chucking up in the bin just cannot believe that anything as daft and profligate as boo.com has been allowed to happen.

By September boo.com was already making a huge splash, despite the fact that it was not even up and running, having missed several launch dates. Lastminute had been in operation for almost a year, but this new company was threatening to snatch its title as the most hyped dot.com in Britain. Everything about boo was big. It was going to be the first global sports-wear site, it was going to use cutting edge technology, it had attracted more investment than any other internet start-up in Europe, and it had already burnt up a lot of money. From its base in London it was going to launch in eight markets simultaneously – a hugely ambitious move for any company, let alone one run by people with no experience of managing a major enter-prise.

The fact that London had been chosen as the headquarters of this new empire was surely a sign that the UK was now the centre of Europe's dot.com industry. If boo's ambitions were to be realized, it would mean that London would have as much right as Silicon Valley, Seattle or New York to call itself a centre of the New Economy.

It was on the slender shoulders of two young Swedes who had met twenty years earlier at kindergarten that so much rested. Ernst Malmsten and Kajsa Leander had come a long way from the small town of Lunn where they were brought up. They had lost touch, then met again in the early 1990s in a nightclub in Paris and started going out together. They travelled together to New York where Leander, a classic if rather severe Swedish blonde, financed her studies in the history of art by working as a model for the Elite agency.

Back in Sweden, Malmsten got a job as a literary critic on one of the country's main daily newspapers. The relationship with Leander ended but they kept in touch. A shared passion for poetry became the basis of their first joint enterprise. With no little entrepreneurial flair and a good deal of front, they convinced Sweden's foreign office to co-operate with them in mounting a festival of Scandinavian poetry in New York. It was literature that turned them into internet entrepreneurs.

They started a small publishing venture that consistently lost money. Then they decided that the Internet was a better playground for their ambi-tions. In 1997 Malmsten and Leander launched an online book retailer, bokus.com, which quickly became the biggest in the Swedish market. Opinions differ as to just how successful bokus was. It never made a profit – but then profits were not fashionable in the online world at that time. But it did make substantial amounts of money for its founders and their backers. In November, just six months after they launched bokus, Malmsten and

Leander went to see a young Swedish investment banker and asked him to sell the company for them. They had decided that they wanted to move on quickly and found another internet company. The banker, Patrik Hedelin, was to be the third member of the triumvirate that founded boo, although his earnest demeanour, conventional appearance and almost impenetrable Swedish accent meant that he attracted a lot less publicity.

By February 1998 Hedelin had managed to sell bokus.com to a traditional retailer at a time when old economy firms were becoming paranoid about the Internet and what it might do to their businesses. This transaction was crucial to the founding of boo. It gave the young Swedes some financial breathing space, but more importantly it provided them with a track record as successful internet entrepreneurs.

Neither of them had extensive experience in either business or the computer world, but both were fired by enthusiasm for the Internet and by a belief that they were a couple who could make things happen. They asked Patrik Hedelin to join them in trying to form their new internet venture. After weeks of research, they closed in on one idea.

In his Stockholm flat Malmsten knocked out a five-page business plan. It outlined a vision of an online retailer selling the hottest items in sportswear – products from companies like Adidas, Converse, Puma and North Face, which had graduated from the basketball court and the running track to the clubs. There would be a head office in London's Soho and branches in New York, Stockholm and Munich. Distribution centres in Germany and the United States would ship the goods and the ultra high-tech site would be up and running in five languages within six months. Turning this vision into reality would require a lot more money than could be got in Sweden. Hedelin, their only link with the world of finance, told them that American investment banks would be far more likely to appreciate their vision – and would put a higher valuation on the concept.

So the golden couple and their rather greyer friend set off across the Atlantic. 'The first thing we did,' says Patrik Hedelin, 'was to book into the most expensive hotel in San Francisco. We knew nobody would take our calls if we were phoning from the Holiday Inn.' They started cold-calling the big investment banks. Amazingly, they struck lucky. During the course of several visits to both the West and East Coast they talked their way into ten of the banks.

It was JP Morgan, one of the best-known names in global finance, which eventually took the bait. Hedelin just rang the switchboard and asked for the name of the man in charge of private equity placings. He got through, arranged a meeting, and after a certain amount of to-ing and fro-ing, the bank was soon talking seriously about doing something quite extraordinary – advising a start-up company founded by people in their twenties. But why did one of the Wall Street giants, an organization whose marble halls were usually welcoming America's corporate aristocracy to talk about multibillion dollar deals, entertain these complete unknowns?

'Ernst and Kajsa were an intriguing couple,' says Hedelin. 'They made a real impact together, sparking off each other.' Malmsten, wearing geeky glasses and ultra fashionable clothes, came across as a dreamy visionary. Perhaps he was talking garbage when he painted a picture of a business which could use the revolutionary technology of the Net to build a global retailer in months – but then again, perhaps he just saw further than investment bankers still trying to come to terms with rapid technological change. Meanwhile, his partner was both alarmingly beautiful and totally businesslike, explaining in minute detail just how it would all work.

What is more, they had done it all before. In late 1998 it was difficult to find anyone with experience of running an internet retailer. Malmsten and Leander might not have run a multinational or even been to business school, but dot.coms were different and they had a track record. So, to the delight of the two Swedes, JP Morgan agreed to come on board as advisors. With its backing, the hunt for the substantial investment they required would be a whole lot easier. The bank saw an opportunity to make a name for itself as the top name in European internet finance. It had been left behind in the American internet gold rush by the likes of Morgan Stanley and Goldman Sachs. Here was a chance to take the lead in the continent that was about to become the focus for the next wave of web investment.

By now some of the biggest names in European business had decided that it was time they made a bit of money from the Internet. So boo's search for backing was well timed. JP Morgan put Leander and Malmsten on Concorde and a private jet for what turned out to be a triumphant tour of the European super-rich. The head of the Benetton fashion empire entertained them in his Italian villa and put up £3 million. The French billionaire Bernard Arnault, who had built the champagne to luxury luggage empire LVMH, also agreed to invest through his new internet fund, europ@web.

The Hariri family of Lebanon, who had made their money in construction, added their weight and eventually became the biggest investors. These were all wealthy people with extensive business pedigrees. But they were not Silicon Valley venture capitalists, experienced in assessing what might turn a bright idea into a big business, and they knew little about start-up ventures. Patrik Hedelin says he deliberately chose not to approach venture capitalists. 'We wanted people from these big retailing brands who could bring expertise as well as money to the business,' he comments. A former boo employee has a different interpretation: 'Kajsa and Ernst couldn't get the smart money on board,' she says: 'So they had to turn to the stupid money.' Venture capitalists usually want to keep a very close eye on their investments, to the extent of removing the senior executives if things go badly. That may have made them less attractive to the Swedes. By the middle of 1999 over £40 million had been raised.

One executive who met the boo founders at this time was amazed at their opinion of their company's worth. His organization – one of the business world's most reputable names – had been told it might just be allowed to invest in a company which was now valuing itself at £150 million. 'Their heads had been filled with crap by JP Morgan. They were crazy – but then everybody was crazy at that time.' As someone who believed first class management was key to any of his organization's investments, he was not convinced by the people he found at boo's Carnaby Street office. 'Ernst Malmsten was very unimpressive – not commercial at all. A very sensitive type with poor social skills. Patrik Hedelin would just start to sweat when you asked him fairly simple questions.' The only one who impressed him was Kajsa Leander. 'She was smart, on top of her brief.' The executive had serious misgivings, particularly because he could not negotiate a seat on the board or obtain the kind of control his organization was used to exerting when it invested in young companies. Nevertheless, he ended up putting a small amount of money into boo. 'It was the equivalent of putting your chips on 36 at roulette,' he told me, with a shrug and a smile.

By now boo was already spending its money with some abandon. The first employees came on board at the end of 1998. Among them was Charlotte Neser, a 25-year-old Cambridge theology graduate who was headhunted from a job in advertising. Like many boo staff, she found her job interview excitingly unconventional. It took place in the bar of the Metropolitan Hotel where she was immediately won over by Kajsa Leander's infectious enthusiasm. 'She showed me press cuttings about the poetry festival they'd organized and said boo was going to be fantastic.'

Neser was thrilled by her new job. Her task was to recruit the companies who would supply the fashionable sportswear on the boo site. She was given a list of chief executives and began cold-calling around the world: 'I had to sell them the concept in a minute.' It seemed a daunting task, but she soon found that many of them were quite easy to haul in. 'They were frightened by the Internet but they knew they had to have a presence there.' What they really feared was that online shopping would be a bargain hunters' paradise and would highlight the different prices they charged in different markets. Neser was able to reassure them. 'Our plan was to launch in five languages and in local currencies, so that it would be difficult for people to spot the price differences.' They were also gratified by the plans for a big marketing campaign.

In the early days the team could all gather around the table in the stylish Carnaby Street office which was boo's headquarters. Alison Conway, an American recruited in January, remembers how impressed and excited she was by the cool atmosphere, the stripped pine floors and the sense of a team of the brightest and best setting out to change the world. 'But within a couple of months, the Swedish minimalism was gone, the place was packed and new staff were arriving every day,' she remembers. By now the original plan to launch in April had been put back, but the boo team were not discouraged. After all, they were working for what was already a cool company, receiving masses of favourable press coverage.

In May the *Daily Telegraph* reported that boo.com would be launched later that month by 'Ernst Malmsten and Kajsa Leander who are already well known in e-commerce'. Then in July Leander and Malmsten were pictured on the cover of *Fortune*. The influential business magazine dubbed boo 'Europe's coolest company', an extraordinary accolade for a firm that was still not operating.

If the world of finance thought boo was cool, so did hordes of ambitious young people looking for a job in e-commerce. Among them was Heidi Fitzpatrick, an investment analyst at Nomura Asset Management. Fitzpatrick, who had been born in Finland, then moved to London and married an Englishman, was earning stacks of money but she was bored: 'I hated the City – I wanted to do something cool and not have to wear a suit any more.' When she saw an advertisement for a job at boo.com she leapt at the chance.

She turned up at Carnaby Street for her interview and walked into an atmosphere very different from that of an investment bank: 'I thought, "This is way cooler than the City." It was manic, desks were virtually piled on top of each other, there were pierced noses and green hair. The sheer energy was breathtaking. You got out of breath just by being there.'

Fitzpatrick was interviewed for a job as a financial strategist by Patrik Hedelin, who at that stage was calling himself Chief Financial Officer. 'A sweet guy,' says Fitzpatrick, 'but pretty inexperienced for that role.' Fitzpatrick took the job, which meant a pay cut, and held a huge leaving party at Nomura, after which she burnt her business suits. For her, and many like her, this was a revolution that had to be joined: 'It was like Woodstock. We thought it would all be in the history books. You just wanted to be there.'

By early June, when Fitzpatrick started work, Patrik Hedelin had become Executive Chairman. She now found herself working for a temporary Chief Financial Officer, Rachel Yasue, who had been brought in on contract from the accountants KPMG. Paying for her services was costing boo £1750 a day. However much Yasue might have wanted to keep the finances on a tight leash, she was regarded as a hired hand rather than a major player in the boo hierarchy. Throughout the company's existence it seemed that the job of overseeing the finances was passed around as if it were a ticking bomb. The investors thought that Hedelin was the man with his eyes on the spreadsheets, making sure the money was well spent. He insists that his was a far more strategic role.

More than 200 people were now on the boo payroll, most of them under 30. On one floor of the offices a team was at work on one of boo's innovations, an online magazine about fashion and culture designed to make the site more attractive to potential shoppers. Elsewhere, the 'boo crew' was in training. These young fashion assistants would be on hand to give telephone advice on sizing and availability when the service finally launched. Everyone seemed to be young, attractive and ultra fashionable. Much of the slightly less fashionable technical team was by now housed in overflow offices in Holborn.

But the member of the team attracting most attention was Miss Boo. She was a savvy, chic woman of the twenty-first century who would be the shopper's companion on the journey down the virtual aisles. She may not have demanded dinner at The Ivy or first class flights to New York but she was to prove even more expensive to maintain than many of the senior staff. Miss Boo was an avatar – a computerized woman who would be the mascot of the site. Shoppers would click on her and she would perform miracles.

Getting Miss Boo right became an obsession for Kajsa Leander, who had now assumed the title of Chief Marketing Officer. She spent many hours discussing every detail of Miss Boo's appearance with her team. A breathtakingly expensive copywriter was hired to write words for her to speak. She even brought in a fashionable hairdresser from New York to redesign Miss Boo's coiffure. 'She's a bit of a laddette, strong and independent,' Leander told the *Daily Telegraph* in a June article, which again had the site launching 'later in the month'.

Boo, its staff were finding, was always a month away from launch. The nuts and bolts of website design were the problem. Miss Boo was to front a site which would make boo's technology the wonder of the internet world. Throughout their presentations to investors, Malmsten and Leander had stressed that their site would take online retailing into a new dimension. Shoppers would be able to spin their Converse trainers through 360 degrees, there would be virtual fitting rooms where you could try your clothes out on a dummy your size, and you would be able to zoom in to see every stitch.

However, making all that happen was already proving fiendishly difficult and very costly. One of the technical team's early members was an Australian, Dave Sag. Balding, forty-ish, and dressed in jeans and an old sweatshirt, he had little in common with the fashion victims in the marketing department. But after twenty years in the computer industry and with a couple of his own businesses behind him, he feels he had a sharper idea of what was going on than the people who were supposed to be steering boo. He joined as a contractor in April 1999 because, as he puts it, 'it seemed an opportunity to do some really cool coding for a client who did not seem to give a shit how long it took or how much it cost'.

In his year at boo, Sag rose to become one of the most senior programmers, but he refused a series of invitations to join the staff, preferring to remain a contractor. Not surprising when you consider what he was earning.

Mounting pressure to get the site launched meant he could be working as much as a hundred hours a week. As the penalty payments stacked up, he found himself taking home £6000 in one week. Sag was working on what were called the micro-sites: promotional areas for individual retailers like Converse or New Balance. He could scarcely believe the way the whole operation was being handled, with outside firms working on other parts of the site and a lack of communication. 'Technically it was a shambles,' he says, 'and it was costing £11,000 just to put one product on the site.'

The technical team, in its Holborn outpost, found itself isolated from the rest of the operation. Back in Carnaby Street, Heidi Fitzpatrick was already having doubts about her dream job. Like just about everyone in her office, she had been issued with a mobile phone, a laptop and a Palm organizer on arrival, but nobody seemed to know what they were doing.

Fitzpatrick is forthright to the point of slander about the abilities of many of the management team at boo. 'A very thick individual,' she says of one, 'embarrassingly incompetent' of another. She found herself surrounded by people in their mid-twenties, fresh from consultancy and with no proper business experience, but all apparently vice-presidents. The atmosphere, far from being the Woodstock she had imagined, was more like a renaissance court, awash with cliques and jealousy. 'It was so political it was untrue – much worse than the City.' Come to think of it, just like Woodstock . . .

At the centre of the court were Ernst Malmsten and Kajsa Leander, each surrounded by a gaggle of aides. Patrik Hedelin had his own clique, albeit rather more modest. The Vice-Presidents then had to establish their place in the court by appointing an Executive Assistant and a PA. Another enthusiastic arrival in the Carnaby Street offices was disturbed by what he found. Gary Varley was selected to join the finance team after what he describes as the strangest interview of his life. He was summoned to a Soho café to meet Malmsten and Leander. They did not seem sure what to ask him or how a job interview should be conducted. 'I thought, "Well they're Scandinavian and that means they are more reserved." But later I realized that they're right at the end of that spectrum.'

When Varley arrived in Carnaby Street in late August, his immediate impression was one of total chaos. But that did not worry him at first. Fresh from the staid surroundings of the accountancy firm PriceWaterhouseCooper, Varley was ready for something different. 'I was enthused by it initially. I thought this was how a dot.com was.' But as he saw how little control there was over costs and over the progress of the technology, he realized that even a dot.com should not be quite so different from a normal business. 'It eventually became clear that this was not a creative chaos but a chaos that was going to bring the company down.'

As summer became autumn and the launch date was postponed again and again, costs were soaring. 'Budgets were a moving target,' says Heidi Fitzpatrick, 'every month people just spent what they wanted to spend.' With offices in New York and across Europe, there was a huge amount of travel, much of it without a defined purpose. Fitzpatrick found herself travelling Business Class to New York and staying in the ultra-cool Paramount hotel for three nights, just to meet a PR agency. Later, Dave Sag from the technical team also pitched up at the Paramount – for two weeks. He had been sent out just to talk to Organic, the company working on developing the website. 'I did a lot of shopping,' he remembers.

The most senior staff, in the exalted positions around the founders, were travelling First Class to New York and staying at the Mercer, described in one guide as 'the trendiest luxury hotel to stay and be seen in'. Room rates at the Mercer started at $400 a night. Back in London the spending was also lavish. There were dinners at The Ivy for the vice-presidents, drinks at the Zinc Bar and Alphabet, paid for by Ernst and Kajsa on their company credit cards.

Some, like Alison Crombie who joined the marketing team in August, believe the extravagance of boo has been overplayed. She felt that everyone was working long hours to build something worthwhile. 'It was the best job I've ever had,' she says, 'there was a strong sense of unity, we were all just working all hours to get it done.' Others saw it rather differently. 'It wasn't a business,' says Heidi Fitzpatrick, 'people were just having fun.' Those who were having most fun were the insiders. One of the company's senior managers puts it like this: 'I was a member of the court of King Ernst – and I had the best year of my life. Those who weren't in his court did not have such a good time.' The American Alison Conway was shocked. In an earlier job she had advised internet start-ups in Silicon Valley, and had not seen spending on this scale. The two Alisons also had very different views of the founders. To Alison Crombie, who later moved to become the company's Press Officer, they were a formidable team, working seven days a week to realize their vision. 'They literally had no time off at all,' she says. But by now Alison Conway was becoming disillusioned with a couple who seemed obsessed with the fun side of the job rather than the nitty-gritty: 'Kajsa's obsessions were PR, fashion shows, all the glamorous and sexy aspects. But retail isn't a sexy business. We didn't need people who looked good on the cover of *Vogue*, we needed people who knew about things like warehousing.'

The founders were also living well at boo's expense. The company paid for Leander's house in Primrose Hill and for Malmsten's flat in Notting Hill. He flew in a designer to change the look and its Swedish minimalism won it a spread in a style magazine. Ernst's flat was the scene of lavish dinner parties for those he favoured. 'I remember going there once for dinner,' says a member of the inner circle, 'and there were four butlers, and silver platters with caviar. Ernst invited people he considered cool, like the marketing department – not the operations people, whom he thought were rather smelly.'

Heidi Fitzpatrick recalls how Leander disappeared on a holiday and ran up big bills on her corporate credit card. When another member of the finance team went through the bill striking out her personal expenditure, she was not happy. It was her company – she could do what she wanted. She only backed down when he pointed out how dimly the accountants who examine a company's figures before any stock market flotation would view such practices.

'These guys needed to be house-trained in terms of what was appropriate,' says one banker who had dealings with Leander and Malmsten. But he believes they were products of a time when banks like his were simply too free with their money. 'For them, capital was infinitely cheap. In a sense they were like rock stars – money was thrown at them and they did not care where it came from.'

To Malmsten and Leander, and many of their senior staff, boo was a big company with big ambitions. 'If I want to go to New York, I'll go to New York,' is how one onlooker sums up the attitude. But by the autumn, with none of those ambitions yet fulfilled, it had already burnt up a lot of its investors' cash. Internal company documents show that just in August $18.5 million went out of the door.

Of that money, $2.3 million went on PR and marketing, and a hefty $9.8 million was lumped together under the heading 'Capital Expenditure'. That was a handy place for various extravagances. It included the purchase of a stack of laptops – more careful companies would have leased them; indeed, boo later tried to stem the red ink by selling them and leasing them back. There were also huge fees for a company in the United States to undertake vast amounts of imaging – picturing a product from every angle so that it could be revolved on a computer screen by the customer.

The structure of a multinational retailer had been built but the shop was still closed for business. So, for instance, call centre staff had been employed from the spring but did nothing until the late autumn, at a cost of almost $2 million. But amidst the continued delays in getting the site airborne, one thing inspired the founders – their vision of the broad sunlit uplands awaiting boo. The spreadsheet containing the forecasts of where the company would be in four years showed it grabbing a big slice of a fast-growing online market.

Back at the end of 1998 JP Morgan had set its best analysts to work on producing sales forecasts for boo. By the financial year beginning April 2003, the analysts agreed, overall sales would climb to $1 billion. This put any worries about a few million dollars here or there on the marketing budget in their proper perspective.

That autumn Alison Conway was part of a team that re-examined the forecasts in the business plan. They decided that the numbers were a little optimistic and revised them downwards. This was not a message Ernst Malmsten wanted to hear. 'He had sold a certain number to the investors,' she says, 'and he wanted to make the forecasts add up to that number.' But the backers, who throughout boo's history were more like absentee landlords, were now getting just a little bit concerned. By September over $70 million of their money had been spent and they wanted to know whether it might be possible to sell the odd pair of sneakers. Boo responded by hauling in more consultants from McKinsey and the Boston Consulting Group to advise on how to get the site launched.

By now the technical team was working extraordinary hours. Mark Deal joined the team at the end of August when he was told that the launch was a week away. It stayed like that until November, and the hours mounted as each deadline was missed. Deal remembers working one 26-hour day – he simply did not go home. In October, as the final push gathered pace, Dave Sag reminded the company that he was about to depart on a long-planned holiday with his girlfriend. 'They offered me £10,000 in cash and promised to promote me if I postponed my holiday.' But he still went on holiday – and was promoted when he returned.

What struck Mark Deal when he arrived at boo was that the site was just trying to do far too much. It was to make extensive use of software called Flash, which enabled spectacular animations to appear on the site. Customers would need to have a web browser that incorporated Flash if they were to get access to boo.com. The market research department had worked out that 80 per cent of internet users had Flash. The people in the technical team, many of whom did not have it on their own computers at home, were not convinced.

'We were told the site was aimed at the cash rich and time poor and they would all have the latest computer equipment,' says Mark Deal. He and other members of the technical team told the people over in Carnaby Street that Flash would make the site very slow. 'But the business just wanted a site that would make a tremendous splash. They had promised that to their investors and we were just told to deliver.' The rift between the technical team and the rest of the business grew wider. 'We just did not understand what was causing all the delays,' admits a member of the marketing team. 'And we thought that the techies were just moaning about the difficulties in the way techies do.'

Finally, on 4 November 1999, boo.com went live. In the run-up to the big day Kajsa Leander's sister had been employed to produce a video giving a flavour of the event. Nowadays many members of the boo diaspora have a copy of it tucked away in a drawer. One tape has been shown to members of a particularly stuffy consulting firm, rather as if it were a National Geographic film about the bizarre rituals of a South Sea island culture.

Boo, The Movie is a cross between an edgily cut rock video and a home movie about jolly japes in the student dorm, but it paints a compelling picture of the company's culture. The video cuts quickly between the wacky guys and girls in boo's various offices as the launch day approaches. Ernst Malmsten is seen being cool and delphic, as his young assistants hang on his every word. Kajsa Leander is being made up for a television appearance. And Patrik Hedelin says something totally incomprehensible to the camera.

The sense of euphoria on launch morning is captured, with staff drinking champagne and a man from Benetton smiling as he sees that his firm's investment is being put to good use. Over at the Holborn offices, where junior members of the technical team gathered round a speakerphone without a camera crew in attendance, the atmosphere was rather different. 'A lot of cynical programmers were standing round saying, "this will never fly",' remembers Dave Sag. One of them stood rolling a huge joint on the rack of servers that would deliver the site to an expectant public.

As the boo crew chanted a countdown in the Carnaby Street office, Ernst Malmsten pressed a button to fire boo into the firmament. And the site promptly crashed. More champagne was drunk while the problem was fixed. Soon the site was up and running again, and the staff were rushing to see who could buy something first. Kajsa Leander went on CNN to trumpet boo's arrival. However, it was immediately clear that the Jeremiahs in the technical team had a point. Charlotte Neser returned to her desk to find e-mails from customers complaining that the site was painfully slow. Gary Varley from the finance team went home that evening and visited the site using his home PC with its 56k modem – the fastest connection most people would have at that time.

The boo experience launched with a dramatic opening – an animation of a hockey player sweeping across the screen. That took five minutes on Varley's computer. It was another three minutes before the home page loaded. Research shows that most people will not wait more than twenty seconds for a web page to load. This was more like eight minutes. And for many computer users the site was completely inaccessible. It turned out that Flash was not as widespread as boo had believed. For Apple Macintosh users – a minority, but one with a big presence in the media – the news was even worse. They could not use the site at all. And the woman at the centre of the site proved a severe disappointment. With a 56k modem Miss Boo just stood there lamely rather than animating as promised.

Across the dot.com industry everyone was agog to see how boo would fare. Its arrogance had won it few friends, but on the other hand everyone was aware that a successful launch would give the whole sector a boost. At lastminute.com the Chief Technology Officer Dominic Cameron was aghast at what he saw. 'It was so graphics intensive it was bound not to work. If you didn't have the right software installed you couldn't get in. It's like inviting guests to your home, then telling them to go away because their clothes aren't smart enough.'

In the days after the launch the technical team worked more long hours trying to iron out the 396 bugs in the site. Meanwhile, everyone waited for the first news about sales. When the numbers began to come in three or four days later they were poor. In the UK orders were in the hundreds, not the thousands that had been expected. In other markets, they were even more sparse. Most of the customers appeared to be buying at around lunchtime – it seemed that only those with access to high-speed connections at work could get into the shop. Not everyone saw this as a problem. 'For an e-commerce site we were doing fine,' one member of the management team told me. 'OK, nothing like as good as the investors had been promised – but hey, those numbers were always designed to sell the company.' Cold comfort for those who had risked large sums on the promise of healthy revenues.

Those investors received a memo from Ernst Malmsten after the first week of operations. He admitted that there were technical problems – 'from the outset we knew the site contained specific flaws' – and said that these had affected sales. He conceded that not everyone could use the site: 'The hi-tech nature of boo.com's web technology – specifically the need for Flash and a recent browser – necessarily means that the site does exclude a predefined audience.' In other words, after months of delays, boo had launched with a site that was both a technical and marketing disaster. But Malmsten remained relentlessly upbeat, promising 'substantial performance improvements' in the site over the coming weeks.

In its first month boo sold about $200,000 worth of stock, from which its profit was roughly $100,000. But that November it spent around $20 million. Unless sales took off like a rocket, the company was going to run out of cash very quickly. Gary Varley in the finance department could see that the situation was grim but was told not to let others in on the bad news.

As the outlook darkened, relations at the top were turning sour. The issue which caused a rift between Malmsten and Leander, and their fellow Swede Patrik Hedelin was those magic letters IPO. The company had always been determined to float on the London Stock Exchange or perhaps on New York's high-tech Nasdaq exchange. For too many dot.coms a flotation, promising waves of cash from eager new shareholders, often seemed the only aim of the business. The original target had been to float in September, but even in these heady days you had to have some revenues to talk about, even if you had no profits. But Hedelin was still telling his colleagues as Christmas approached that an IPO would be coming soon and it would value boo at $2 billion. For staff with stock options based on a valuation a fraction of that figure, there was the prospect of bumper profits. Life in Carnaby Street might be gloomy now, but think of the upside.

When I called Hedelin in Sweden a year after his departure from the company he told me he was coming to London to seek funding for a new venture. We arranged to meet at the Sugar Club, a restaurant a few yards from the boo offices and another favourite of its executive class. Between mouthfuls of the restaurant's trademark fusion food he told me how he had grown unhappy with JP Morgan, boo's original fairy godmother. 'I was displeased with the service we were getting from them during the second round of funding. And I was not sure they were the right bank to take us through IPO.' As early as the summer of 1999, boo was being courted by rivals like Goldman Sachs: 'Goldman told us that they were so excited that someone at last understood that e-tailing was a global business,' says Hedelin. So he talked to Malmsten and Leander and they agreed to hold a beauty contest, inviting the big banks to show off their best frocks and talk about their ambitions to travel and meet people – or in this case sell boo to a willing investment community.

The banks were told that they would have to pitch in New York. 'We thought their American divisions had more experience,' explains Patrik Hedelin. But Credit Suisse First Boston ended up sending its London team out to New York to make their presentation. One of the bankers found it bizarre to travel so far to talk to people based just a few miles from his office.

Nothing came of this process because even investment bankers desperate to launch any company onto the market could see that boo was in no shape to sell shares. But during the beauty contest a JP Morgan banker tried to ring Hedelin on his mobile phone and found that it was being looked after by a Goldman Sachs security man. The bank, which had done so much to give boo a start in life, was furious about this disloyalty. 'They were under the mistaken impression that I had promised them the IPO,' says Patrik Hedelin.

In any case, JP Morgan and the investors were becoming increasingly agitated by what they saw as Hedelin's failure to exert control over boo's finances. They pressed for his removal. By now, Ernst Malmsten had also begun to decide that his old friend and backer was something of a liability. Hedelin was told he had to go. The company dressed up his departure by stressing that he had a wife and two children at home in Stockholm and had grown tired of commuting weekly to London. Even in the dot.com world, 'he wants to spend more time with his family' was a useful euphemism. Later, Hedelin and JP Morgan were keen to blame each other for what happened to boo. But as one of the investors wryly puts it, 'There was plenty of blame to go round – enough for both of them.'

Ernst was falling out with a lot of people. Tony Barsham had been involved with boo almost from the start and was now Vice-President for Operations. He was an experienced consultant who had been rung by Malmsten and Leander back in the summer of 1998 for advice on the systems that they would need. He had joined them and had been an enthusiastic exponent of the boo vision. At 41 he was a good ten years older than just about everybody else at boo and was seen by many as a calm and steady influence. But by December 1999 he had had enough. Others say that he had a huge row with Ernst Malmsten – all that he will confirm is that there were differences of opinion: 'We agreed mutually that it was time for me to go. I was feeling pretty worn out by it all.'

By now the company's headquarters had moved into spacious new offices around the corner in Regent Street, allowing the whole technology team to be together in Carnaby Street. But morale was sinking. Gary Varley and Heidi Fitzpatrick, who had both arrived with such high hopes, were disillusioned. In January Varley was concerned that that the company could run out of money any day. 'We'd get money in from the investors and it would go straight out to the creditors.' He had no faith in the ability of Leander and Malmsten to turn things round: 'They just had no leadership skills.' By February, more people were leaving and many of the rest had decided there was not much point in working. 'We were out every lunchtime getting shit-faced,' is how Heidi Fitzpatrick puts it. 'There was no management and we all went home at six instead of working all hours.'

Then came the first sackings. Desperate to work out what could be chucked overboard to keep the ship afloat, executives focused on *Boom*, the online magazine. Seventy people were made redundant. Some of their colleagues were envious. 'They got a decent package,' says Alison Conway, 'people were saying can I go too?' The company was at last trying to show that it was making a real effort to trim costs. Unfortunately, the job cuts sent a different message to the media and to the investors. They saw it as a signal that confidence in the eventual success of the project was ebbing away.

Another problem was that boo was sitting on $15 million worth of stock – and in the highly perishable world of high fashion sportswear some of it was already going out of fashion. Sitting on valuable merchandise had not been part of the company's original business plan. The idea had been that products would speed their way from the supplier through the boo operation to the customer with barely a pause for breath. But that meant that boo was asking the fashion business to move its logistics into the twenty-first century. It was difficult enough making boo's own systems work. Asking suppliers, which often had creaking systems, to move at internet speed, was too much. So if customers were to receive their orders within days of clicking on the site, boo had to hold plenty of stock.

But there were some reasons to be cheerful. Sales improved towards the end of January after some barren weeks. By offering discounts of up to 40 per cent, boo persuaded more people to start buying. It was a dangerous move for a company that wanted to be a destination shopping experience, not a bargain basement. 'The whole basis of their original agreement with suppliers was that discounts would be very limited,' says one of the investors. But Ernst Malmsten took the best day's figures and trumpeted them at a First Tuesday meeting as evidence that boo was on the way up.

And in February the man many hoped would be boo's saviour arrived in Regent's Street. After Patrik Hedelin left, JP Morgan pressed for the appointment of a Finance Director who could finally instil the discipline that boo so desperately needed. The man chosen was Dean Hawkins, the Finance Director at Adidas. Now the backers hoped that a grown-up executive from a grown-up company would make all the difference.

'The investors wanted someone with grey hair or no hair – and Dean was losing his fast,' says Charlotte Neser. By now she had risen to the post of Vice-President Europe, and was still convinced that the boo idea could work. She hoped that the balding Mr Hawkins could instil some financial discipline while her marketing team set about boosting sales.

His new colleagues were enthused. 'Everyone wanted to work with Dean,' remembers Heidi Fitzpatrick. But it soon became clear that Dean did not want to work at boo. He just sat in his office with his head in his hands, looking like a man who could not quite believe what he had walked into. He told one banker close to the company that he had been sold a pup and should have done his homework more carefully. Within weeks Hawkins had gone to a job at another internet company. For some who had steadfastly believed that all was well this was a grim moment.

By this time Gary Varley from the finance department had also left the company. His colleagues saw his departure as another bad sign. After all, Varley had seen the figures and knew the true state of the company's finances. Boo had always planned to come back to its investors to seek new funding in the spring and that need was getting ever more urgent. Suppliers were beginning to ask difficult questions about when they were going to get paid. For Heidi Fitzpatrick it was also time to go: 'I could see that this was just going to be a horrible disaster.' Fitzpatrick left and returned to the City as an investment analyst covering internet stocks. Her dream of relinquishing the rigid framework of a traditional workplace had been abandoned. Perhaps somewhere with structure and discipline might not be such a bad place after all. In any case, things had changed while she was away. She didn't need to replace the suits she had burned; her new employer, Lehman Brothers, had decided to adopt the dress-down culture of the dot.coms.

As March ended, boo's press office was getting ever more calls from journalists enquiring whether the company was going to get the funding that it needed to keep going. Alison Crombie was putting on a brave face. 'I told them the money was coming. I was 75 per cent sure that was the case. After all, it seemed ridiculous to think that the investors who had put so much money in would just pull out.' For boo's investors, the time had come to play double or quits.

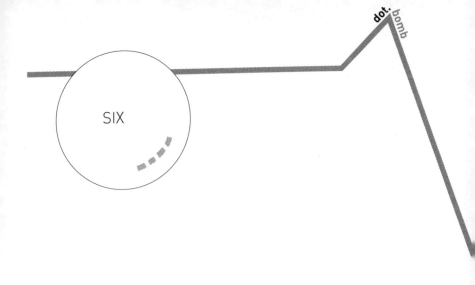

Party time

IF SOMEONE EVER DECIDES to erect blue plaques marking the historic sites of Britain's dot.com revolution, then the Alphabet Bar in London's Soho should be their first stop. On the first Tuesday of October 1998, 80 people gathered here for a cocktail party. They chatted, drank a few glasses of wine, swapped business cards and agreed to meet the following month. And so First Tuesday was born.

From that original meeting grew an organization that was to spawn many of the dot.com investments of the following eighteen months and itself grow into a multinational business. The excitement attending its rapid expansion, the ever higher valuations put on its business, followed by the bitter break-down in relations between its founders and its eventual disintegration also make it a handy metaphor for the whole dot.com phenomenon.

The four people who came together to create First Tuesday were typical of the dot.com generation. They were young overachievers, desperate for their skills to be recognized and impatient with any organization that could not offer them rapid advancement. They wanted to kick-start the online revolution in London; they were also quite interested in making substantial amounts of money.

Adam Gold read history at Cambridge and then became an investment banker with Credit Suisse First Boston. 'I hated it,' he says, ' I was a fish out of water.' In 1998, still in his mid-twenties, Gold quit banking. He decided to try and use some of his contacts in the internet world which he had garnered while at CSFB to start his own business. He flew to San Francisco and spent a month networking furiously. He met a lot of the movers and shakers in Silicon Valley's dot.com scene – people like Mike Moritz, an expatriate Welshman who was a senior partner at the venture capital firm Sequoia Capital and had given Yahoo its initial funding. 'It was the right time and I'm the right kind of guy to just have the guts and go and speak to these people,' says Gold.

Before he flew to San Francisco in August, Gold had met Nick Denton, then starting his own dot.com in London. Denton was a journalist who had got his first break by simply turning up in Eastern Europe in 1989 just as Communism was collapsing, and volunteering his services to various British newspapers. His career had taken him to the *Financial Times*, where he had covered the collapse of Barings. Later, he moved to a job as the paper's technology correspondent in Silicon Valley. Denton was another of that breed of journalist who eventually found it just too frustrating to be interviewing people of his age who had gone out and started multimillion-dollar companies. 'I remember meeting this guy in Silicon Valley who was 25 and whose internet company had made him a multimillionaire,' he says. 'I thought he was smart – but no smarter than me.' By the time Denton met Gold he had left the *FT* to launch a venture called Moreover.com, which aimed to be a kind of digital news agency, tailoring news from different sources and channelling it to websites which needed a news feed.

Gold and Denton hit it off. Their ambitions meshed, and they spent lunch talking impatiently about why London could not be more like Silicon Valley where everything happened at the speed of light. Why, for instance, were there no networking organizations like the Valley's 'Digital People'? Events where entrepreneurs and venture capitalists could meet in relaxed surroundings provided the social glue which made Silicon Valley work. In London, there was nothing like that.

In September Gold returned from his trip to the West Coast, inspired by the buzz of the fastest moving place on earth. He caught up with Nick Denton and they agreed to have a go at setting up their own network. They co-opted another friend of Nick's, someone who did not really need to work. Mark Davies was a social anthropologist by training and an early beneficiary of the dot.com boom. In New York in 1995 he had started Metrobeat, one of the first city listings sites. He had quickly beaten the traditional media in the race to establish the city's most comprehensive online entertainment guide. Metrobeat was then bought by another online listings company, CitySearch, making Davies an internet millionaire. He stayed with his new bosses for a couple of years, but in the autumn of 1998 he had come to London and had some time on his hands.

The three of them set to work putting together a guest list for their first meeting. 'The list was basically people we knew,' says Adam Gold. 'But the whole idea was that as it grew it would be open – not invitation only – and it would be relaxed in that Californian style.' The trio decided they needed extra help. Adam Gold called an old friend from his student days, Brent Hoberman, and asked him to get involved. But Hoberman was far too busy preparing for the imminent launch of lastminute.com's website. He suggested someone he thought would have the contacts and sheer undiluted energy to make a difference.

Julie Meyer was an American who, at the age of six, had told her father that she wanted to be the first female President. As she grew up in California and Chicago, it was one ambition that had faded. It was replaced by a determination to make a mark in the business world – an ambition that was reinforced by a devotion to the works of Ayn Rand, the American novelist who became a guru for believers in a meritocratic capitalism. She had come to Paris to study at the Sorbonne, and then worked as a consultant for high-tech companies like Motorola and Hewlett Packard. An MBA at INSEAD, the ritzy business school at Fontainebleau outside Paris, had given a final sheen to her CV. She remains in touch with many of her MBA class – just one of the networks which this intense, voluble woman manages to maintain.

Meyer arrived in Britain late in 1997. 'I met this guy who said, "The people you need to know in London are Tim Jackson and Brent Hoberman."' Tim Jackson ended up offering Meyer the job that Hoberman had just left after their falling out. Instead she started work as Tom Teichman's first employee at New Media Investors, the venture capital firm set up to invest in internet opportunities. There, in the summer of 1998, she did meet Brent Hoberman as one of the NMI team helping to get lastminute.com established.

When she got the call from Adam Gold, Meyer was excited by the invitation to help plan this dot.com party. She could add a lot more names to the list, and as a venture capitalist at a company desperate to track down new investment opportunities, she stood to benefit. Meyer claims that as soon as she joined the team she adjusted the direction in which it was heading. 'Adam wanted it to be just cool, hip people – the "digerati". I said it should be more inclusive.'

They chose the Alphabet Bar as a venue simply because it belonged to a friend of Nick Denton. It was one of the hippest bars in Soho, the venue earlier that year for the first official absinthe tasting session in London since the 1920s. Now all they had to do was hope somebody turned up. Anybody who has ever organized a party knows that feeling of dread as the hour on the invitation arrives and you find out just how popular you are. But this event fulfilled all their expectations.

Out of the 120 people who had been invited, 80 packed into the small basement bar. Just as an extraordinary number of people claim to have been at the Cavern when the Beatles first played, so everyone who is anyone in the dot.com world believes they were at the Alphabet Bar that night. But among the guests were venture capitalists like Vic Morris of Atlas Ventures, later to fund the ill-fated Clickmango, and Dafna Ciechanover of Excite, the internet portal. 'There was a real buzz, there was something in the air,' says Adam Gold. He climbed on a table and made a short speech. It felt like the start of something that London had been waiting for.

Afterwards, the four founders headed off to dinner at Circus, a restaurant that would later be the scene of many an extravagant evening for the people behind boo.com. Then they went back to Mark Davies' West End flat to discuss what should happen next. All were agreed that they would do it again. 'We discussed how exclusive it should be and we decided we needed a speaker,' says Julie Meyer. 'We said, "Let's get Brent Hoberman and Martha Lane Fox – they're just launching their dot.com."'

The next party was to be on the first Tuesday in November and the event would be called First Tuesday. There was a new venue, the offices of Syzygy, a web design agency. 'A friend had shown me round Syzygy's really funky offices near Oxford Circus,' says Adam Gold. 'The owner, John Hunt, let us use the place for nothing. It was really instrumental in helping First Tuesday grow, having somewhere trendy like that which everyone wanted to go to.'

Hunt was soon to start a business with Gold and play a controversial role in the First Tuesday saga.

Brent Hoberman and Martha Lane Fox gave what one observer describes as 'the worst, yet most effective presentation I've ever seen' at First Tuesday's second meeting. They shared a microphone and continually finished each other's sentences as the story of lastminute.com's birth tumbled out in a rather incoherent fashion. 'But the audience was gripped because they were all thinking, "these are people just like me – and they've done it",' says that observer, John Browning. The former editor of *Wired* UK had missed the first meeting because he was abroad. His magazine had folded eighteen months earlier at a time when Britain's internet revolution was stubbornly failing to ignite. Now, as he surveyed the First Tuesday crowd, he sensed that the fuse was at last about to be lit.

Browning soon found himself asked to help guide First Tuesday's progress. Mark Davies had been talking to his tax advisor. He was told he had a choice between staying in the UK and paying over a large slice of his fortune, or leaving the country for a while. Davies decided to go travelling in Africa. His departure deprived First Tuesday of the one founder of whom all the others still share a good opinion. 'Just a really, really sweet guy,' as Julie Meyer puts it. Perhaps he was wise to get out when he did

The three remaining founders asked John Browning to join them. He was something of a contrast to them – in his forties, settled in an elegant Islington home with his wife and two children, plugged into the internet scene but in a more donnish, laid back kind of way. He was enthusiastic about the project but it did not threaten to take over his life.

His arrival was to bring the first real clash about who actually owned First Tuesday. While just about everyone else saw it as a cocktail party, nothing more or less, Adam Gold says he always had an inkling that it might become a business: 'Two weeks before we even started we were sitting around and I said, "Listen, this could turn into a business, so lets work out how to parcel out the equity right now." The others said, "Bugger off – you can't be serious."'

Later, there was to be a lively discussion about what stake John Browning should get in the venture. Browning insists that when he joined he had no inkling that this was more than the hottest party in town; any discussion of equity would have appeared outlandish. But Julie Meyer says that she had to put up a fight with Nick Denton and Adam Gold to ensure that the new man got a fair stake. John Browning says he eventually became aware that something was going on behind the scenes. 'When the equity discussion started I just said, "You guys go away and figure what you want to give me" – I was really not that bothered.' The four of them each ended up with about 20 per cent of the company.

In all the arguments over money and strategy that were to cripple First Tuesday later on, Adam Gold always had one trump card. It was he, after all, who had come up with the original idea. But one person disputes that. Jim Clark was an American who had worked for the Clinton administration and then came to London, where he ran a non-profit organization called the World Technology Network. In 1998 he started planning a new institution that would aim to encourage high-tech entrepreneurship in Britain. In a briefing paper on the idea he talked of how the emergence of New York's Silicon Alley had in part been due to the Friday beer-drinking evenings organized by the city's New Media Association. Then in the summer of 1998 he came across Adam Gold, and decided that this was a young man with the qualifications and energy to make it happen. He offered him the job of running his new organization. Gold said he needed time to consider the move.

Gold prevaricated through the autumn months. Even in November, the month after First Tuesday launched, he was still e-mailing Hunt about the job offer. He said he had not reached a definitive conclusion but was not sure that he want to be involved in a non-profit organization: 'I have always imagined that the optimal time to work in a non-profit organization is after having "made the bucks", and with this, the associated experience.' Soon afterwards, Clark was invited to a First Tuesday event and was surprised to find that Gold was one of the founders. 'I went up to him and said how great the event was – and he was literally just speechless with embarrassment. He just gulped and walked away.' However, Clark was relieved that he never employed Gold. He felt that Gold was solely intent on becoming an internet millionaire rather than changing the climate for entrepreneurship in Britain.

By early 1999 First Tuesday was getting bigger and bigger and was making a difference to that climate. A system had been devised to identify what role you played in the dot.com world. As they filed in, guests were given a sticky label – entrepreneurs had a green dot on theirs, venture capitalists had a red dot, and for the fee-hungry consultants, lawyers and others desperate to feed off the new industry there was a yellow dot. Amongst the speakers at the early meetings were Louise Kehoe, the respected *Financial Times* Silicon Valley correspondent, and Rikki Tahta who was in the process of setting up a venture capital fund with Simon Murdoch, the man whose business had become amazon.co.uk. But the speakers were not what attracted an ever larger crowd to First Tuesday.

'Right from the start, people were using it as a platform for doing business,' says John Browning. 'The speeches were not that interesting, but deals were getting done.' It grew by word of mouth – or viral marketing as the digerati liked to call it. Just as a hot nightclub becomes the place to be seen, word got out in the tiny dot.com community that First Tuesday was the hottest ticket in town. If you were a young entrepreneur, you knew it was the best place to go to meet people who might fund you. If you were a venture capitalist, here was an easy way to find out where the technology was heading and who had the brightest ideas.

At most parties, certainly British ones, guests circle the room, looking nervously for a familiar face, and then spend most of their time in one small group. At business functions there may be a hidden agenda – a deal to be done, information to be extracted – but it usually stays hidden amidst the formalities. At First Tuesday everybody's cards were on the table – they were not just here to schmooze, they wanted to be millionaires like those they had read about in the United States. They surged around the room, forming and reforming into different groups. There seemed to be no wallflowers. The different dots helped to break the ice. All over the room, you could see the red dots – the venture capitalists – surrounded by a sea of green dotted entrepreneurs, furiously pitching.

The crowd would be young, casually dressed (except for the lawyers), and in-your-face. I remember leaving one meeting with a stack of business cards and a condom. A young man was handing them out as a promotional tool for his online consumer opinion site. Adam Gold makes big claims for the impact that the organization had: 'First Tuesday has been instrumental in changing attitudes in the UK. Everything from the dress-down culture, to the pushiness, to the open exchange of business cards.'

By spring the Syzygy office where the parties were still taking place was bursting at the seams. Nick Denton used his contacts at the *Financial Times* to get the first major press coverage of the event and interest took another quantum leap forward. Now John Browning was becoming aware that this was more than a hobby: 'The attendance figures were soaring. I said, "We're going to have to start tracking this." We were having to control entry at the door. We needed to turn it into a business.' The parties moved to the shiny headquarters of Bloomberg, the financial news service. Soon the crush was getting dangerous once more – and then the caravan moved on to even bigger venues like Lord's Cricket Ground. The location of each meeting was e-mailed to guests just a couple of days before the event – but still plenty of gatecrashers managed to find their way in.

It was in April 1999 that Julie Meyer began to realize that dollar signs could soon be attached to First Tuesday. At this time, say friends, there were growing strains between Meyer and her boss Tom Teichman at New Media Investors, partly because she was devoting so much time to First Tuesday. So she was looking around for an alternative employer. Meyer herself refuses to talk about this.

However, she does confirm that she had a breakfast meeting with Christopher Spray of Atlas Ventures, one of the most influential figures in London's venture capital industry. He told her that First Tuesday was a business and that he would consider investing $1 million for up to 40 per cent of the company. 'I didn't even think about it as a commercial venture until Christopher Spray made that offer,' she says, her eyes lighting up with excitement. 'It hit me right between the eyes. I said to myself, "Good lord, this man thinks I'm backable, that's unbelievable!"' According to John Browning, Spray, who had been a frequent visitor to First Tuesday, had understood the value of a network: 'He said, "You have the attention of the 3000 most important people in my universe. I am sure you will find some way of making money from that."'

The next year of First Tuesday's life was to be spent puzzling out just how the hottest party in town could start making money. The problem was that the founders seemed incapable of uniting around one vision – instead they spent much of their time at each other's throats. The absence of the two people who had come up with the original idea did not help. Adam Gold and Nick Denton were each working to start their own internet firms – and over the next few months both were to depart for San Francisco. Gold left in April with John Hunt to set up a web technology business, Obongo. Denton had gone by September to establish a San Francisco base for Moreover.com, his news feed company that was now up and running.

Both were living proof of the power of First Tuesday, in that they had received backing from venture capitalists who had attended the parties. Moreover.com was backed by Simon Murdoch and Rikki Tahta, partners in the new Episode 1 venture capital fund. Obongo received funding from Atlas Ventures. So from now on Julie Meyer and John Browning would have to shoulder most of the work. The first project was to take First Tuesday across Europe. 'We had been getting calls from people around the world asking whether they could stage an event using the name,' says Browning, 'and at first we were thinking, "You're asking *us* permission to stage a cocktail party in your own city?!"'

Where all the founders agree is that from the summer of 1999 Julie Meyer was the extraordinary force which turned First Tuesday into a global business. She threw in her job at New Media Investors in July and put all of her energy into expanding the organization. From here on, though, Meyer's resentment against her co-founders would grow by the day. Trying to piece together what happened is like talking to the partners in a failed marriage. They see it from very different perspectives.

Late in 2000 I arranged to meet Julie Meyer at Home House, the London club favoured by the dot.com aristocracy. I was her 2.15 appointment in a schedule that was always strained to breaking point. Home House, in a Regency house on Portman Square, is at first sight like any other traditional London club – all wood panelling, high ceilings and discreet staff. Then you notice that the man paging through the *Wall Street Journal* is wearing sandals, shorts and a T-shirt. As I sat in the bar, where large TV screens were tuned in to MTV and the rolling financial news station CNBC, the club's steward arrived from time to time to pass on messages apologizing for Miss Meyer's tardiness. Finally she arrived 45 minutes behind schedule – as ever, in a smart suit rather than dressed down First Tuesday style – and apologized profusely for her lateness.

Immediately it was as if she had been bottling up her resentment about the last eighteen months and was now determined to remove the cork. 'First Tuesday would never have happened as a business if I hadn't left my job and ·

put £50,000 of my savings into it,' she began, and went on to suggest that her absentee colleagues in California had only begun to take an interest again when they realized that they could be sitting on a fortune.

It is impossible to overestimate the destructive role played by personal relationships in First Tuesday's problems. Julie Meyer's extraordinary energy and passionate commitment to First Tuesday are impressive. Nonetheless, you can understand why her colleagues may have found it a little tiring. There were cultural differences between an American who took herself and her role very seriously – and was always ready to say just what she was thinking – and the more reserved, ironic frame of mind of a Nick Denton. Even the American John Browning, a long-term London resident, seemed to have an understated Englishness compared to Meyer. And First Tuesday was not unusual in being rocked by personal antipathies. After all, dot.coms are classic people businesses – and if the people do not gel, neither does the business.

At our meeting Julie Meyer outlined her frenzy of activity in the summer of 1999. She had given herself a September deadline to establish First Tuesday in fifteen cities across Europe – recruiting volunteers to staff each city group, arranging sponsors and making sure that everyone could launch at the same time. 'I was running it from my living room. I'd have piles of paper all over the floor I'd be going round the corner to the internet café to send e-mails. Some Saturday nights I'd sit there having worked maybe a 100 hours that week and say, "Julie, you're doing all this and maybe nobody cares. People are going to laugh at you for thinking that taking a cocktail party across Europe is such a smart idea."'

Then on 7 September the launch of the new pan-European First Tuesday appeared on the front page of the *Wall Street Journal* and nobody was laughing at Julie's big idea.

'It was the most amazing piece of organization I've ever seen,' says John Browning admiringly. The events in London and now across Europe were attracting ever more media interest, which fed through into ever greater numbers of people wanting to be there.

This, remember, was the time when the dot.com boom was beginning to roar. Freeserve had floated, lastminute.com was talking of following it and venture capitalists had huge sums for internet investment burning holes in their pockets.

Julie Meyer, with her blonde hair and blue eyes, was becoming a media star. But relations behind the scenes had not improved. There was still no agreement on how to turn First Tuesday into a proper business. There was a range of ideas. Some of the founders thought it could become an incubator, a newly fashionable type of investment company taking small stakes in dot.coms and helping them to grow. Others believed the future lay in taking a cut from any deal hatched during a First Tuesday event. There was also a view that the real priority was to become a portal – an online presence which internet start-ups would quickly see as the place to go for information and services like recruitment. Ironically, the company that preached the dot.com gospel was slow to establish a credible presence on the Web.

Venture capitalists were already enthusiastic about putting money in. 'We loved First Tuesday,' says Simon Murdoch of Episode 1. 'It had built a global brand without spending any money.' Even in September, when the dot.com boom was just beginning to accelerate, there was already talk of a $20 million valuation on the company. But nobody was going to come up with cash until First Tuesday came up with a clear explanation of its strategy.

And there was now a serious need for cash. First Tuesday had survived this far on a shoestring. It had been given services free or at a discount from people who saw the benefit of being associated with this revolutionary idea. However, staff were now being employed and costs were mounting.

In October another of the key characters in First Tuesday's drama arrived on the scene. It had become obvious that this chaotic but promising adolescent company needed a chief executive if it was to be transformed into a proper business. Reade Fahs had contacted Julie Meyer after First Tuesday's August event offering his services. Fahs, a 39-year-old American, had time and money on his hands, having just retired with a big pay-off after a successful stint at the helm of the opticians Vision Express. He had been enthused by a visit to First Tuesday and, as an experienced manager who had worked in major companies like General Foods, he believed it had an immensely valuable brand. 'It was commerce plus a cause, and I found that tremendously attractive,' he recalls.

Julie Meyer did not follow up the call from Reade Fahs, but at the following month's event he met John Browning who thought he was just what they needed. After a series of interviews with the founders and with

Christopher Spray at Atlas Ventures, Fahs was made chief executive. It was Spray's views that were decisive in the decision to appoint someone whose managerial skills might now give the organization some direction. The hope was that a newcomer could act as a referee between the bickering founders.

Another of the venture capitalists watching from the sidelines says Fahs was just what the organization did *not* need: 'He was a consensus builder – what those people needed was a dictator.' But Fahs was hamstrung from the start by the fact that he was not on the Board. The idea was that this would happen as soon as the company got funding. He now believes there was a simple explanation for that decision. 'There was a power struggle going on between London and California. The guys in California did not want to give London a casting vote by putting me on the board.' The end result was that over the next nine months the man who was supposed to be in charge was not even allowed to vote on what should happen next.

Fahs, John Browning and Julie Meyer all agreed to forego any salary until the funding had been completed. For Meyer that became an increasing strain. 'Not getting paid was a serious problem for me. I'd had big debts from business school and I'd spent the money I took from my New Media Investors job on First Tuesday.' Browning says that, while he would rather have been paid, he did at least have an alternative income from consulting and public speaking.

Relations worsened between Meyer – who felt she was giving her all to First Tuesday – and both Browning and Fahs, whose contributions she regarded as inadequate. The relationship between Fahs and Meyer was difficult from the start, and soon became impossible. She did not like his Midwestern accent or what she regarded as his ignorance about venture capital. Colleagues say she resented the fact that he had been brought in by Christopher Spray who had decided that she would not make a suitable chief executive.

There was also a generational problem between the fireball Meyer and the laid-back Browning. Meyer, single and in her early thirties, could not understand how John Browning could go away on holiday in August when the European launch was imminent. For Browning, in his forties with two children at school, there was a limit to how much he would let his family life be disrupted.

Another relationship was becoming tense. The independent-minded people who had set up First Tuesday events in cities across Europe and further afield were beginning to ask the London headquarters where they stood. The 'city leaders', as London called them, felt they were doing much of the work in building the First Tuesday brand – but where was their payback?

In an attempt to deal with the rising tide of discontent, the city leaders were summoned in December 1999 to a meeting at the Hempel, an ultra chic hotel in West London. After some amiable and enthusiastic discussion about their common ambitions for First Tuesday, they got down to the serious business of money. When Reade Fahs told them that he was prepared to offer them 8 per cent of the equity to share out between them they were not impressed. David Burden, who ran the Birmingham event, recalls the reaction of his colleagues: 'We all felt that First Tuesday was all about the network – London just did not recognize the effort we were all putting in.' The city leaders stormed out of the minimalist Hempel with its maximalist prices and went to a Greek restaurant down the road to nurse their grievances.

Nevertheless, as 1999 drew to a close, First Tuesday's star was shining even brighter. New events were starting around the world, increasing sums were being raised, and the organization had become the first port of call for anyone wanting an insight into the dot.com boom. As well as the monthly free-for-all, which had begun to resemble Freshers' night at a student union, there were now more exclusive events. Discreet dinners were arranged where top names from the subscriber list could meet in a less frenzied atmosphere. So vital was First Tuesday becoming to the dot.com world that its power and financial standing seemed certain to multiply over the coming year.

But Julie Meyer was restless. She knew that Christmas meant London would shut down for a week and even she might be forced to slow down a little. So she headed for Tel Aviv. 'I figured Israel would be one place I might get some work done over Christmas,' she says. She met the local First Tuesday group and also held talks with an internet investment company called Yazam. 'I sat across the table from these Orthodox Jews with big visions who said, as I described what First Tuesday was doing, "Yes, we're doing that too and we've got millions in the bank."'

Meyer recommended to her colleagues that they keep in touch with

Yazam with a view to co-operating in the future. Later, however, she would fight tooth and nail to try to prevent the Israeli company from taking over her baby. She returned from Tel Aviv in a deep depression about the state of First Tuesday, which she believed was facing a serious crisis. 'I wrote an e-mail to the Board on 31 December saying, "We have under £12,000 in the bank, we have no proper website, and we have not achieved any consensus on our strategy." I warned that if we didn't get our act together, we'd end up having to sell ourselves to the highest bidder.'

So in January the company at last started getting serious about pitching to venture capitalists – just what its members had been doing at every party for the last fifteen months. But by now the organization had what was known in the dot.com world as a fast 'burn rate' – in other words, it was eating cash at an alarming speed. With money running low, First Tuesday turned to one of its suitors for some temporary help. Reade Fahs negotiated a $1 million bridge loan with Episode 1, in return for which Rikki Tahta and Simon Murdoch were guaranteed a seat at the table as the venture capital deal was hammered out. The conditions attached to the loan appeared reasonable at the time, but, as a fundraising process which should have been completed in weeks dragged on for months, they eventually gave Tahta and Murdoch the power to close First Tuesday down.

By the middle of February negotiations were delicately poised. The city leaders, still angry over what they regarded as the derisory stake offered to them before Christmas, had driven through a deal which could give them up to 20 per cent of the company. The agreement had been negotiated by Reade Fahs and Julie Meyer. However, it still had to be sold to the other founders who would see their stake in the business diluted. Meanwhile Meyer's relations with John Browning had reached breaking-point, again over his absence. In the middle of the month Meyer e-mailed Adam Gold in California with this startling message about their colleague: 'I would like to propose relieving John Browning of his operational responsibilities at First Tuesday.' She went on to complain that Browning was on holiday again, and that the website – his responsibility – had been dramatically mismanaged. She concluded: 'I cannot continue to work with people who do not understand how competitive this market is, and who believe that it is appropriate to take holidays at a time like this.' Gold replied saying he'd been thinking exactly the same thing and would try to convince Nick Denton that

Browning's role must be downgraded. The idea seems to have been quietly dropped as the horse-trading over the funding deal intensified.

At the end of February Atlas Ventures and Episode 1 were on the verge of signing a deal that would have put $15 million into First Tuesday, valuing the company at an extraordinary $62 million. The day before a key meeting with Atlas, Julie Meyer sent another emotional e-mail to her co-founders pleading with them to accept the concessions that were needed to keep the city leaders onside and finalize the deal with Atlas and Episode 1: 'I've totally and utterly given my life to this company for 8 months and 3500 hours. I really need you both to bend to help me get through this stretch; obviously you can stop me dead in my tracks. We can argue all day long about what is right and what should have happened, but I am near the breaking point, and need to finalize this round so that we can all breathe in and out, and get the job done.'

Denton sent a conciliatory reply: 'I know that I would accept concessions – if you advise – that would otherwise make me fume,' he wrote. 'You are the driving force behind First Tuesday and I trust you to make the right calls.' It seemed that a successful conclusion was now in sight. Atlas and Episode 1 said they were ready to sign up at a price, which even one of the First Tuesday insiders describes as 'higher than we deserved'. But there were to be more twists in this tale.

While Julie Meyer was leading the drive to get funding, Reade Fahs as Chief Executive had to be involved in the presentations to the venture capitalists. Meyer says she became convinced that he was just not up to the job. 'He's a nice guy but he just could not articulate any strategy and he did not understand venture capital at all. People wanted to invest but every time I wheeled Reade out the guys would go cold.' Fahs insists that he always had a clear view of what First Tuesday was about – an organization that had become a vital source of deals for venture capitalists and which could make money out of its role as an intermediary between the entrepreneurs and those who might finance them.

Nevertheless, Meyer was determined to get rid of him. So furious did she become after an internal staff meeting in London early in March that within four hours she was on a plane to San Francisco to talk to Gold and Denton about demoting Fahs. The Chief Executive says there was a different reason for Meyer's anger. 'That meeting was the first time I had overruled Julie –

and she was furious.' Fahs says she then told him that she had to leave to visit a sick relative on the West Coast.

The meeting out in California was also attended by John Hunt, Adam Gold's partner at Obongo, who had a small shareholding in First Tuesday and from now on was to play a bigger part in events. Everyone agreed that Fahs should be moved – perhaps to a job as chief operating officer. The issue of how to shift their Chief Executive rumbled on for the next few months, with all the founders except John Browning agreeing that it was necessary, but failing to unite on how to achieve it.

A few days after the meeting Gold pressed for John Hunt to be brought in as a consultant with a brief to push through the funding deal and move Reade Fahs. Meyer says she was unhappy with this arrangement, especially given the nature of the contract Gold was proposing. 'John Hunt was going to do a month's work in return for shares which at that time were valued at $5 million.' But she says her co-founders outvoted her. Hunt saw his role as trying to sort out a company which was in crisis, with its leading figures at each other's throats and no clear strategy. He laughed when I quoted that $5 million figure at him, maintaining that it was based on a fanciful valuation. He says he deserved some payback, not just for the work he was undertaking in the spring of 2000 but for his role in First Tuesday's early months: 'I was the first person to actually put his hand in his pocket. I not only gave them my Syzygy offices, I paid for the drinks, the microphones, everything.'

The California contingent now proposed a radical change in the search for venture capital. They had decided they did not like some of the conditions in their existing deal and they would now approach a legendary name in Silicon Valley finance. Benchmark Capital was one of the venture capital firms that had made huge sums spotting internet talent in the mid-1990s. The auction firm Ebay was one of its many success stories and its partners were themselves as rich as many of the entrepreneurs they had funded.

In dot.com circles Benchmark had rock star status – if you could drop into conversation that you were talking to them it was like saying Madonna was popping round for tea. The approach was made easier by the fact that one of the senior partners at Atlas, Eric Archambeau, had by now left the London firm to join Benchmark. Nick Denton insists that this was more than a case of being star-struck. They were offering Benchmark a lower valuation than had been sought from Atlas because they thought the West Coast venture capitalists would inject the management skills needed to give the company a real future. The team geared themselves up for what was going to be the presentation of their lives. In early April First Tuesday came to pitch at Benchmark's offices in Sand Hill Road – the Mayfair and Park Lane of Silicon Valley venture capital. It seemed to go well. Again, there were hopes that the prize was at last in their grasp.

Then the Benchmark partners came to First Tuesday's offices in London and everything began to unravel. The venture capital firm was confronted with a series of incoherent presentations from a bunch of people who seemed to have no clear idea of where they were heading. Afterwards, Eric Archambeau of Benchmark went to lunch with Julie Meyer and emerged convinced that this was not a deal his company should do. 'This company has got fucked-up DNA,' he told another of the founders. Meyer insists that the real problem was that Gold, Denton and Hunt were concerned that they would lose too much of their equity under the deal proposed by Benchmark.

The next day John Hunt e-mailed his colleagues with what he called a 'Benchmark Hymn Sheet', a common approach to be taken in response to any awkward questions from journalists about what went wrong. They were to stress that they not been 'comfortable' with Benchmark's approach and in particular what it offered the city leaders but that they looked forward to working with the firm in the future. Some hope.

And now Julie Meyer was at daggers drawn with John Hunt. In mid-April, after the collapse of the Benchmark deal, he circulated a document outlining what he had achieved so far in his consultancy. She sent it straight back with comments in the digital equivalent of red ink. Hunt wrote that the key issue hampering First Tuesday was communication: 'There is a significant element of mistrust and misunderstanding all round, which is driven by people being selective, slothful and occasionally disingenuous in their communications.' Meyer fired straight back: 'I think you should add the impact of some of us living with others' greed and selfishness.'

In his list of achievements Hunt wrote: 'Restore Julie's faith that she would not be fired post-financing!' Underneath, Meyer penned ten furious lines accusing Hunt of contributing to the atmosphere of mistrust: 'If there has been a civil war you have helped to create it.'

Later she tore into him over his failure to sort out her future position and salary: 'It seems rather unbelievable to me for you who have charged $5 million for one month's worth of work to be nickel and diming me who has worked 4000+ hours with no pay for 9 months which has had the unfortunate result of throwing my personal financial situation into ruin.' Friends of Hunt say his task had been made impossible after Meyer's lunch with Archambeau of Benchmark.

So it would be fair to say that as May approached, with money running out and no funding agreed, all was not peace and light at First Tuesday. And in the real world things had started to turn nasty. In the weeks after the last-minute.com IPO, shares in internet companies started tumbling. Venture capitalists, intent on recouping their initial investments through quick stock market flotations, were wondering nervously whether that exit might now be barred. And there were rumours that one prominent dot.com in the online fashion business was close to collapse.

This is how Julie Meyer summarized her position: 'I'm dealing with greed in the founders, incompetence in the management team, the market is correcting on itself and the network is wondering where the leadership is.' And, surprise, surprise, when they knocked on the doors at Atlas and Episode 1 again, they found a rather frosty atmosphere. The British venture capitalists were not amused to have been left at the altar in favour of some flash Harrys from across the pond.

'It was a bit like being dumped on a date,' says Simon Murdoch. 'They got seduced by the glamour of a Silicon Valley firm – and then they came back to us cap in hand.' It was all the more remarkable that Christopher Spray of Atlas agreed to resume negotiations, albeit at a lower valuation. Not only had Atlas been jilted, but the affair had also involved one of its own former partners, Eric Archambeau.

As the negotiations with Atlas and Episode 1 stumbled on through May, the market in high-tech stocks took further sickening lurches downwards. Venture capitalists were losing their appetite for a firm that was still hazy about whether it was going to be an online jobs market, an international network of dot.com people, or an investment vehicle. Then Episode 1's backers in New York, Chase Manhattan, suddenly started telling Rikki Tahta and Simon Murdoch to hold back. As they watched their American dot.com deals turn sour, Chase had little appetite for this British adventure.

Both Atlas and Epsiode 1 decided to walk away from the table. Not only had they tired of the constant bitching between the founders, they had also begun to question whether the whole First Tuesday idea worked as a business. 'It seemed to be a great idea, the kind of concept a consultant might come up with,' says one of the venture capitalists. 'But it breaks down on the detail. Who owns the intellectual property that is First Tuesday? Who owns the guy who turns up to the event in Johannesburg?' Questions were also being asked about the sky-high price that Julie Meyer was seeking: 'Julie was just pulling these ridiculous numbers out of the air.'

By now some of the dot.com movers and shakers were deciding that First Tuesday was no longer a priority entry in their electronic organizers. Mark Simon, an entrepreneur who had just sold his computer company, visited a First Tuesday event in the summer of 1999, and like many others, ended up starting a new internet business. But his was a rival organization called thechemistry.com. Its pitch was that it was more exclusive – you had to be screened by the organizers before you could attend. Soon you were more likely to bump into leading venture capitalists at thechemistry than at First Tuesday.

Even worse for Julie Meyer and her colleagues, Episode 1 now wanted its loan repaid. Suddenly First Tuesday was not just in danger of missing out on a good funding deal, it faced liquidation. 'I went to sleep for two months with Simon Murdoch's words ringing in my ears,' remembers Meyer. 'He said "Do you think I have any problem throwing you into liquidation, Julie? I have no problem."' Episode 1 accepts that it was obliged to 'put a gun to First Tuesday's head'.

By now the organization was looking for what was described in the minutes of a board meeting as 'salvage financing'. Just about every source of funding in London and around the world was canvassed, with no result. At the end of May the company had negative net assets and its lawyers were warning the directors that there was a danger that they could soon be trading while insolvent, a serious offence.

John Browning felt that the end could be nigh: 'The clock was ticking.' But Browning was philosophical about the situation. He had not joined First Tuesday expecting to make a fortune from it. 'I was not that upset – so a wine and cheese party had ended up not making any money.'

That was not the view of the other founders who felt that an awful lot, financially and emotionally, was now at stake. At a board meeting on 27 June they agreed that the most likely option was now a sale to the highest bidder, just as Julie Meyer had warned six months earlier. There were several potential candidates, including the internet news magazines *Red Herring* and *Industry Standard*, and the Israeli company which had earlier been considered as a potential partner, Yazam.

A sale would mean that the founders' dream of building a viable business on their own terms was over. But if First Tuesday collapsed, their reputations would suffer. Adam Gold and Nick Denton, concentrating on building their own businesses in California, must have been acutely aware of that issue. John Browning, formerly of *The Economist* and *Wired*, remembers a discussion with Denton, the one-time *Financial Times* writer: 'We were talking about what happened if First Tuesday went broke and we said to each other, "Ooh, I'd love to write that story!"'

But there was one last venture capital avenue open. Venture Partners was a Norwegian-based company run by Karl-Christian Agerup, who also ran the First Tuesday event in Oslo. His company had stakes in lastminute.com and another prominent internet start-up, Stepstone. He had been in talks with Julie Meyer for some time.

Suddenly, by the next board meeting on 2 July a deal was on the table. Agerup and another venture capital fund Catalyst, which had been approached by Reade Fahs, were talking of putting in $7 million. 'Discussions went well,' said the board minutes, 'and a term sheet was agreed and signed this morning. Closing expected early on this week, with money in the bank shortly thereafter.' Phew! At the last minute it seemed that an independent First Tuesday with a healthy bank account was a reality.

Regardless, there was still time for some more bloodletting. Straight after the board Julie Meyer fired off another sizzling e-mail to Nick Denton, complaining that he had failed to deliver on a promise that they would finally act to remove Reade Fahs as Chief Executive. 'Pretty much every strategic move that continues to need to be made in this company whether it's hiring of city leaders to country managers or raising a co-investment fund I proposed aeons ago, and nobody listened to me,' she thundered. 'I'm beginning to think this is a gender issue, and frankly there have been a LOT of observers to the situation who have been saying that for a long time, and I have always tried to say it wasn't.' E-mail may be a marvellous new communications tool – but, as these missives burning their way across the ether between London and California show, its instant nature often serves to inflame passions rather than cool them.

On 12 July Karl-Christian Agerup of Venture Partners called Julie Meyer to say he had just had a meeting with his colleagues at Catalyst and they had agreed to delay the deal by a week, just to get some details sorted out. According to Meyer, this caused unnecessary panic in the First Tuesday offices, which had seen so many potential saviours walk away over the preceding months.

Reade Fahs admits that he was worried by this turn of events. 'We were close to running out of money. We needed options.' He had been keeping in touch with Yazam, and now he called the Israeli company and told its executives they needed to act fast. Separately, Lucy Reis, who was First Tuesday's Chief Financial Officer and also shared a flat with Meyer, was also extremely concerned. After a shouting match with her flatmate, Reis called John Hunt in California to tell him there was a problem. Hunt then called Israel and worked to convince Yaacov Ben-Yaacov of Yazam that a deal could be done.

The one thing that Julie Meyer was determined to avoid was an outright sale of her baby – and that was what a deal with Yazam would mean. 'I felt that we had a real chance to build a sustainable business on our own,' she says. But it is also clear that this was more than business, it was personal. She had an emotional commitment to First Tuesday and did not want to let go. Over the next few days Meyer and Reis passed each other in their shared flat without speaking. Their relationship was never to recover from the tensions of mid-July, and a few weeks later Reis moved out.

Hunt's call to Israel had a speedy effect. By the following weekend Yazam's executives and a dozen Israeli investment bankers were in London to examine First Tuesday's books. They quickly had a deal on the table. It valued First Tuesday at $50 million. Given that the business had been seeking a $68 million valuation in February, this looked a respectable sum in July after the crash in the dot.com market. It was not as good as it looked. Most of the money was in shares in the Israeli company, and Yazam had given itself an extraordinary valuation of $450 million. A few months later that figure would seem like the product of very wishful thinking.

Crucially, however, there was some cash, around $6 million, which would be shared amongst the founders. Now there were two offers on the table, both of which appeared to have merits. The Yazam deal would place First

Tuesday under the wing of a more powerful organization, supposedly with better management, which could establish a business model to take the organization forward. It would also provide what many other cash-strapped dot.com people were now frantically seeking – a lucrative exit. The alternative proposed by Venture Partners would allow First Tuesday to survive as an independent organization – and it might appeal more to the City leaders as it was being led by one of their number. The issue would be decided at a board meeting on 19 July.

The final scene was to be played out at the Institute of Directors just off Trafalgar Square, a great marble temple in London's clubland and an ironically conservative venue for the players in a dot.com drama. As he sat in a taxi on the way to the meeting, John Browning suddenly realized that he was wearing jeans and would not be allowed in. He phoned the office and got a colleague to go out and buy some more respectable trousers. He met her halfway and changed in the taxi.

Browning arrived at the board meeting in an uneasy state of mind: 'I felt like mine was the swing vote. I like Julie and it was clear that she would feel immensely betrayed and unhappy if it went to Yazam.' The meeting lasted two hours, almost all of it taken up with attempts by Julie Meyer to change everyone else's mind. Her case was that First Tuesday was simply trying to hand over its management problems to someone else instead of solving them itself. She argued passionately that the organization could thrive on its own with the backing of the venture capital money. Perhaps too passionately. 'It was an emotional presentation not a rational one,' says Simon Murdoch of Episode 1, who also attended the meeting. 'The only way to persuade these people was to convince them that it would produce more money for them. She failed to convince them.'

Meyer's was the only vote against the sale to Yazam. She refused to sign the agreement at first, until she was warned that she would not get any of the cash unless her signature was on the deal. That evening she returned to First Tuesday's deserted offices in St James's Square. She saw that Reade Fahs had left his laptop on his desk and checked to see whether his e-mail was protected by a password. It was not – and when she examined the messages he had sent, there was evidence of his contacts with Yazam. Searching through his desk drawers she found the draft of his deal with his new employer. From Reade Fahs' point of view there was nothing wrong with all this. He had managed to save First Tuesday by maintaining contact with the organization's eventual saviour. But to Julie Meyer, increasingly convinced that she was the victim of a conspiracy, here was more evidence of treason.

Later Meyer had to go and break the news to Karl-Christian Agerup at Venture Partners. He had been alerted to the threat a few days earlier, but had assumed it would be impossible for his rival bidder to push a deal through so quickly. 'He was furious, incandescent,' says Meyer, 'he wanted to know why they had put in six weeks' work for nothing.' There was talk of legal action, but eventually Agerup walked away, bitter at the way his approach had been treated. The City leaders were also concerned about a sale which appeared to offer them very little.

'We were in two minds about the Yazam deal,' says David Burden of First Tuesday Midlands. 'We hadn't realized how much money the centre was burning and how poorly it was funded. But on the other hand, there was some bad feeling that the founders were getting cash out and we were getting nothing.'

For Adam Gold the deal just made sense. 'We took a dispassionate decision on what was best for First Tuesday,' he insists. Even if they had taken the Venture Partners money in July, they would have needed more funding soon – and by the end of the year the climate would have made that impossible.

For Gold and Denton this was the end of the affair. They had to concentrate on keeping their own dot.com vessels afloat in stormy seas and now had £1 million in cash to help them. Julie Meyer stayed on for a few month's under Yazam, nursing her grievance about the way the sale had been handled. By Christmas she had gone on to start her own firm, Ariadne Capital, using her windfall to try to spin her extraordinary web of contacts into a business offering help to start-ups. John Browning was the only one you were still likely to see at First Tuesday events.

The new owners quickly found that they had bought a pig in a poke. By October the manager appointed to run First Tuesday was sending furious e-mails to Yazam's head office about the situation he had inherited: 'I sense a place out of control,' he wrote, 'and am unhappy that my team are beginning to look down at First Tuesday as a joke outfit (along with the rest of London by the way).' He was battling to clear up a lax financial regime which had included, 'Lack of expenses control (expense for beauty treatments etc. going through the books)' and 'expenses being paid for people who are neither employees nor consultants of First Tuesday'.

The First Tuesday deal turned out to be a disaster for Yazam. The Israeli company ran into serious cash problems in the autumn as its stakes in other internet firms dwindled in value. By Christmas the men who had done the deal, the President Phil Garfinkle and the Chief Executive Yaacov Ben-Yaacov, had both resigned and First Tuesday was up for sale again. In January 2001 the networking club was sold to the City leaders for about £1 million. They had at last triumphed in their quest to have their voices heard in the organization that they had helped to build. The only problem was that little of it was left.

The whole sorry saga of First Tuesday is an object lesson in how any kind of organization can be driven off course when relations between its leading figures do not work. We have all seen the same thing happen, in anything from a political party to the local bowls club. But at First Tuesday it was money that helped to magnify those tensions. Perhaps if the organizers had been content to run it on a non-profit basis, something more sustainable could have been constructed. Only in late 1999 could the hosts of a cocktail party have believed that they were on their way to creating a multimillion pound business. Looking back with a little more perspective, those aspirations seem far-fetched. The strange thing is that for a few months they were realistic. Venture capitalists really were intent on throwing money at Julie Meyer and her colleagues.

'Everything that happened to the dot.coms in general happened to First Tuesday as well,' says Adam Gold. The difference was that, unlike many British dot.com pioneers, the party hosts who were briefly the toast of the new media era walked away from the experience as millionaires.

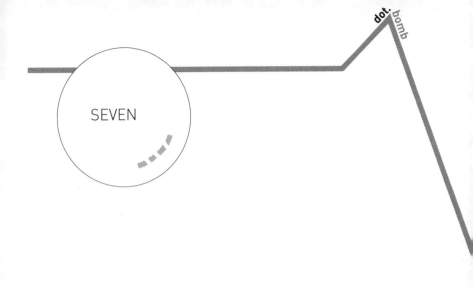

SEVEN

The kids are alright

ONE THING MAY HAVE struck you so far about the people jostling and shoving their way into Britain's new dot.com industry. They are, almost to a man and woman, under 40. The Internet had turned out to be the weapon that allowed the young to force their way into business and prove that you did not need to spend twenty years climbing the corporate ladder before you could run something.

Take Michael Smith, for example. When I came to visit the Chief Executive Officer of Firebox.com in his offices near Vauxhall Bridge I found a 25-year-old in a T-shirt. He was surrounded by a group of even younger people, who could have been the staff of a student newspaper. In the room where we talked there was a Play Station 2, at that time the hottest games machine around and not available in UK shops. Smith explained that he and his team would pop in here between business meetings to relax with a quick shoot-'em-up game. Although Firebox was still a small business, it had already won the backing of some very grown-up venture capitalists. That funding was won on a visit to First Tuesday, but the company was born because Michael Smith wanted to run a business and the Internet gave him the chance.

His father was a teacher, his mother a chiropodist – there was not a lot of business in his background but he had always been interested in making money. As a teenager he got a computer and started producing address labels for people. When he was given some money on his eighteenth birthday he spent it not on a motorbike or a hi-fi system but on buying some shares. He had studied geography at Birmingham University, then got a job managing company car schemes. One of his clients was the investment bank Goldman Sachs, where he would present young executives with the keys to the new Porsche. The smell of money emanating from Goldman Sachs was invigorating, and he decided that he wanted to get into investment banking.

Smith was still in touch with a university friend, Tom Boardman, who had studied artificial intelligence. He had taken his expertise to a company that programmed Breathalysers – not a bad job, as it involved getting drunk to calibrate the equipment. Smith and Boardman had much in common. They wanted to start a business, they both liked a beer or two, they were in love with gadgets and they were subscribers to *Loaded* and other lads' mags. They decided that there was a gap in the market for a company selling toys to boys like them.

A £1000 loan from Michael's mum paid for two computers and a printer. Office space was out of the question, so in the spring of 1998 they persuaded Tom's parents to let them occupy the loft of their home in Penarth, just outside Cardiff. After starting with only a paper catalogue, they quickly realized that it was a good idea to go online. They registered a domain name, hotbox.co.uk, and waited for customers to come clicking.

People came, but for the wrong reason. What Smith and Boardman had not realized was that hotbox.com was an American porn site, and soon they were getting a lot of dubious traffic. 'Tom's parents thought we were porn barons,' Smith remembers.

Real business was very slow. They were bombarding the men's magazines with news about their site but were getting two orders a week. Then came their salvation in the form of the shot glass chess set. This was a chess set made up of glasses which players would fill with different kinds of alcohol. Each time you took a piece, you drank a shot. Perfect for a boys' night in. This time the free publicity they managed to get in *Loaded* and *FHM* worked, and orders started to arrive in Penarth.

Firebox, as it was now known, was a very primitive e-commerce operation. Customers had to print a form from the website and then fax it to Penarth. Somehow the two young entrepreneurs had managed to persuade their bank to give them the equipment to process credit card orders. As the business grew, the house began to fill up with their stock. 'Parcelforce vans were turning up all the time,' says Michael, 'Tom's mum was not impressed.' But it was still a very small-scale operation. 'We were just experimenting and we felt pretty isolated. Nothing like First Tuesday existed at that time – we'd have given our eye teeth for the chance to meet people in a similar situation.'

By early 1999 the Firebox office in Penarth was home to three people – another former university friend had joined Smith and Boardman in the loft. They decided they had to move if the business was to grow. There was only one place to be if they wanted to raise the funds that they needed. 'We had to be in London to get venture capital – and anyway, most of our customers were in the South East,' says Michael Smith. 'We just had this picture of London as the pulsating heart of the new economy.'

Two more friends joined Firebox and they rented a three-bedroom flat in London. Five young men, living off pizza, in increasingly sordid surroundings which doubled as a living and working space. It could have been the plot for a dodgy sitcom. But they quickly got down to the serious business of raising money. Within a couple of weeks of arriving in London, Smith heard about First Tuesday and decided they should all go. They put on their suits – later they realized ties were not required – and set off for that month's meeting at the London Business School. With them they took a ten-page business plan. 'It was very vague. We'd researched on the Internet how to do a business plan but we didn't really know what we were doing. We didn't even really understand what venture capital was.'

However, it was at this time that First Tuesday was swarming with venture capitalists desperate to find someone to fund. The Firebox boys talked to five different companies at that night's meeting and one of them ended up as their first investor.

New Media Investors, the firm that had backed lastminute.com, was at First Tuesday. It was in the process of turning itself from a company that just invested money belonging to its founder Tom Teichman and his family and friends, to something far more ambitious. New Media Spark, as the new company was called, would raise £10 million on the Alternative Investment Market that autumn, and then build a much bigger fund. So Teichman had money burning a hole in his pocket, and when he met the lads from Firebox he liked what he saw: 'They were the kind of people who would never have dreamed of starting a business five years earlier. Suddenly they could see what was happening in America where people were making huge fortunes – and they were prepared to work to make it happen.'

Michael Smith believes that Firebox had an edge because the people behind it were different from the usual types who pitched up at New Media Spark, armed with spreadsheets and slick presentations: 'They were meeting loads of business school graduates and consultants, and although we had little experience of the business world, we had shown entrepreneurial flair.' Their real ace was that they had actually created a business. Many of those seeking funds had 50-page business plans containing detailed forecasts of how they would spend investors' money to grow compelling internet offerings – but they did not have as much as a website. 'We had revenues and we were profitable because we had to be.'

In Michael Smith's mind it all happened in a blur. They arrived in London, pitched up at First Tuesday, and emerged with seed funding of £500,000. In fact, there was a long process to go through and the money, which gave New Media Spark a 27 per cent stake in Firebox, did not arrive until late in 1999. But Smith and his flatmates had chosen the perfect time to look for venture capital. Any earlier, and a bunch of likely lads flogging gadgets would never have got a meeting. Any later, and their ambitions would have been seen as too limited for a fund like New Media Spark.

Half a million pounds was not a huge sum but it enabled Firebox to move out of a flat and into some proper offices. By Christmas, sales were doubling every week, fuelled by ever more press coverage. It was now spreading into the Sunday supplements and the women's magazines – 50 funky gadgets to buy your man this Christmas. The company would later feature in a BBC documentary about dot.coms. They had learnt their lesson well. If you cannot afford to advertise, get your name known for nothing.

The five who had started in London were still living together, now in a house in Kennington. 'We've had three cleaners and they've all given up on us,' says Smith. They were working extraordinary hours at an age when they could have been in a safe nine to five job and enjoying their free time. 'It's been the only thing in our lives for two years,' says Smith. 'The hours don't matter. I'd rather be at my computer answering e-mails, watching the orders come in, than slumped in front of the TV.'

By the spring of 2000, at the height of the dot.com frenzy, it looked as though Michael Smith and Tom Boardman had made the journey from a Penarth loft to seven-figure riches in just two years. They raised another £1 million from investors that summer. But the mood was changing and they knew they now faced an uphill struggle.

From a tiny operation which made just enough to keep them in beer and rent, the business had grown into something more ambitious, employing eighteen people. They were spending money on the basis that new funds would be available in the coming months – that was the way a dot.com thought. The internet bubble had given them the chance to become entrepreneurs. However, investors had now decided that there was nothing magical about selling goods to consumers over the Net. What was Firebox but a catalogue retailer with nothing unique to defend itself if a bigger fish should decide to enter its pool? Harder times would test the durability of young men with little experience of the wild swings of the business cycle.

Michael Smith is a relative veteran compared to some of those who used the Internet to barge their way into business. Across Britain it was teenagers who were among the first to wake up to the possibilities of the new technology. They often caught the industry itself unawares. When text messaging was launched by the mobile phone networks, they thought it would be a minor addition to the phone's capabilities. But soon teenagers were finding that messaging was an entertaining and cheap way of staying in touch with friends. Soon ten times as many messages were being sent as had been forecast, the majority by people under twenty.

For Tom Hadfield it was e-mail which changed his life and promised at one stage to make him into a teenage internet millionaire. In 1994 he was a bright twelve-year-old growing up in Brighton, interested in football and hoping to sign up one day with Brighton and Hove Albion. Then a friend got on the Internet. Tom found himself spending every hour online at his friend's house, until his parents got a phone call demanding that he spend a little time at his own home.

So Tom's parents agreed to get him an internet account. It was the early days of the Web, but he soon found himself joining online discussions, talking to people in Australia and exchanging football results by e-mail. He still believes he was not that different from many of his contemporaries:

'There was a whole generation of us doing exactly the same – and adults knew nothing about it.'

But Tom turned his internet obsession into a business. Within a few months he had started his own site and was thinking about a bigger project, based on his interest in football. 'At that time there were plenty of amateur sites,' he says, 'but nobody was doing it commercially.' He had been e-mailing football results to ex-pats desperate for news of Wycombe Wanderers or Everton, and unable to find it in their local newspapers. The twelve-year-old was learning a key business lesson. Offering people information they desperately want but cannot get elsewhere is a compelling proposition. One morning in 1995 he shouted through the bathroom door at his father to ask him if it would be alright to start a company called Soccernet. As he concentrated on shaving, a distracted Greg Hadfield said that would be just fine.

Now Tom did have one big advantage. Greg Hadfield was a journalist who had worked on the *Sunday Times* and the *Daily Mail*. Hadfield Senior remembered that Sir David English, chairman of Associated Newspapers, had just made a speech at a new Media conference and had talked of encouraging 'little people with big ideas'. Hadfield took his son's idea to his bosses at the *Mail* and asked them to back it. While they mulled over the question of putting £5000 into a schoolboy's venture, the family went on holiday to France.

'We got the phone call giving the go-ahead from the *Mail* when we were on a ferry home,' Tom remembers. 'I ran up and down the boat shouting, "We're going to be millionaires."' There are some who have suggested that Tom is just a handy media front for his father's business ambitions. Both Greg and Tom insist that Hadfield Junior has been the driving force. He has come up with the ideas that have transformed both his and his father's lives. The day that Soccernet launched in August 1995 was the first time that Greg Hadfield had ever used the Internet. Tom and a couple of friends had spent much of the school holidays designing the website. It was an instant hit. 'I woke up three days after launch and told Dad that 20,000 people a day were looking at the site. It was mind numbing for a twelve-year-old.'

For the next three years Tom was to spend most of his waking hours working on his website. The big breakthrough came with Euro 96, which Soccernet helped turn into one of the first major sporting events to make an impact online. With England hosting the tournament, the frenzied interest in football reached new heights, and the growing internet population turned to sites where they could get news and vent their feelings about that Gascoigne goal or that Southgate penalty miss.

Before the tournament Tom Hadfield had managed to get in e-mail contact with Jerry Yang, one of the founders of Yahoo. He ended up with an agreement to provide the search directory's coverage of Euro 96. In return, Yahoo took £1000-worth of advertising on his site. 'They didn't know they were doing business with a thirteen-year-old,' Hadfield told me. 'It's the old joke, on the Internet nobody knows you're a dog.' A presence on the world's busiest site drove a lot of traffic to Soccernet. Tom was staying up way beyond his bedtime to update the site, with his father coming in at 2 a.m. from the *Express* where he was now working.

By the time the tournament was over the Hadfields were both exhausted. Running Soccernet was just occupying far too much of their time and they decided to close it down. But while they were on a family holiday on a Greek island, Greg Hadfield's mobile phone rang. It was Guy Zitter, the managing director of his former employers, the *Mail*. Zitter said he would pay Hadfield £40,000 a year to run Soccernet full-time.

For a man who was tiring of the politics of newspaper journalism, it was a great opportunity to be his own boss. Hadfield leapt at it. He also reached a gentleman's agreement with Zitter about the family's stake in Soccernet, 'I said, "When it's worth a million I'll get my mortgage paid off." He laughed at the idea that it could ever be worth a million.'

Father and son, who had seen little of each other over the years when Hadfield was travelling the world as a journalist, now spent many hours together developing Soccernet. Tom's life was becoming very different from that of his school friends. He travelled to Fort Lauderdale in Florida to talk to the internet sports division of CBS about providing their coverage of World Cup 98. It was a classic business trip, there and back in 30 hours. 'He told his teacher, "I'm going to America on Monday",' Greg Hadfield remembers. 'She said, "You can't do that, you've got some important course work on Thursday." He told her he'd be back by then.'

He was becoming a media star, with interviews in the national press and an appearance on Esther Rantzen's chat show. But he carefully avoided talking to the local papers. 'I just didn't want to get the mickey taken out of me on the way to school,' he says. He was trying to be average, meeting his mates in the evenings, buying CDs, playing in goal for a local football club, although Brighton had by now told him he was not going to make it as a professional.

However, there were now some difficult commercial decisions to be confronted, along with his GCSEs. The Hadfields had developed a closer relationship with CBS Sportsline, which was now hosting their site. The company had brought in $1.5 million of sponsorship for the France 98 coverage. The sponsors would only pay out if the site achieved a million hits per day, which seemed an ambitious target. But as the World Cup got underway, it was soon getting 5 million hits a day.

The Hadfields hatched a plan to get Sportsline to buy Soccernet and then float it on the London and New York stock exchanges. 'Tom had been reading about all the internet floats in America,' says Greg. Sportsline was interested in the idea but the *Daily Mail* made it clear in the summer of 1998 that it did not want to sell.

Father and son were becoming disillusioned. They knew that there would need to be some serious investment in the site as the world's media groups woke up to the promise of sport on the Internet and prepared to steamroller the pioneers. 'We weren't getting the support we wanted. We were doing lots of hard work for no return,' Tom remembers. There were tense discussions about the site's future and just what stake the Hadfield family now had in the business. The night before his GCSEs started, Tom found himself talking to lawyers about the negotiations with the *Mail*.

In 1999 Tom and Greg Hadfield left Soccernet. Shortly afterwards, the *Daily Mail* changed its mind and sold up. Walt Disney's internet division, eager to move into the fast-growing sports website business, paid £15 million for a 60 per cent stake in Soccernet. The following year they bought the rest of the business. Greg Hadfield insists they could have got a better deal: 'Sportsline was offering $43 million just for the name.' But the *Daily Mail* had made a huge profit from a business created by a twelve-year-old. The Hadfields did get something. When the deal came before the board, Guy Zitter reminded his fellow directors that they had promised to see the family right. Tom and Greg ended up with around a quarter of a million pounds. If they had been a bit more careful about giving away ownership of Tom's idea, they could have been multimillionaires.

But by then the teenage entrepreneur and his father were profiting in other ways from their experience in building Soccernet into a successful business. They had started a new internet company aimed at the education market, something they felt they knew a lot about. After all, Greg Hadfield had been an education correspondent, his wife was a teacher and Tom had spent more than ten years in the system. But it was their track record as dot.com pioneers that was to be their calling card when they set about looking for funding.

Schoolsnet's aim was to become the place teachers, parents and pupils would come for information about education. It would carry reviews of every school in the country, with links to information about local house prices. It would carry adverts for teaching jobs, and, by providing up-to-the minute coverage of the latest news from the chalkface, it would overtake *The Times*' Educational Supplement as the profession's forum. It would become indispensable to head teachers, who had just been given more power over budgets, by allowing them to buy school supplies online.

This was the picture painted by Tom Hadfield when I visited Schoolsnet's London offices, near St James's Park in December 2000. As he walked me through an office housing 40 staff, he was an engaging mixture of gangling schoolboy and self-confident entrepreneur. He could certainly talk the talk, as he explained that Schoolsnet was a 'hugely revolutionary concept with a compelling B2B revenue stream'.

The investment community had also been impressed – the Hadfields had raised £700,000 from angel investors in the summer of 1999. In the spring of the following year they had raised a second round of funding to the tune of £5.75 million. Earlier, exaggerated accounts of what Tom was worth had appeared in various newspapers, which had assumed that he had cashed in when Soccernet was sold to Walt Disney. But now the Hadfield family had a majority stake in a business valued at £40 million.

Tom really was a teenage dot.com millionaire – on paper at least. He had just learnt that he had become the youngest Briton to be selected by the World Economic Forum in a list of 100 global leaders for tomorrow. He would be travelling in a few weeks time to Davos in Switzerland for the Forum's annual meeting, where prime ministers and presidents rub shoulders with business giants like Bill Gates of Microsoft and Steve Case of America Online.

By now he had spent six years as an internet entrepreneur – which made him one of the most experienced people in the industry. He was still trying to keep his feet on the ground, studying for A-Levels and managing to get to the pub in the evening. He was hoping to get a place at Oxford but first he wanted a breathing space, a gap year to recover from the stresses of business.

Tom Hadfield has remarkable self-assurance and drive and would no doubt have ended up in business if he had been born twenty years earlier, although he might have had to wait rather longer. 'As a teenager I could never have set up a factory,' he said. 'It's the Internet which has made all the difference.'

As the dot.com frenzy began to take hold in the latter half of 1999, journalists were desperate to uncover stories of instant fortunes and the younger the beneficiary, the better. But some of the teenage internet millionaires were the result of a certain amount of creative thinking – on the part of both journalists and the teenagers themselves.

In September 1999 *The Times* carried an article headlined 'Jewish Website Nets London Schoolboy £5 million'. The piece by Ben Hammersley described how seventeen-year-old Benjamin Cohen from North London had started a website, jewishnet.co.uk, which was attracting the attentions of big business. He was now thinking of buying a Porsche with his millions. Hammersley was careful to attribute the valuation to Benjamin's father, Richard Cohen. But to journalists who followed the story up, Benjamin Cohen was a gold-plated teenage hero with £5 million in the bank. Within hours he had appeared on local radio, on BBC television and on CNN. Soon he was featuring in lists of the young dot.com rich.

A year later Benjamin gave me a lift to a North London tube station in his second-hand Vauxhall and laughed about the £5 million teenager tag and the Porsche plans. 'Most of the journalists didn't really believe I was worth £5 million, but funnily enough the businessmen did.' He said he was not sure how Ben Hammersley had got hold of the story. Hammersley says it was Ben Cohen himself who repeatedly rang *The Times* with news of his ambitions.

There was some truth behind this tale of youthful enterprise. It had all started because Ben suffered from the debilitating disease ME. He had always been interested in computers but now he went online. 'I was off school for a whole year and it was a way of keeping in touch.'

Nevertheless, he began to find the Net a frustrating place to navigate with no proper roadmaps. 'I decided there weren't any good search engines, so I'd build something better.' He taught himself some basic programming and ended up creating a product he called Hermia. He wanted to turn this into a business but could not work out how to make money from a search engine.

Instead he decided that there was money to be made from providing a site that would make compelling reading for the Jewish community. Unlike Tom Hadfield, Ben was in touch with business from an early age. His grandfather had been managing director of Ladbrokes, and his father was a director of a software firm, Epoch. 'There was always a lot of talk in our house about shares – what was up, what was down. I was reading the *FT* from an early age.'

So it seemed natural for Ben to want to turn his interest in the Internet into a business. It was to be called Jewishnet, and Ben borrowed £150 from his father to buy the domain name and get the site going. Ben Cohen poured all his energy into Jewishnet. The site was to take advantage of what was one of the Internet's great selling points, its ability to bind a community together by offering it a new means of communication.

Jewishnet offered a directory of Jewish businesses – plumbers, electricians, lawyers – but its real selling point was that it provided a place where the community, and particularly its younger members, could talk about whatever was on their mind.

Ben employed his own rabbi as a Cyber rabbi. He would visit him once a week with e-mailed spiritual queries and then post the responses on the site. There was also an agony aunt to handle the emotional problems of Jewish teenagers. The whole operation was run from Ben's computer at home with the aid of a few friends.

By May 1999 the Jewish community's traditional noticeboard had woken up and started asking questions about this upstart. 'The *Jewish Chronicle* rang my dad, who was listed as company secretary, and said, "What's going on? This is competing with us." They asked him if it was an American company. He said, "No, it's just my son running it from his bedroom."'

The *Jewish Chronicle* became the first of three businesses that talked to Ben Cohen and his father about buying Jewishnet. Ben quickly decided that the *Jewish Chronicle* was not the right partner. 'It was like trying to do a deal with the BBC. It's set up as a charitable trust and so it's not really commercially minded.'

Then came a call from a company called Totally, which ran a similar site to Ben's, Totallyjewish.com. That led to a meeting at a hotel in Elstree where Totally's executives were slightly taken aback to find themselves dealing with a seventeen-year-old. 'They offered me a couple of per cent of their company and I went away to think about it.' The teenager was not going to be overawed by talk of lucrative share deals.

After all, he was now getting advice from the man who was the leading light in internet finance at that time. Waiting for his father in reception at his offices in Colindale, Ben had got talking to Geoffrey Chamberlain. The head of Durlacher, the internet investment company, was also a director of Richard Cohen's software company Epoch. Ben performed the legendary Silicon Valley elevator pitch – the twenty-second hard sell to a venture capitalist you meet in the elevator – except that the two never actually made it into the lift. He told Chamberlain about his plans for Jewishnet and got him to agree to help find backing. In the end, on the advice of Durlacher, Ben Cohen did a deal with the free newspaper *London Jewish News*. A new company called Sojewish.com was formed, in which the young entrepreneur, now eighteen, would have a stake of around 17 per cent. The deal was concluded in January 2000, and within days Ben had a new angle for the press.

This time it was a plan for Sojewish to float on the Alternative Investment Market. According to the *Daily Telegraph*, 'the web site was conservatively valued at £5 million several months ago and – given the enormous demand for internet shares at the moment – could quickly reach a market capitalisation of £50 million or more'. But a few weeks later Totallyjewish, the company that had missed out on the deal with Ben, announced its own float on AIM. However enormous the demand for internet shares, another company serving the Jewish online community would be too much for the market to digest.

Ben Cohen was still managing to keep his name in the public eye. In February an announcement came that he had been voted sexiest webmaster in the Internet Awards, and had taken second place in the Internet Icon category behind Martha Lane Fox. The only problem was that none of the journalists who received news of these awards was able to trace the

organization behind them. Cohen told the online news service The
Register that he had only found out about his success when he was
informed by e-mail. Unfortunately, he could not say who had sent the e-
mail.

Disappointingly, by October 2000 his company had not floated on AIM.
Instead it had been sold to Totally, which paid Ben Cohen for his stake in
shares worth £310,000. Over the coming months, as everything internet
went out of fashion, those shares would be worth a lot less. The internet icon
was not downhearted. According to the *Daily Express*, he now planned to
spend his gap year 'running his much larger internet business CyberBritain'.

This was the organization I came to visit in December. A woman called
Lisa, described as personal assistant to the chief executive officer, Mr Cohen,
found me a space in his diary. One of the strengths and weaknesses of the
Internet is that you are never quite sure about the scale and credentials of
the organization behind a website. A look at CyberBritain's website indicated this was a substantial business. 'The company has recently been
reorganized to become a holding company with a number of subsidiaries
operating in a number of B2B and B2C areas.'

But when I arrived for my appointment, I found two teenage friends of
the CEO in a tiny storeroom in his father's offices. Ben was out, his PA had
departed the company with his diary, but the teenagers assured me that
CyberBritain was going to be huge. It was a portal powered by its own
search engine, it had its own music magazine. How could it fail? When Ben
turned up he was similarly ebullient about his plans. His company had
already recorded an extraordinary 420 million page impressions, and the
unique search technology Hermia, designed by the founder, was going to
turn this into a very significant business.

A few weeks later it turned out that that the teenage tycoon's plans were
heavily dependent on the Internet's oldest business and the only one that
had always made money. Into my e-mail inbox came a press release from
CyberBritain boasting that it had received 56,000 registrations for a new
service. 'Hunt4Porn' was a search engine that did just what it said. No
longer would impatient internet users have to wade through all sorts of
perfectly innocent sites – Essex County Council's homepage, the Chicken
Breast Information Bureau – to find some genuine pornography. I rang Ben
to ask him why he had become a porn baron. 'I'm not selling pornography,'

he insisted, 'just acting as a guide.' I wanted to know what his parents thought. 'My dad is OK because he thinks it will make money, but my mum doesn't like it.'

Whatever you may think of Benjamin Cohen, you have to admire his ability to manipulate the media. The increasingly outlandish values put on his flimsy company merely reflected the mood of the time. But then some of the bigger dot.coms, which managed to sell shares based on even more outlandish valuations, were to prove equally flimsy.

Many of the young entrepreneurs who started companies in bedrooms and lofts across Britain are likely to come to grief. After all, survival rates for new businesses have always been low. That does not mean we should under-estimate the impact the new technology has had on the eagerness of young people to have a go. There does seem to have been a real change, particularly amongst young science graduates, who in the past would have meekly accepted that their future lay somewhere halfway up the ladder of a corporate giant.

Adam Twiss and Damian Reeves decided while they were studying computer science at Cambridge that they would rather be their own bosses. They started an internet software company, Zeus, which developed a product enabling websites to handle greater numbers of visitors. Their business expanded as their studies continued and so when they came to graduate they did not have to start filling in application forms. 'It was more fascinating than going to work in the IT department of some City bank,' Twiss told an interviewer. By the spring of 2000 the firm was employing 46 people and was valued at £600 million.

But if the dot.com boom helped open doors to careers in business for thousands of young people, there was a more unfortunate aspect to this obsession with youth. If you were over 40, nobody seemed interested. Rob Simon, marketing director for an e-commerce recruitment agency called Raw Carrot (and there must be a thesis to be written on the proliferation of daft names in the dot.com economy), admits that ageism was rife. 'I was advising a venture capital firm which was looking to recruit a chief executive for a dot.com they were funding. They made it clear that they did not want anyone over 35 – they said older people just would not have the hunger to make the business work.'

A survey by the online news service for the IT industry Silicon.com found huge amounts of resentment amongst older workers. At a time when the demand for computer skills was at its peak, they were finding that nobody wanted their experience. One e-mail described the challenge he faced: 'When applying for jobs through agencies, I am often asked my age. After supplying it (I am 54) I always ask if this is a problem. I am always told that age is no problem. That is the last I hear from them.'

Of course, the computer industry has always favoured the young. Bill Gates dropped out of college to start Microsoft. Steve Jobs and Steve Wozniak created Apple in their early twenties. It is the young who are the most receptive to new technology and most prepared to work crazy hours in pursuit of the new, new thing. Besides, you had to be young and fit to fight your way to the bar at First Tuesday.

Nonetheless, as pictures of the dot.com generation crowded out the old corporate knights on the business pages of the newspapers, some began to question the trend. When the going got a bit rough, might it not be an idea to have someone with a few grey hairs who remembered that share prices could fall as well as rise?

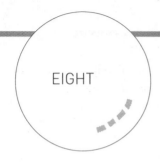

EIGHT

Smart money, stupid money

IN THE 1960S, FOR those who were young and in touch with what was happening in the world, VC stood for a ruthless and focused band of people who would destroy anything in their path if it threatened their objective. For the dot.com generation of the late 1990s, the initials stood for something similar. But for them VC meant venture capital not Vietcong.

Venture capital was the rocket fuel that powered any internet entrepreneur who wanted to turn a brilliant idea into a viable business. The psychology of the VCs – as they were universally known – became an obsession for the people gathering at events like First Tuesday in search of funding. There was constant talk about which of the VCs were on the lookout for new investment opportunities, what were their likes and dislikes, and how exactly the protracted courtship ritual which led to funding should be conducted. The vocabulary of VC was haltingly exchanged by people who did not yet speak the language. What did it mean to sign a term sheet? What exactly was an 'anti-dilution clause'?

There were two views of the individuals who ran venture capital funds, most of which were structured as partnerships, with each partner going out to hunt down opportunities that would have to be approved by his colleagues before any money was committed. Some felt the VCs were smart, well-connected individuals who often had the technical background to understand the ideas brought to them by hopeful entrepreneurs, combined with the financial and managerial acumen to guide them through their growing pains. Others saw them as venal and ignorant money-grabbers who would demand a huge slice of your company in return for miserly funding, and then try to push your business in directions which you knew to be ill conceived.

I got a flavour of this at a networking event that brought together a group of entrepreneurs and venture capitalists. A young Australian who had got his company off the ground after a long and tortuous journey through the offices of every venture capitalist in London complained bitterly at the sheer rudeness of the people he had met. 'Look at that guy over there,' he said, pointing to a young man in a pinstriped suit, whose badge revealed that he worked for a company called Durlacher. 'I met him on a Friday. He told me to block off time the following week for meetings. I got in early, spent all day phoning and e-mailing him. Nothing. And I never heard from him again.' For a moment, I worried that the young man was going to seek out the venture capitalist and take a swing at him. Instead he went on to tell me of his contempt for the whole VC crowd, which moved herd-like every few months from an obsession with one kind of internet firm to a new craze. He had distributed a list of rude, ignorant VCs to friends in the dot.com world.

A venture capitalist across the room had just been describing to me the level of technological expertise and careful analysis that went into his every deal. When I mentioned this to the Australian he curled his lip. 'They think they're smart money, but very often they're so stupid.'

Which view you took of venture capital probably depended on whether anyone had shown an interest in your business plan lately. What was not in dispute was that clearing the series of hurdles from initial contact with a venture capital firm to signing a contract was a lengthy and painful business.

Except, that is, in the autumn of 1999. For a few brief moments it seemed that the tables were turned. Instead of hordes of desperate start-ups besieging the venture capitalists and trying every means possible to get an audience, it was the VCs who were fighting to win the right to fund a company. The Freeserve IPO had shown everyone that billion pound companies could be created in a matter of months. Suddenly the venture capitalists examined their portfolios and realized they were sadly lacking in anything with a dot.com on the end of its name. The 'me too' spirit of the dot.com boom infected them as much, or even more, than anyone else. Having apparently ignored what had happened in the United States over the previous five years, they suddenly woke up and said '150 per cent return on capital? I think I'd like some of that too!' One particular case seemed to exemplify this transformation.

On 1 October 1999 two young men with no great track record in business suddenly achieved fame by raising money in record time. The *Financial Times* reported that Toby Rowland and Rob Norton, founders of a company planning to sell health products on the Internet, had raised £3 million from venture capitalists in just eight days. The story was soon being repeated in other newspapers and on television, and made dozens of other young hopefuls believe that they too might find that getting funding was child's play. The company at the centre of this extraordinary piece of generosity from the VCs was Clickmango.

Of course, their progress from the dot.com drawing board to millionairedom was not quite as smooth and speedy as it appeared in the media – but it was still a remarkable tale. They started with just a few advantages. Toby Rowland was the son of one of the most colourful British business figures of the twentieth century. Tiny Rowland, who had built the mining empire Lonrho and fought an epic battle with Mohammed Al Fayed over the ownership of Harrods, died in 1998, leaving his son Toby a very wealthy young man. Rob Norton, also from a prosperous if less high profile background, had met Rowland at Oxford.

Toby had run the University's French society at Oxford, which had proved to be an irresistible magnet to other male students because it had a reputation as a dating agency for sloanes. Rowland took over the job from Brent Hoberman of lastminute.com fame, later to choose Toby as best man at his wedding. Oxford in the early nineties was bringing together a group of prosperous and privileged young people who would soon play a big part in the dot.com bubble. At the same time, Cambridge was turning out brilliant young engineers who were to build more sustainable businesses.

After Oxford Toby Rowland had worked as a management consultant at KPMG – where he had been miserable – and had then joined Disney. Meanwhile Rob Norton was making a career in journalism with Reuters before leaving to work for America Online. From there he had moved to

Paris to work for an internet company called Nomade. The two of them kept in touch, and when they met and played computer games together in Rowland's Sloane Square flat they chewed over the idea of starting their own internet company.

In the summer of 1999 they both decided that it was time to quit their jobs and have a go at a dot.com idea. Norton, whose stepfather ran a health farm, had been talking to Rowland about an idea for an online health products business. The market for health foods and health treatments was growing rapidly, and Norton felt that a website which offered consumers advice and showed them where they could buy the best products would prove both compelling and lucrative. He set off from Paris for London – and within hours the two of them were sitting with their first focus group.

The first thing they needed for their company was a name; they decided to try out various options on two groups of women from their target audience, aged between 35 and 55. 'We had about 50 names, of a fruity, watery, leafy kind,' says Norton. 'Fruity names tested well – but there were problems with a lot of them. "Pear" was difficult – and "cherry" had lots of awkward connotations.' Eventually they narrowed it down to mango; 'It was the only "non-confrontational fruit",' says Norton. With click on the front to give the name a cyber edge, they had created a typical internet brand – striking, memorable and slightly ridiculous.

So they had a vague business plan and a name. Now all they needed was some funding. On a summer's night in August 1999, just days after they had given up their jobs to work on their business, Rowland and Norton set off for First Tuesday. That month's event is the one that many now remember as the blissful dawn of Britain's dot.com age. It was held at Home House, the fashionable club in Portman Square, and on a sweltering summer evening the seething crowd spilled out into the garden. Just a couple of weeks after the Freeserve IPO, everybody was suddenly aware of how great the opportunity was for those who could stake their claim right now.

'We didn't know what to expect that night,' says Rob Norton. 'We thought we were just going to a party, but it was clear the moment we arrived that there was a frenzied pitching atmosphere. So we thought – let's go for it.' So ill-prepared were they for an approach to the big names in venture capital crowded on the lawn at Home House that they had not even had business cards printed. So they rushed back inside, tore a corner each off a paper tablecloth and scrawled their names and an impromptu daisy logo next to the word 'clickmango.com'.

They set about doing their double act in front of every venture capitalist they could find at the party. And if ever there was a perfect conjunction of greed and fear amongst the VCs, this was it. Greed because they had realized that the enormous sums being earned over in Silicon Valley might well be mirrored in Britain now that Freeserve had floated. Fear because if they did not move quickly those smart American venture capital firms would be catching a plane over to seek fresh meat in Europe.

Norton and Rowland emerged from their frenzy of pitching with one firm lead. Atlas Ventures agreed that they could come and talk about Clickmango at some stage. This was a big fish to have tugging on the end of the line. Atlas had a solid reputation in the United States and Europe as a venture capital fund investing in young technology companies. Now its London office, open for less than two years, was building a name, going aggressively after dot.com business. But the Clickmango duo knew that they had to have a little more than names scrawled on a piece of paper to show Atlas. For the next three weeks they sat in an office in the East End, trying to pull together a convincing business plan. Toby Rowland, with his KPMG training, wrote the financial model. They asked friends at QXL and last-minute.com to examine their numbers and make sure that they added up – although at that time all forecasts for dot.com revenues were based on a lot of wishful thinking. They spoke to two media doctors, Thomas Stuttaford and Michael van Straten, and got their agreement to lend their names to the site.

From 24 August they began an intense campaign for funding. There is always an intricate dance between the entrepreneur and any venture capitalist who is vaguely interested. The entrepreneur desperately needs the funding but does not want to give away too much of the company at an early stage. The VC wants to get in at an early stage but does not want to pay foolish sums, and would like as much control as possible over the infant business. Norton and Rowland set off on their funding quest with what appeared to be very ambitious aims. They wanted to raise £3 million but they were determined to keep control, so that £3 million would give the investors less than 40 per cent of Clickmango, putting an overall value on the company of £7 million.

They had thought through their tactics carefully. Their campaign involved seeing all the venture capitalists who would entertain them over as short a period as possible so as to build a sense of momentum. 'We wanted to do it quickly,' says Norton, 'and we wanted to have multiple offers so that we could force the price up. There's nothing that gets an investor as interested as finding that his rival down the road is interested.'

The next ten days were a blur as they sped across London in taxis with bundles of documents, packing in three or four presentations a day. Rowland and Norton, two young men of extraordinary self-confidence, made an impressive double act. They had a background in e-commerce – or at least as much of a track record in those innocent days as anyone else – and they talked a very good game. 'It was a crazy time,' Rob Norton says. 'Toby had this neck brace because he'd been in a car crash – he kept taking that off for the presentations. And I was feeling pretty dreadful from sheer exhaustion. It was a very emotional experience – when we came out of a successful pitch we'd hug each other in the lift on the way down.'

Their schedule took in Jacob Rothschild, Apax, Elder Street and Atlas – some of the hottest names in venture capital. On the first day at their very first appointment they were offered £1 million just 40 minutes into the meeting. At lunchtime their next appointment at Quaglino's produced an offer to buy the whole company. The final meeting later that afternoon also ended with promises of cash.

On the second day of their campaign they performed for Atlas and it was immediately clear that there was huge enthusiasm for the concept and for the way it had been researched and presented. Norton and Rowland knew that despite the multiple promises of cash that they were now receiving, it was vital that someone volunteer to lead the funding. 'We had begun to understand that the whole thing can drag on unless you get someone who wants to lead – someone who says they are committed to putting money in whatever anyone else does,' says Rob Norton.

Atlas indicated that it was prepared to lead – a huge boost for Norton and Rowland. The company had an enviable reputation built up over nearly twenty years that had seen it play a part in the creation of dozens of high-tech firms in the United States and Europe. 'It was a first tier company and it was great to get them on board,' Rob Norton comments.

Over the next week and a half there were four more meetings with Atlas as the venture capitalists and the two young entrepreneurs headed helter-skelter towards the altar. There was also one encounter with a venture capitalist that did not go quite so well. When they turned up to see Amadeus Partners they quickly discovered that their hosts had already funded another company called ThinkNatural.com. Its business was selling health products online through a site that would also offer consumer advice. Just a tad similar to Clickmango. 'We would have preferred to have known that before the meeting,' says Norton. The two young men quickly ended the discussion and left in a huff. Hermann Hauser of Amadeus has a different view of the encounter. 'Clickmango might have seemed more glamorous than ThinkNatural,' he says, 'but we were not happy with the team.'

However, by the following Thursday Clickmango was on the verge of turning itself into a multimillion pound company in record time. Atlas had drawn up a term sheet, the marriage contract at the centre of any venture capital deal. Another 24 hours were spent waiting for the lawyers to produce documents, but by 6 p.m. of Friday 4 September the deal was done. Atlas had been prepared to provide all the funding itself, but Jacob Rothschild had lobbied strongly to be involved and was allowed to put in some cash.

Rowland and Norton say they were taking mobile phone calls from the other eager suitors right up until that Friday evening, begging them not to walk away with Atlas. So why were they such hot property? Timing was all. A similar online health company in the United States, mothernature.com, was about to float on the Nasdaq, promising a mouth-watering return for the venture capitalists who had backed it. B2C – online retailing to consumers – was red hot, with feverish talk of high streets being deserted as millions of shoppers clicked their way round virtual malls. 'There was tremendous optimism at the time,' says Rob Norton. 'The traditional retailers seemed to be nowhere as far as the Net was concerned. There were forecasts that 10 per cent of the market was going to migrate online and we were going to get a large chunk of that.' Clickmango's business plan did not envisage the company making any profit for three or four years. That meant that the company would have to attract another round of funding the following summer, but as lastminute.com had shown, that should be no problem.

The deal done, the next priority was to tell the world. At the First Tuesday event in August the Clickmango team had met Narda Shirley, the woman who had helped to put Martha Lane Fox's name on the lips of every

City editor. They had begged the dot.com sector's hottest PR person to take them on. She told them they would have to get some backers first. Now she was ready to help – and saw immediately that the speed of their funding would make a good tale.

They could not go public until the end of September because Atlas and its lawyers were going through the due diligence process. Every detail of the business plan had to be examined, from the contracts with suppliers to the amounts that Rowland and Norton were going to pay themselves and the all-important stock options programme which would be vital in hiring the right staff. The one thing that could not be assessed with any accuracy was the revenue forecast.

While the lawyers did their work, Rowland and Norton trained for their media campaign. A former tabloid journalist spent a day with the two entre-preneurs, bombarding them with aggressive questions about the business and their personal lives. They knew that Toby Rowland's background would attract intense interest. Then Narda Shirley set to work – and found no diffi-culty in getting coverage for Clickmango. It was the lottery winners' angle that attracted journalists, the idea that £3 million could be raised in such a tearing hurry.

Some did question how wise the venture capitalists were to rush in. 'Are we mad? We don't think so,' Vic Morris of Atlas Ventures told the *Independent*. He stressed that Atlas did not just put money into any Tom, Dick or Harry.com: 'You have to have the mixture of the right marketplace, the right people behind you and a clear merchandising strategy. It's not enough just to set up a site and hope someone will buy you out and make you rich.' Although at this stage, Clickmango had not even got as far as setting up a site.

The coverage in the broadsheets was followed by a ten-minute slot on BBC 2's respected financial strand, *The Money Programme*. The next six months were to see Clickmango's name crop up time and again in the press, before it sold as much as a jar of ginseng. With £3 million in the bank the firm was able to move out of a mice-infested cubicle in a converted brewery and into a large warehouse space just off Brick Lane in London's East End. An area stretching from Brick Lane through Shoreditch and Clerkenwell had become home to dozens of small web companies. Some wags were dubbing it Silicon Ditch.

They set about building the business, hiring writers who would provide compelling content to bring customers to the site, and working on what they described to journalists as 'sophisticated database technology', which would allow them to track their customers' preferences and then sell them additional services. Eventually 25 people were to fill the big white space that was now Clickmango's headquarters. As they hunted around for services, they found that lawyers, accountants, designers wanted just one thing – equity. The dot.com mania they had helped to generate had convinced everyone that a stake in an internet firm was the equivalent of a winning lottery ticket.

The aura of cool attached to Clickmango was increased when the company got itself some new furniture. The pink inflatable room dividers that turned a corner of their office into a meeting-room seemed practical – but later on the blow-up boardroom was to seem an apt metaphor for a company whose inflated ambitions were quickly punctured.

One person was to become even more associated with the company than the two founders. Rowland and Norton pulled off a tremendous publicity coup by getting one of Britain's most popular celebrities to put her name on the site. Joanna Lumley, now forever linked with the Bolly-swigging, chain-smoking Patsy in the long-running sitcom *Absolutely Fabulous*, was a clever choice to front a site dedicated to healthy living. Getting her onboard involved three months of delicate negotiations with the actress and her agent. 'She checked it out with friends, wanted to see what the artwork looked like, she was very professional,' says Norton. 'She wanted to know exactly what we wanted her to do and how much work it would involve.'

When her link with the company was unveiled in March 2000, another wave of publicity crashed over Clickmango. A report in the *Sunday Times* said that Lumley's stake in the company would be worth up to £5 million at flotation. But she had been wiser than many of those who did business with the company. As well as shares, she negotiated a sizeable fee.

By February there was talk in the advertising industry weekly *Campaign* of an agency winning a 'ten million pound media planning and buying account from Clickmango' for a campaign which would include television adverts in the summer. By this time, however, Clickmango had spent a sizeable chunk of its initial £3 million and the site had not even launched. Worse, their rivals ThinkNatural.com, while making far less impact in the media, had at least been up and running and selling products since November.

Clickmango finally launched in April, but with the money running out Norton and Rowland now had to devote most of their time to chasing up their second round of funding. And when they returned to the scene of their whirlwind triumphant tour of the previous August, they found a very different reception. A month after the lastminute.com IPO, a chill wind was blowing through the dot.com world. The share prices of those companies that had managed to float were falling quickly. The bank balances of those that had not made it that far were being examined with rather more scepticism by their backers.

B2C, so popular in the autumn, was now as welcome in a venture capitalist's offices as a smoker in a health food shop. The VCs had moved swiftly on to another acronym – B2B, business to business – although even this was looking tired around the edges as share prices in all kinds of internet ventures disappeared off a cliff. 'There was no problem actually seeing people,' says Norton, 'but they all repeated the same thing, parrot-like, "we're not into B2C, we're into B2B now". That kind of acronym chasing by the VCs was rather depressing.'

This time the company was looking for £10 million, which, said Rowland, would take them through to profitability in about three years. Sales were running at £100,000 a year, but the company was getting through £100,000 a month. It would take time to close that gap. Suddenly venture capitalists had woken up to the idea that 'profit' was not such a dirty word, and they wanted it now. 'We couldn't just say, "yes, we'll make a profit next week",' says Norton.

After being cold-shouldered by funds that had been begging to invest six months earlier, they tried every other avenue – from old-fashioned retailers to health insurers. There was no interest. Even their biggest fans at Atlas Ventures did not want to know. What was bizarre was that their backers did not accuse them of failing in any way. 'They kept on saying, "You've executed well, you're ahead of your business plan,"' says Norton, '"but we think you are wasting your time."' They changed their strategy and begged for just a few hundred thousand pounds to change Clickmango into a B2B firm. No more of that tedious online shopping – instead they would become an advice site, generating cash through advertising. There was a company waiting in the wings to act as partner in this abrupt change of direction.

But it became clear that Atlas was not going to put its hand back in its pocket. Norton and Rowland knew the game was up when they showed the people at Atlas a presentation featuring the Joanna Lumley cartoon on their site rising phoenix-like from the flames. 'So,' asked Christopher Spray, the senior partner at Atlas, 'is Joanna rising from the flames or falling into them?' The next day Rob Zegelaar, the Atlas partner who had first backed them, told Rowland and Norton at a short meeting that they were not going to get the cash they needed.

Unlike many a dot.com failure, the Clickmango founders were realistic about their impending demise and determined not to go down in a messy implosion of lurid headlines and unpaid debts. 'We wanted just to fade away quietly,' says Rob Norton. Unfortunately, the *Daily Telegraph* got wind that something was up and warned the founders that unless they talked, the paper would run a story saying Clickmango had gone bust. At this point Narda Shirley set to work to spin the story in a better direction. She advised her clients to talk to the *Sunday Times* and stress that they were doing the responsible thing, gradually winding the company down over a couple of months. Journalists eager to write about the humbling of brash young dot.com millionaires pounced on the failure of Clickmango, but the gradual rundown of the company over a period stretching to the end of September dulled the impact of the story.

So what does the brief, if spectacular, life of Clickmango tell us about the nous of the venture capitalists who funded them? The VCs liked to think that theirs was the smart money in 1999, but Clickmango was just one among a number of investments which looked pretty stupid by the end of 2000. In essence, two young men started a health shop, made less money than my local Body Shop rakes in from peppermint foot balm, and then closed down.

So why were they hot in August 1999 and rot in May 2000? It was all about what is known in the VC business as the 'exit strategy'. Venture capitalists will tell you at length about their detailed assessment of business plans, the long hours they spend assessing the capabilities of aspiring entrepreneurs and examining the markets which their companies intend to enter. But in the end, their business is all about getting in at one price and getting out at another, hopefully many times greater.

In the autumn Clickmango was valued by Atlas at £7.8 million because it could be compared with similar ventures in the United States that were achieving astronomical valuations. Atlas was betting its money not on a view of the intrinsic worth of an online health shop but in the hope that within eighteen months Clickmango would be selling shares on the public markets, enabling its backers to cash out at a huge premium. Even in the UK some venture capital firms were making extraordinary returns from investments in dot.coms. Apax Partners had invested £12 million for 30 per cent of QXL in the spring of 1999. By the end of the year, when the online auction firm floated, that stake was worth £45 million.

But by the following May it was becoming clear that investors were not going to stomach any more dot.com IPOs for a long time. 'At the seed round you have to make the assumption that the market and the way it values companies will not change,' says Vic Morris of Atlas. 'When it comes to the second round it is not just about how the business has performed – it is about how comparable firms are now being valued. Entrepreneurs assume that because you've backed them once, you won't want to throw it away by refusing to spend more. It doesn't work like that – with every incremental dollar you ask yourself whether you'll make money.'

I heard Vic Morris speak at a meeting of the networking organization thechemistry.com in September 2000. An audience of entrepreneurs, desperate to know how to squeeze money out of venture capitalists who were now battening down the hatches, hung on his every word. Morris told them that the lesson of recent months was that dot.com businesses were just like any other business – if they were retailers they should be valued on the same basis as other retailers. 'I'm no longer convinced that there are any new business models on the web,' he said. He mocked dot.com buzzwords: 'Disintermediation – cutting out the middleman – isn't that what Tesco has been doing with its suppliers for years? Demand aggregation – isn't that what the Co-Op did?'

He talked of dot.com blather from entrepreneurs. 'I sit down with people who say, "we have a diverse revenue stream". That means they don't know where their money is coming from.' In other words, Morris seemed to be saying that all of the thinking behind his firm's decision to back Clickmango and a string of other dot.coms had been faulty. For Atlas had valued a corner shop as if it were a budding Microsoft, and backed entrepreneurs who seemed unsure of what they were selling. When someone in the audience questioned him about that investment, Morris was defensive. He went out of his way to stress his continued faith in Norton and Rowland: 'If they came to me with another business plan, I'd back them in a heartbeat.'

At least Vic Morris was prepared to examine the dot.com experience and try to draw some lessons from it. Other venture capitalists who had been only too eager to bang the publicity drum during the good times were strangely reclusive as times became harder. The woman in charge of publicity at one of London's premier venture capital firms told me that her job was 'to protect the partners' bandwidth', and she thought it very unlikely that that any of them would have time to speak.

I talked with Vic Morris early in 2001 as he was preparing to leave Atlas Ventures. He was no wet-behind-the ears city slicker, pushing cash in and out of businesses he barely understood, but a computer industry veteran. He had started working life as a mainframe programmer for British Leyland at Longbridge in 1975, then moved into management in the computer business, both in Britain and in Silicon Valley. In October 1998 he had returned to Britain from California to become a partner at Atlas. As he looked back – just two years in real time but centuries in internet time – it seemed a golden age of innocence.

'I came back to London and was impatient at first because I could not find the dot.com buzz I'd experienced in the States. Then I went to First Tuesday and found the buzz was there.' Venture capitalists – an obscure breed in Britain until then – were suddenly very fashionable. 'We felt like rock stars,' says Morris. 'At First Tuesday I did not circulate – I just stood in a dark corner and people would gravitate towards me.'

Critics suggest that Atlas, whose UK operation was fairly new, got carried away on this tide of adulation and helped inflate the dot.com bubble by throwing its money around indiscriminately. The firm, under its senior partner Christopher Spray, was known to some as 'Spray and Pray'. Vic Morris insists that the perception is unfair – dot.com deals were only a small part of what Atlas did, and most of them fared better than Clickmango. But he admits that he and his partners did get very excited by the promise of the Internet, and also saw a chance to boost the profile of Atlas. 'Christopher Spray and I decided it was a good way of marketing the firm. And it worked – we soon became one of the best-known firms in London, and because of things like Clickmango, lots of more obscure deals came our way.'

It was 1999 when venture capital in Britain suddenly woke up to the promise of the new technology. Over a billion pounds was invested in high-tech firms, four times as much as in 1995. After years of timidity about risking money to turn bright ideas into solid businesses, the tide seemed to have turned. So who were the people importing this risk culture from the United States?

The pioneer of internet finance in Britain was an unlikely figure. In my travels through the dot.com companies and their backers I found a couple of constants – table football machines or pool tables seemed present in every office, and ties were nowhere to be seen. At the offices of New Media Investors, the founder Tom Teichman came gliding across the foyer on a micro-scooter to greet me. So it was something of a shock to come across Geoffrey Chamberlain at Durlacher.

Chamberlain, an understated man in his fifties, wore a standard pinstriped suit, a sober tie and in the corner of his very functional office in the heart of the City was a shoe-shining machine. But this was the character who had given his backing to companies like IMVS and 365 Corporation when every other venture capitalist would not let them through the door.

However, Chamberlain was not a standard venture capitalist. He was a City veteran who had helped create the derivatives market in London after observing the way that complex financial instruments were revolutionizing American finance. 'The common thread in everything I've done is to see a big picture agenda in Europe from what has happened in the USA,' he told me.

In the early 1990s he spotted the emergence of specialist technology investment banks in Silicon Valley, which were doing intensive research and then using their expertise to get involved with the new companies at an early stage. He decided to try something similar in London and his vehicle was Durlacher, a poorly regarded and ailing stockbroking firm.

One of the first pieces of investment research on the new economy was a Durlacher report at the beginning of 1996 called 'The Investment Implications of the Internet'. 'Research was vital,' says Chamberlain, 'everything was changing so rapidly it was frightening.' His company wanted an intense involvement with the people it backed. Its ideal was to create a company from ideas spun out of its own research and then take it all the way to stock market flotation.

That is what happened with 365 Corporation, a business where Durlacher provided both the initial funding and one of the founding directors, David Tabizel. The idea was that a collection of websites devoted to football, music and other interests could be spun into a digital business where content was available across a whole range of media. Early in 1999, 365 needed to raise £10 million to acquire a telecommunications business. It was a time when the American internet scene was already boiling over and 365, as one of Britain's pioneers, should have been attractive. But nobody seemed to want to take a punt. 'It was a hell of a struggle,' says Geoffrey Chamberlain. 'None of the city institutions was interested.' By the end of the year, when 365 floated, those same institutions were fighting to get a piece of it; £1.5 billion was chasing just £50 million worth of shares. 'It went from total scepticism in the spring to a crazed gold-rush in the winter.'

By the height of that gold-rush Durlacher had taken stakes in more than 30 internet companies, and the man who had transformed a dull and uninspiring stockbroking firm into a high-tech investment powerhouse was being hailed as a genius.

The work of venture capitalists is all about a proper balance of risk and reward. Out of every ten companies they back they expect one or two to be outright failures, six or seven to produce very mediocre returns – 'zombies' as some VCs call them – and one or two to be the shining stars that will provide the returns needed to keep the fund's investors happy. But as the 1990s drew to a close the whole game suddenly appeared to be a lot easier, as internet firms produced a galaxy of stars for the venture capitalists. Hermann Hauser, a very different character from Geoffrey Chamberlain, was another person to profit while the going was good.

Hauser is an extraordinary combination of high-powered scientist and entrepreneur, with a career that has encompassed its fair share of triumph and disaster. He co-founded the Acorn computer company, which blossomed and faded in the 1980s, then worked for Olivetti before moving into venture capital.

Hauser is an amiable, engaging character with piercing blue eyes. When I met him in his London office he strode over to a whiteboard from time to time to flesh out some of his ideas in a series of rapid sketches. But one phrase stuck in my mind. We were discussing the future of medicine, an area where he believes his venture capital firm may profit. I mentioned how attractive I found the idea of having my eyesight corrected by laser surgery, but said I was put off by the prospect of paying over £2000. 'There are many constraints in my life,' said Hauser with a slight smile, 'but money isn't one of them.'

The firm in which he is a partner, Amadeus, specializes in what he calls 'deep technology'. Hauser, who lives and works in Cambridge, keeps a close eye on what emerges from the University's laboratories. By funding companies with cutting edge technologies, which he is well qualified to understand, he helped grow his investors' capital by as much 75 per cent a year in the late 1990s.

Amadeus also invested in a range of dot.coms – companies like last-minute.com, getmapping.com, and Clickmango's rival, ThinkNatural. But like every other VC I met after the bubble had burst, he was keen to stress that this had been a very small part of his business. 'We never got so seduced by dot.coms as others did. We were always into deep technology. But yes, we participated in it – VCs just could not ignore it.'

The venture capitalists like to paint themselves as deeply rational and omniscient individuals. Nevertheless, at the height of the boom it was difficult to be rational. Partners in venture capital firms arrived at their desks each day to find their in-trays and their e-mail inboxes choked with more business plans. Simon Murdoch of the Epsiode 1 fund remembers joking with colleagues about the most outlandish proposal to arrive on their desks. 'It was a toss-up between justlightbulbs.com – a site which did just what it said – and a business providing underwater maps on the Net for scuba divers.'

In this feverish climate it was difficult to assess the abilities of the entrepreneur. 'It was much easier to fake expertise in the dot.com area,' says Hermann Hauser. 'Nobody was a real expert – anybody could hold forth if they knew the buzzwords. If someone wants you to discuss microprocessor architecture that is a lot harder to fake.' But in late 1999 you did not need to be clever to make money from funding internet companies. You gave them some seed capital, their valuation grew, and a year later a grateful stock market would take them off your hand. Or so it seemed to a new breed of investment companies that entered the fray.

They were called 'incubators' or 'accelerators', and they painted themselves as venture capital firms cum finishing schools for aspiring entrepreneurs. They would provide their young charges with seed capital, premises, access to web design agencies and a host of other services – and, best of all, they would give them the benefit of their own management skills. Companies with names like Brainspark, Antfactory and Speedventures claimed that they would offer more than just cash in the bank. Their expertise would be crucial in helping young companies take their first faltering steps.

The river of money began to flow faster and faster, and much of it was going round in circles. The biggest splash was made by a firm called Jellyworks whose investments included a stake in Antfactory. Jellyworks was backed by a colourful city dealer, David Rowland (no relation of the Clickmango founder), and run by his 25-year-old son Jonathan. When it was floated on the Alternative Investment Market in December 1999 its shares quickly soared from 5p to £1.20, as investors flung their money at an internet business which was flinging its money at other internet businesses.

A company born just a couple of months earlier was now being valued at nearly £250 million, yet most of the £17 million it had raised was still sitting in the bank. Investors were betting that Jellyworks could soon multiply its money through the alchemy of internet investment. Nine months later Jellyworks was sold to another hi-tech investment firm, Shore Capital, for just £60 million – and all of that in shares.

Another internet investment firm with famous names attached to it followed a similar trajectory. Oxygen Holdings, which aimed to nurture the dot.com ideas generated by students, was backed by the celebrity PR man Matthew Freud and his then-girlfriend Elisabeth Murdoch, daughter of the media magnate. On the day it hit the stock market in February 2000 its shares rose from 2p to 57.5p. A dot.com dish served up with a dash of celebrity had driven investors to new heights of lunacy. By the end of the year the shares stood at 3p.

The irony is that by the spring of 2000 the flood of venture capital for which internet firms had been crying out had arrived onshore just as the

bubble began to burst. Come the end of the year, many venture capitalists were sitting on their hands, and some were asking whether it would be
more sensible just to return the money to their backers. Even some of those
who had seemed so perceptive in their investment strategy a year earlier
were looking a little sick now. On the day I visited Geoffrey Chamberlain,
Durlacher's share price stood at 20p. Nine months earlier the company's
share price had hit a high of £4.47 after announcing that annual profit had
risen tenfold to £5 million. Durlacher, which five years earlier had been the
smallest company on the Alternative Investment Market and was valued at
less than £1m, was worth £2 billion in March 2000 and stood just outside
that gallery of the corporate great, the FTSE 100.

Even its chairman knew it was madness. 'Our stock got carried away to
completely ludicrous levels,' he told me, 'We knew we could never achieve
the revenue to justify it. We were supposed to match the Shells of this
world.' Now that the market had realized that Shell-style revenues might not
be available to every dot.com, their prices had fallen back to earth, bringing
the companies that had invested in them down with them.

At least some of the venture capitalists had been able to make healthy
returns while the going was good, although in Britain it was the companies
which understood and backed groundbreaking technology rather than
dubious dot.coms that did best. Amadeus got its money back 30 times over
when a chip designer, Element 14, was sold to an American firm just twenty
months after its initial investment.

But often what had looked like smart money in 1999 seemed pretty
stupid by the end of 2000. So what are the secrets of VC success? Jon
Moulton, the man who briefly put venture capital onto the front pages in the
spring of 2000, has a few ideas. Moulton grabbed plenty of headlines when
his company Alchemy made a bid to take the ailing Rover car company off
BMW's hands. That offer was later withdrawn, but Alchemy had made
excellent returns, often through turning round dull old engineering firms.
Before starting Alchemy, Moulton had been at Apax Partners, another
unshowy venture capital firm that had a long track record of backing
winners.

I saw Jon Moulton shock an audience of entrepreneurs and venture capitalists by claiming that most of his success was down to a combination of
pure luck and a steady nerve. 'The only reason that I've survived for twenty

years is that I'm a nerveless bastard,' he said with a slight smile. The audience kept pressing him to reveal the secrets that helped Alchemy turn base metal into pure gold. But he insisted that much of his success had been down to pure chance. Bookham Technology, his best investment, which had earned his firm 300 times its original stake, had come to him not after careful research but because an acquaintance had said his brother had a clever idea. The brother was Dr Andrew Rickman whose fibre-optic components maker soared into the FTSE 100 in 2000, before making a speedy exit.

Moulton said there were some obvious mistakes to avoid. 'Don't back the guy who says he has a new operating system which is going to take on Microsoft.' The quality of the people was vital: 'Really good business ideas are regularly wrecked by bad management.' But his best advice seemed to be about the factor that is at the heart of any market: price. Alchemy had done hardly any deals in the dot.com sector, not out of distaste for the companies, but simply because the entrepreneurs were demanding too high a valuation. As a result, Alchemy's performance was ranked in the bottom quartile of VC funds at the beginning of 2000 but in the top quartile by the end of the year. So the simple answer to success in venture capital is buy low, sell high. Easy really, isn't it?

In November 2000 I visited Rob Norton in the offices of Clickmango for a television interview about the state of e-commerce. The dot.com had shut up shop by now, having at least achieved a graceful exit, paying off its creditors and making sure that staff had plenty of notice. But it was a dismal scene nevertheless.

Norton sat at a desk in one corner of the large white space that had once been home to his and Toby Rowland's ambitious project. He was tapping away on a laptop, putting together a plan for what he hoped would be his next venture. A group of serious, sober-suited people clustered at the other end of the office – new tenants gradually taking over the place. A noticeboard propped up in one corner featured newspaper cuttings from the day Joanna Lumley announced her involvement with the site. In another corner was the last fragment of that famous pink inflatable boardroom. 'Don't film in that direction,' pleaded Norton as my cameraman composed a wide shot of the cavernous office, 'it looks so sad.'

He then proceeded to tell me a tale that seemed to sum up the

Clickmango experience. When Norton and Rowland got their £3 million from the venture capitalists they did not even have a bank account in Clickmango's name. They went into a branch of the Royal Bank of Scotland in the City and talked to the member of staff who dealt with new business clients about opening an account. 'The guy asked us whether we would like some help with a business plan, he asked what sort of revenue we were expecting to make,' said Norton, shaking his head. 'He seemed to think we were just a typical small business. Even when we deposited the £3 million, he didn't return our calls. He probably thought it was dodgy.'

The bank official, it appeared, had treated them as if they were two guys starting a corner shop, in need of advice on how to manage their cash-flow, rather than serious players who had won the backing of some very smart financiers. Norton painted the man as a frightened little bank clerk who was out of his depth when it came to dealing with the industry of the future. But despite its grand ambitions, Clickmango ended up as a business with corner shop revenues. Perhaps the man from the Royal Bank of Scotland, proffering his starter pack for small businesses, was a little smarter than the venture capitalists.

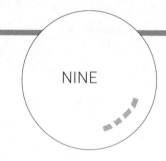

NINE

Everyone's doing it

IT SEEMED DURING THE period between the summer of 1999 and the spring of 2000 that half of the population of Britain had an idea for their own dot.com scribbled on the back of an envelope. The other half was fantasizing about leaving their dull old job to work with some funky people in a Clerkenwell loft on an internet idea that was going to be huge. Nobody would give you too many details about their dot.com concept – there was always a danger that you would run off with the idea and make the millions destined for them.

We have heard about the people who became the celebrities of the dot.com era – Martha Lane Fox, Julie Meyer, Kajsa Leander – but while they were appearing on CNN and on the covers of *Newsweek* and *Fortune*, thousands of more obscure people were joining the revolution. At every level of old economy companies restless staff were wondering whether the Internet might be the escape route that could take them to the better job and income they knew they deserved.

Students looking for their first job were asking themselves whether they wanted to disappear into some giant, faceless organization or whether it might be better to take a risk and start their own business. The self-employed, who had always had an eye for the latest trend, were quick to latch on to dot.com opportunities. Schoolkids – often with the active encouragement of their parents – were discovering that a website that had previously been a mere hobby might just turn into something more serious.

I began to realize quite how widely the bug had spread when I bumped into a neighbour in the summer of 1999. In our West London street where most people exchange little more than a nod as they climb into their Volvos, Geoff was different. Endowed with all the enthusiasm of one of life's natural salesmen, he knew everyone and was always keen to stop and chat.

In a varied career he had seen a lot of business's rich tapestry of triumph and failure. He had sold a photocopier business in the late 1980s for close on a million, invested the lot in a factory in St Helens and then gone bankrupt. He had got back on his feet, running a couple of pool halls and doing a little light chauffeuring, and the last time we had talked he was selling conserva-tories. 'Best business I've ever been in,' he confided. 'Lovely product, lots of customers.'

However, when I met him that morning and asked how the conservatory business was going there was a very different message. 'Given up that rubbish,' he said. 'Nothing but grief. Never got my commission, then found out the franchise owners were dodgy. I'm doing the Internet now – best thing I've ever done.'

Scanning the Franchises section of the small ads in the *Mail on Sunday* he had seen this: 'The Business for the New Millennium. Fastest growing industry in the world. Everybody Wants It. No Competition.' Well, who would not be interested? It turned out to be a franchise business called Net Traders whose aim was to make money by putting thousands of small firms on the Internet. They would be given a domain name, an e-mail address and advice on selling their products online.

Geoff and a partner decided to take on the West London franchise. Soon he was pounding the streets, calling in at every butcher, baker and candle-stick maker to tell them why they needed to be on the Net. Geoff knew little about computers and less about the Internet but he has always been a quick learner. At that time you could not open a magazine without reading the warning from Andy Grove, the chairman of the computer chipmaker Intel, that 'in five years time you'll either be an internet business or you won't be a business at all'.

Geoff took that as his mantra as he bustled through the doorways of dozens of small businesses and unleashed a Power Point presentation on the laptop he had been given as part of the franchise agreement. A few deft clicks and he was showing bewildered shopkeepers just how easy it was to get their business known on the web. For a £195 down payment and £40 a month he could give them www.joesironmonger.com and build them a three-page website.

Even those without a computer could benefit from a web presence. If customers clicked on their e-mail address, they might think they were e-mailing joe@joesironmonger.com but in fact they were triggering a fax which would soon be coming out of Joe's machine.

Soon he had signed up estate agents, motorcycle shops, a firm making Indian pickles and an Ealing restaurant. Geoff was telling his clients that the Web was the way to get their products to a worldwide audience. As ever, his enthusiasm was catching. One day he stopped me in the street and asked me if I could get him the e-mail address of Alex Allan, the government's newly appointed E-Envoy. 'I'm going to be an internet guru,' he insisted, 'I can tell him what's going on at the sharp end.' For Geoff, like many of those drawn into the dot.com world, this was the biggest thing that had ever happened to business, a technology that was going to change the world.

As I drove along the suburban streets in the spring of 2000, I wondered whether Geoff might be right. Everywhere it seemed that small shops and businesses were changing their signs and shopfronts to add three w's to their name. The local plumber's merchant seemed to be called bathsmart.com, the motorbike shop had a website and the mini-cab firm was promising that we could book online. The fact that my computer took five minutes to log on to the Internet and then frequently crashed halfway through loading a web page while I banged my head against the monitor, mouthing obscenities, was obviously a minor wrinkle that would soon be ironed out. Britain was going online in a big way. Geoff never got to meet the E-Envoy, but Mr Allan and plenty of senior cabinet ministers were surely pushing plenty of business in his direction with their constant exhortations to small businesses to get connected.

One summer evening in 2000 I had a long chat with Geoff over a glass of wine. While his enthusiasm had cooled slightly – 'My hopes and ambitions of making a quick million have gone' – he was still sure he was in the right business. He was no longer advising his clients that they could sell their products online. One, who wanted to sell her African textiles, had not had a single hit on her website in months and had chucked it in. But he had some success stories. A man who dealt in antique fireplaces and saw most of his profit go to what Geoff described as 'a bunch of Nigels in shops in the King's Road' had managed to sell one chimney-piece direct to a wealthy American who had seen his website. Geoff had concluded that the Internet could be a brilliant way of talking to your customers. However, he was warning his clients not to expect miracles.

But as the evening wore on the picture darkened. Winning new business had been a lot harder than he had imagined. Each franchise was supposed to have a target of 240 sales a year. Geoff and his partner had managed the best performance with 150 – the next best had signed up 68. Converting Britain to the Web was a harder road than he had imagined. 'The Net is all a bit over-hyped and under-used at the moment,' he admitted.

Then, quite suddenly, he revealed what had obviously been on his mind. 'Actually,' he said, 'Net Traders went skint on Monday.' The managing director of the business had filed for personal bankruptcy. Now he confessed that he'd had some initial doubts about this entrepreneur who had made his money as a publisher of 'adult material'.

When they had signed up they had travelled to the MD's home in Mansfield. 'He told me, "You won't have any trouble finding it – it's the one with the powder blue Jaguar and the Saab convertible parked outside." The house was very ordinary – and I'm never too sure about someone whose cars are worth more than their house.' Geoff remembered from his days in the photocopier trade that a flash new motor was always a sign of a businessman who was trying a little too hard to impress. He had visited the company's offices just a month ago and found that the MD had ordered a pink leather three-piece suite, a huge new desk and £20,000 worth of artwork for the walls. 'All fur coat and no knickers' was how he described it.

Now everything hung in the balance. A new owner had taken over Net Traders and had promised to keep things going. A notice had appeared on the website promising that nobody would suffer as the result 'of an unfortunate series of circumstances resulting in the bankruptcy of their former Internet Services Provider'.

A few weeks later Geoff was out of the internet business, after deciding that there was not a profitable future in it for him. He and his clients were the victims of another dot.com collapse where inflated ambitions and exuberant spending had led to predictable results. For Geoff, though, there had been a bonus. He and his family had fallen in love with the Internet. When I last visited, his teenage daughter was looking up the Education Act of 1944 as part of her history homework, and earlier the family had spent an hour searching out obscure song lyrics. 'Whatever happens,' he said, 'we've all learned an awful lot about this technology and that'll make a difference to our lives.'

Right at the top of British business, senior executives were following the same path from naivety and ignorance about the Web, through blind enthusiasm about its potential, to a more realistic view of what the technology might offer business in general and them in particular. One of London's top headhunters watched that journey.

Aliza Blachman O'Keeffe was a senior consultant at Spencer Stuart, a recruitment agency – or rather 'a leading management consulting firm specializing in senior-level executive search and board director appointments', as its website puts it. An American who had settled in London after working for the World Bank and McKinsey, she was a key player as the dot.com bubble inflated. For her task was to track down the kind of people who might leave grand jobs at the highest levels of British business to run a dot.com.

Headhunters appear to sign the same secrecy agreements as MI6 agents, and Ms Blachman O'Keeffe will not name her clients; industry sources say she was responsible for recruiting many of the chief executives who migrated to internet companies such as the online recruitment firm Stepstone.com and the portal Excite Europe. Headhunters keep up a constant dialogue with people who may be happy in their current jobs but want to know what is happening in the market. It was early in 1999 that she realized these clients had got the bug. 'Suddenly I had successful corporate players interested in one job with a firm started by a 26-year-old. My colleagues at Spencer Stuart were amazed by who was on the list. One was number two at a media firm, another was Chief Financial Officer at a FTSE company.' It was as if the manager of Manchester United had applied to run a park football team.

Blachman O'Keeffe says her clients' attitude to the kind of jobs that she was offering evolved as the dot.com boom accelerated. 'At the beginning I had to explain to people why they should even consider giving up a big job at a £200 million company to come and work for a start-up. Then in the second stage, at the height of the boom, I would ring up and say, "We need a chief executive for a pre-IPO dot.com," and they would be there by lunchtime.' Later they wised up to the fact that moving to a dot.com might not be the no-brainer that it had seemed for a few months.

The jobs might involve moving from a corner office in some corporate tower to a desk in the middle of a Clerkenwell loft, but that did not mean the headhunters were looking for second-raters. 'Some of the people who were ringing were reasonably senior executives at FTSE 100 companies who were never going to make it to the top,' says Blachman O'Keeffe. 'What they did not understand was that in this new world we were looking for stars.'

But the people who were identified by the headhunters as stars were getting dozens of offers. 'There's a real shortage of talent here in the UK,' says the headhunter. For these stars the attraction was not just the possibility of becoming very rich. 'It was about more than money. They liked the cappuccino machine, the energy, the table football in the corner of the office.' And because they were waking up to the fact that business did not necessarily have to be conducted in formal surroundings by sober-suited people, her clients were also interested in personalities as well as profits. 'For the first time in my life I was getting people saying to me, "I don't want to work with assholes."'

To anyone trapped within the confines of a traditional organization, the possibility of escape not just from the assholes but from all the tedious para-phernalia of corporate life is very attractive. The endless meetings, the carefully graded promotion ladder, the elephantine pace of decision-making, the memos, the back-stabbing, the politics – who needs them?

Suddenly there was an alternative. Yvette Ruggins was one who made the leap. By 1999 she had spent six years with the multinational company Kimberley Clark as European marketing director for a fast-growing brand of disposable nappies, Huggies. Then she was offered a move to a new area – female incontinence products. 'I just couldn't see myself describing my job at dinner parties,' she says. But it was not just the potential for social embar-rassment that brought her career at Kimberley Clark to an end. Ruggins was fed up with the politics that dominated her working life. 'There were all sorts of cliques and if you were not male you were not part of the clique. It got in the way of business, and politics was a game I was just not prepared to play.' On a 'ludicrous' trip to Miami for a three-hour meeting she made up her mind. 'It was time for a change, and female incontinence wasn't the answer. I'd worked for a number of multinationals and didn't want to do it again.'

She took redundancy from Kimberley Clark and prepared to spend a long summer relaxing and thinking about what to do next. Within days, though, she got a call from William Burton, a distant acquaintance who had heard about her departure from the corporate world. Burton was a former sales director at Thomson Holidays and he and his wife were now starting a dot.com. They persuaded Yvette Ruggins to join and soon she found herself working in a very different environment from the one where she had spent most of her career. Holidayexpert.com aimed to become an upmarket online travel agent. Yvette Ruggins became its marketing director and spent the next eighteen months living a typically manic dot.com experience.

Instead of the huge corporate offices of Kimberley Clark, she found herself in a bedroom in Burton's parents' home in Richmond that had become the temporary headquarters. The woman who had been handling multimillion-pound budgets was soon in a local office supply store buying a flipchart. 'I compared the prices of three models very carefully. I suddenly realized that I did not have the infrastructure which I had when I was working for a big company.'

Holidayexpert.com travelled the same roller coaster of hope and despair as many other dot.coms. It was another small business with big ambitions. There were dozens of tiny specialist travel agencies scraping by on their commission income – but Holidayexpert's founders believed that the rocket power of the Internet would enable it to grow quickly into a major business. This would be the site where the more discerning, affluent traveller would come to put together their own holiday, choosing from a selection of hand-picked hotels, and then getting the flights, car hire and anything else they needed. Holidayexpert signed deals with the upmarket travel firm Kuoni and with a series of airport hotels. But in an online market already crowded with travel sites, they needed the resources to grow quickly.

William Burton's experience as a senior travel trade executive allied with

Yvette Ruggins' track record in marketing gave the company plenty of credibility and they managed to pitch to many of London's ritziest venture capital firms. At Atlas Ventures they knew things were not going to work out when the senior partner fell asleep during their presentation. Time and again they thought they were about to do a deal with the likes of Durlacher or Goldman Sachs, and on each occasion there was a last minute hitch. 'One guy was all set to sign,' Yvette Ruggins remembers. 'Then he came back and said his boss didn't like travel sites. Another firm had actually signed a term sheet – then their American headquarters told them they weren't to do any more B2C deals.'

In the end it became clear that Holidayexpert was not going to take off in a big enough way to need a marketing director, and Yvette Ruggins parted amicably with the company, as the husband and wife team tried to turn it into a smaller scale venture. But Ruggins still feels that it was a positive experience. 'It showed me that I could never work for a big firm again. I worked incredibly hard for both Kimberley Clark and for Holidayexpert – but at the dot.com it did not feel anything like as arduous.'

It was the different lifestyle that made the long hours much easier to take. 'In a dot.com you can work from home, you can work long hours but to your own schedule, and you can wear what you like – all things that were not possible at Kimberley Clark. And it is not boring. You had highs and lows on a daily basis.'

For Yvette Ruggins, as for many others, the dot.com bubble failed to deliver on its promises. But she has no regrets. 'It was such an intense time. There was a revolution going on and you could not have forgiven yourself if it had worked and you had not been a part of it.'

Inside the marble temples of commerce there was growing unease in the boardrooms about rebellion in the ranks. Suddenly many of the brightest and best of their younger troops were being lured away by the promise of dot.com freedom. Accountancy firms like PriceWaterHouseCooper and KPMG, investment banks like Lehman Brothers and Credit Suisse First Boston suffered defections. The big management consulting firms, such as McKinsey, Andersen Consulting and Bain, were worst hit. Whole armies of consultants headed off to dot.com land, eager to prove that a twenty-something with an MBA could run a business as well as tell others how to do it.

You could not walk through a dot.com office without tripping over a former consultant or banker.

One of those who made the journey from consulting to e-commerce spoke to me at the end of 2000. He did not want his name published because by then he was wondering whether he should have bought a return ticket. By 1999 he had been with one of the big consulting firms for three years and was in his early thirties. He was earning £100,000 but in the next couple of years he stood a good chance of becoming a partner and that would mean as much as £500,000 a year. But he was fed up.

He was working on an e-commerce business set up within the consultancy and he was exasperated by the hierarchical nature of the firm. 'There were just seven of us working on this project, but there were twelve partners on its board. They wanted to make sure they got a share of any dot.com money.' Unfortunately the business was not making much progress because it took so long to decide anything. 'There was an awful lot of anal decision making – "How will this reflect on the partnership and on me?" I just wanted to say, "Get your frigging cheque-book out!"' He felt that the dot.com world was all about being quick on your feet – and he was going to get nowhere riding on this elephant.

That was what pushed the young consultant to look elsewhere. The pull came from meeting a former colleague who was starting a dot.com. He was offered the chance to join a venture entering what was becoming the hottest area of e-commerce. Already the internet gurus were saying that the big money was to be made not from selling to consumers – B2C – but from acting as an online middleman between businesses – B2B.

The project he joined aimed to provide a digital marketplace for construction businesses, somewhere for a notoriously inefficient and sometimes corrupt industry to buy supplies and organize projects. Looking for the best price for cement? Come to our website. Want to hire project managers? We've got a database. My young consultant friend drew me a sketch illustrating a popular theory of the time. It showed a very fat butterfly. The wings were the construction companies on one side, their suppliers on the other, and the body was the online marketplace, grown chubby on the flow of cash between the two.

What none of the other bright young people behind the site seemed to ask themselves was why the industry would let the fat butterfly come and turn things upside down. The suppliers, for instance, were used to high margins. Were they really going to sit back and watch some young upstarts come in and cut their prices? However, in the summer of 1999 that was old economy talk for those who did not understand that the Internet changed everything.

'It was a time when there wasn't any bad news about the Internet,' said the consultant. 'You did not think of failure. It was landgrab time.' He left his post at the tired old bureaucracy and set off for the dot.com that soon established itself in offices just off Piccadilly. By this stage jobs in online companies were deeply fashionable. 'You were not going to get a laugh at a dinner party if you said you worked for a dot.com. Whereas if you said you were a management consultant, you always got the old joke about being the man who got hired to tell someone where the hands on his watch were pointing.'

There is no doubt that it became cool to work for a dot.com – so cool that the makers of the BBC's cult drama series *This Life* followed it up with a new drama set in a dot.com, *Attachments*. It was all there – the tense meetings with the smug venture capitalists, the bitter rows between the founders, the sex in the office toilet. Somehow one cannot imagine a similar drama being set in the offices of a small travel agent, although that is all many a dot.com amounted to. Every small business I have ever visited has tales of triumph and despair, great teamwork and bitter disputes, but it took the arrival of the dot.coms for most people to realize that business does not have to be dull.

Working in a dot.com was little different from sitting behind a desk in any other office – but it felt better. David Anstee, an Australian in his early thirties, put it like this: 'Everyone's young, it's a new industry and we've got a new take on it. It's a fun environment to work in.' He was talking about his company ihavemoved.com, which finally struck gold in March 2000 after a dispiriting trek round London's venture capital circuit. The funding from NM Rothschild came just as BT was about to cut him off, and would have been impossible a few weeks later when the market went into freefall.

Anstee had packed a lot of experience into a few years. He had left a job with an investment bank for a spell as an assistant cameraman with National Geographic. One shoot off the Norwegian coast had seen him carrying a rifle to frighten off polar bears. His next stop was London Business School where he started an MBA and spent a summer on an exchange at the University of California at Berkeley. He had been thinking of sliding back into 'the darker side of investment banking' as he puts it, but Berkeley changed his mind. Helping some fellow students with a start-up, he caught the dot.com bug and decided he just did not want to be a banker or a consultant: 'Those guys don't improve anything, they don't add value. They hate it, they get paid stacks of cash and have golden handcuffs, but it's *so* not the answer. Even if this all blows up, I've still learnt eight times more than they have.'

His big idea came to him when he and a friend, Niko Komninos, returned to the flat they shared after a trip and found a stack of post, not only for them, but also for the previous three owners. What was needed – both by the movers and by the companies that serviced them – was an online service that allowed you to let everyone know when you changed address. Anstee, Komninos and two other friends from London's tribe of aspiring dot.com entrepreneurs started ihavemoved.com. Luckily, at a time when B2C was going out of fashion, the firm was selling itself as a B2B, collecting its revenue from businesses. Typically it cost the utilities £2 to £5 to alter the records every time someone moved house. Ihavemoved.com was going to charge them £1 per customer. There were also opportunities to sell other products to people using the site. The firm signed a deal with the Domino's pizza chain that would give every customer a free pizza when they moved in.

Once the long march to funding had reached a successful conclusion, everything changed. Now they could get offices and computers and start recruiting. By the summer they had an office in Westminster above a web design agency and the workforce was growing quickly. 'We were perceived as being a cool business and the CVs came flooding in, although only about one in four were from women,' says Anstee. But the former MBA student was adamant about the kind of person he did not want in his dot.com. 'We didn't recruit MBAs – business is about work, not talking about strategy.'

Anstee and his three co-founders found the pace unrelenting, even after the money arrived. 'There are now 30 hungry mouths to feed and there's pressure on us to get new financing. We spend a lot more time than we'd like just schlepping around VCs and that just means less time to put into the business.' But to be working in a small team, in a hot industry with people your own age in pleasant surroundings seemed a better deal than had been available before. Until then, many of the cleverest graduates had to choose between buying the smart suit and joining the regimented ranks of high finance or entering the more flaky world of media and design companies, where clothes were casual but the rewards were less attractive. Now, it seemed, you could wear a T-shirt and still make a million.

Like many of London's dot.coms, ihavemoved was extraordinarily cosmopolitan. A company founded by an Australian, two Greeks and an Italian had a workforce with nine nationalities and twenty languages between them. London's diversity – greater even than could be found in Silicon Valley – was one of its great strengths when it came to founding companies which often had global ambitions.

Anstee was keen to stress the importance of the casual atmosphere. His company has the inevitable pool table in the office and no dress code. 'Everyone wears what they want – the odd one out is the girl who wears a suit every day. We have pizza delivered every Tuesday for lunch, and it's compulsory to go to the bar on Friday. The only way to work out what employees are really thinking about is to get a few beers down them.'

It is a fascinating irony of the dot.com start-ups that so many of its employees were, in a sense, living contradictions of the presumptions about the future their business models depended upon. E-commerce envisaged a world in which people would be content to access all their needs sat in solitude at a computer screen inside their own home – but what the people who actually worked for the dot.coms found most liberating about their new work environment were the old-fashioned pleasures of sociability and human interaction.

Nevertheless, companies like ihavemoved.com had to show that they could keep that sense of fun while growing rapidly. Young companies are by their nature smaller, nimbler and more exciting than the lumbering old beasts of the corporate jungle. The real test for the dot.coms was whether they could maintain the revolutionary zeal that had been present at their birth. As companies grow, they inevitably acquire a lot of baggage, much of it unnecessary. Somebody decides the company needs to hold a weekly planning meeting, then it becomes a daily event and soon decisions have to be made about who should be present at the meeting, and that leads to an assessment of the hierarchy of the company and each person's place within it. Before you know it, you're ICI and you're hiring consultants to come and tell you how to make the organization more responsive to change. At the other extreme dot.coms that had never thought about managing their growth were threatened with the kind of chaos that engulfed boo.com.

For many in the dot.com world a business became a cause, but for others a cause became a business. The Internet was a glorified noticeboard where people with shared interests and passions could publish material for everyone else to share and argue about. As the dot.com bubble inflated, some of these shared interests were rapidly turned into businesses.

I came across just such a case when I went to film a sixteen-year-old schoolboy in a Suffolk village. Oli Watts was a bright, talkative boy who had seen everything turn sour eighteen months earlier. He had been bullied severely, so much so that his life had become a misery. It was not so much physical as mental abuse. He felt that all of the 150 children in his school year were ganging up against him. After a while, his parents, who were both teachers, started worrying that Oli always felt ill in the mornings and kept finding reasons to miss school. They sent him for counselling and eventually he was moved to another school.

Although his life improved radically, Oli decided that he wanted to make something out of his experience. He had been mucking about with a computer at home ever since he was ten, and had got a book out of the library called *Web Design in a Nutshell*. He had designed several websites for bands he had been involved in and now his father, David Watts, suggested he create a site about bullying.

Oli set to work on something he called pupiline. The idea was a site that would provide a forum for youngsters to share their experiences of bullying, but also a light-hearted online magazine dealing with teen issues. His father bought the domain name for pupiline.net and Oli worked into the small hours to make it happen. In February 2000 the site went live and rapidly attracted plenty of visitors. Children who had suffered similar ordeals to Oli's were eager to relate their experiences on the site's discussion boards. Bullying was an untold story and for many teenagers the Web provided the perfect means to share it. Such was its impact that Oli was invited onto chat shows, featured in newspapers in Britain and abroad, and even won an endorsement from Tony Blair.

On the face of it, a heart-warming tale of triumph born out of adversity.

But what was different about Oli's story was that his anti-bullying campaign had developed ambitions to become a business within days of its launch. And this only happened because it was February 2000 and Britain was in the grip of dot.com mania.

A few days after pupiline went live, Oli's parents had some friends round for dinner. Phil Brightie worked at the Sixth Form College that employed David Watts, and his wife Fiona Garrington was a former journalist who now worked from home as a public relations consultant. Naturally conversation turned to young Oli and his website. David Watts took the guests upstairs to the computer and logged on to pupiline. He asked for advice on how the site could be promoted. Phil said he would mention it to a friend who lived in the village.

The friend was Edwin Hamilton, the Business Development Director at the privatised nuclear power company British Energy. His job involved managing the company's e-commerce ventures and he had been involved in sponsoring First Tuesday events in Glasgow. Within days he had met David and Oli Watts and agreed to put some of his own money into pupiline.

Hamilton informed the sixteen-year-old that he had created something that was more than just a website: 'I told him, "What you've got here is a pure natural brand" – when kids came to this site they knew just what it stood for, unlike many of the commercial youth sites.' Hamilton advised Oli and his father on the mechanics of turning the site into a business – forming a limited company, registering the different variants of the name, getting to grips with online security. Eventually Edwin Hamilton left British Energy and became pupiline's chairman.

He introduced the Watts to a branding company, Design Bridge, which revamped the site and was happy to take its £100,000 fee in equity rather than cash. Pupiline also got investment and an office from an Internet service provider in Ipswich. For David Watts this was the opportunity he had been thinking about for years. 'Our family has always believed that we have the combined energy to do just about anything. I'd always thought we'd have a business one day – perhaps a restaurant – and then this came along and we thought, "Hey, we can do it right now."'

When I visited the pupiline office in the autumn, Oli and a group of his friends were diligently preparing content for the site. Every now and then, one of them would disappear to the local Burger King, which sponsored the site, and return with some chips. Oli even had an employee – a 22-year-old Manchester University graduate who was editing the online magazine.

David Watts explained that his knowledge of business had been 'zip' back in February, but by this stage father and son were both talking like veterans of the world of dot.com finance. Seed funding and angel investors, VCs and B2C tripped off their tongues. Oli, who was studying business as one of his GCSE subjects, told me he would quite like to become a dot.com entrepreneur and move to Silicon Valley. And his father insisted that his son played a crucial role in deciding the direction of the company. 'He is a forceful voice in meetings. We had a meeting with one potential investor in his fifties who wouldn't talk to Oli – he addressed everything to me. We didn't do business with him.'

With traffic building, sponsors coming on board and more investors ready to back them, a middle-aged teacher and his teenage son appeared primed for business success. The website, with its slogan 'by us, for us', was going to tap into a global teenage market which was already spending a lot of money online.

Only during the dot.com bubble could this have happened to the Watts family. They may have been saved from letting their ambitions become too grandiose by what began to unfold in the rest of the dot.com world. When I spoke to Edwin Hamilton again in February 2001, he was keen to stress the modesty of pupiline's operations. The venture capitalists had decided they were no longer interested in B2C sites, especially if they were run by sixteen-year-olds. But that was OK – the site was cheap to run and would not be burning up cash at the rate of boo.com.

Oli Watts had become a minor dot.com celebrity, invited to address conferences and winning awards, but he was still at school and his dad was still a teacher. Their vision of rapid business success was now on hold but they still had big ambitions. 'The first wave may have gone, but the swell is beginning to rise again,' David Watts told me a year after his son started pupiline. 'We're going to be in a strong position to catch the next wave.'

It may have seemed that everybody in Britain – from Martha Lane Fox, to Oli Watts, to my friend Geoff – was starting a dot.com. But this revolution was more defined by geography and social background than its proselytisers would have you believe.

Next time you find yourself in central London you might wish to take in some of the historic sites of dot.com land. Start at Home House, the digerati hangout on Portman Square. Head across Oxford Street down Park Street, past the offices where Martha Lane Fox and Brent Hoberman took lastminute.com through its notorious IPO. Now walk east for a while, cross Regent Street to Glasshouse Street where you can pop into the offices of New Media Investors, lastminute's first backers, and see if they are still taking business plans. A few steps will bring you to the Alphabet Bar, where you can get a quick drink in the birthplace of First Tuesday, before completing the pilgrimage a few hundred yards on in Carnaby Street where Ernst Malmsten and Kajsa Leander spent a fortune on their plan to make boo the world's coolest online retailer.

The point of this little exercise – which should not take more than twenty minutes – is to prove that geography matters in the online world. The majority of the people who saw themselves as leaders of the UK's dot.com revolution were concentrated in a small area and bumped into each other fairly frequently. Most of the dot.coms took off in London, with small clusters in the Thames Valley and in Cambridge. There were exceptions – Blackstar, a successful online video retailer, was born in Belfast and managed to stay there. Peter Wilkinson's Planet Online was determinedly Yorkshire-based, and when Freeserve put much of its operations into offices in Leeds, a sprinkling of internet firms gathered around it.

One of the great myths of the internet age is that location is unimportant now that we can communicate with each other at the speed of light. For at least a decade, we have been told that millions of us will soon be tele-working – setting off each morning to the shed at the bottom of the garden to log on to our job, rather than getting the 7.12 to London Bridge. Even though the technology exists to make the office redundant – and some people even use it – most of us still pitch up in some steel and glass edifice to moan about the boss, gossip by the coffee machine and do a little light work. Why? Largely because face-to-face communication is still the means by which most of us conduct our lives and our businesses.

In fact, in the dot.com world, human contact seemed to be even more important than in older industries. Businesses that were little more than a smart idea had to be built on trust, and trust cannot be constructed entirely by e-mail. And, crucially, just about all of the money was concentrated in

London, and venture capitalists who were prepared to fly across the Atlantic on a whim were not often found tooling up the M1 to Doncaster to scout out some likely prospects.

So Michael Smith and his friends moved from Cardiff to London to find the venture capitalists who would fund Firebox. Simon Murdoch believes that even Gerrards Cross 15 miles outside London, where he started book-pages.com, was too far away from the metropolis to be an ideal location. 'I should have spent far more time networking, getting to know people, and Gerrards Cross was too far out of London to be convenient for that.' When Murdoch started the venture capital fund Episode 1 with his partner Rikki Tahta, its offices were just off Oxford Street, a few hundred yards from Home House.

I got an interesting perspective on the question of location when I first met one of First Tuesday's founders, Nick Denton. Our encounter was not in London but San Francisco where I was filming a television report about Britons who were making it big in the heart of the dot.com world. Denton had shifted much of his company Moreover.com from London to San Francisco. Here was a business with global ambitions to send news content to websites – surely it could operate from anywhere?

But Nick Denton thought differently. 'We need to be in the global capital of the Internet, which is not just San Francisco but these couple of streets around South Park.' South Park was not the location of the profane cartoon series but a patch of grass fringed by cafés. *Wired* magazine had been founded just round the corner, and now dozens of dot.coms had moved into every loft space, their inhabitants emerging at lunchtime to lie on the grass and swap tales of successful funding rounds and soaring stock options. Nick Denton believed that his firm had to have an address in this location before the American venture capitalists and customers crucial to his business would find him credible.

Those who felt that they did not have to go all the way to San Francisco still saw the need to be close to those with a shared vision. That was why First Tuesday took off at such speed. It was not just a place to meet the venture capitalists who might fund you but somewhere to try out ideas on others following similar paths. Metcalfe's Law, which states that the power of a network increases by the square of the number of computers connected to it, works for people too. And London seemed to be creating a dot.com network that would suck in more wealth and talent to an area that was already seen as too powerful by the rest of the country.

The First Tuesday gospel did spread across the UK, with events held in a number of cities. However, many of them were getting going just as the dot.com bubble was bursting and the venture capitalists were retreating into their shells. After the spring of 2000 it was difficult enough to extract funding for a company in Clerkenwell – getting venture capital to come to Bolton was nigh on impossible.

Surely what the new economy did was provide encouragement to young entrepreneurs of a different breed, breaking down the class barriers that have been a constraint on British business? That may have been the case at the more technology driven companies. Certainly if you were a computer games software genius in your early twenties, you got a hearing from the investment community in 1999 when you might have been turned away five years earlier. Scientists who had long complained of the British bias against ideas which needed long-term funding were now getting more respect from the City, and building companies like Autonomy and Bookham Technology.

But when it came to the pure dot.coms, many of the people who leapt on the bandwagon had a head start in life. Brent Hoberman and Martha Lane Fox, Toby Rowland and Rob Norton were all at Oxford together. Jonathan Rowland was bankrolled by his wealthy father when he set up Jellyworks, and when Emma Edelson founded another internet investment company, Oxygen, it was her father Michael's City connections which proved crucial. Even Trinny Woodall and Susannah Constantine, the *Daily Telegraph*'s Sloaney fashion columnists, got in on the act with their site ready2shop.com.

In the dot.com world the key skill was not the ability to write elegant software, or understand the latest microprocessor architecture, or even draw up a convincing business plan. It was the people who knew how to network who stood the best chance – and an Oxbridge education and a healthy bank account are great confidence boosters. If the bubble had lasted longer, a far wider group of people might have burst through the barriers to business success. But in the brief dot.com boom, it was the networking skills of the old establishment that flourished.

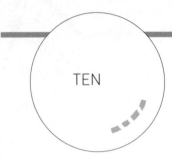

TEN

Fifteen minutes of fortune

IN THE ATTIC OF his home in West London, a bearded man in his late forties spends long hours parked in front of his computer, engaged in an obsessive hunt for wealth. In the early months of each year the hours become even longer as the hunt nears its conclusion. Philip Beresford has spent a decade examining records at Company House, ringing contacts and perusing annual reports in his quest to track down the wealthiest people in Britain and rank them according to their millions. Every March his efforts result in the publication of the *Sunday Times* Rich List, a supplement which adds as much as 20 per cent to the circulation of Britain's most successful Sunday broadsheet.

Beresford started compiling the Rich List when he was a journalist on the staff of the *Sunday Times*. He now describes himself as a 'wealth consultant', and has turned the examination of the rich into a full time occupation. In the early months of 2000 his work suddenly became a lot more complicated. As he rushed to complete that year's Rich List, he found it virtually impossible to keep track of the burgeoning wealth of a new class of entrepreneurs – the dot.com millionaires. As share prices in internet enterprises soared ever higher, their founders climbed their way up more rungs of the wealth ladder. People who had not even been on Beresford's radar a few months earlier were suddenly challenging for places in the chart.

What really astounded Beresford was a new attitude amongst the newly rich. He had grown used to having to squeeze information out of millionaires who thought that appearing in his list was either vulgar or just annoying. Painstaking detective work was needed to find his way through the maze of family trusts and shell companies that led to the pot of gold. Each year he would receive angry calls from people complaining that he had massively overstated their wealth.

But in 2000 people were demanding to be in the list, not out of it. A month or so before publication Beresford took a phone call: 'This guy rang and said, "I have got an internet business with my partner and it is going to be worth £300 million." I said, "Send me something to prove that."' Nothing arrived to substantiate the claim, so the caller was not included in the list 'He rang two days before publication and said, "Are we in?" When I said no he was livid and he ended up slamming the phone down.'

When the list appeared in March it still included a whole raft of dot.com names. In 1999 ten places had been occupied by internet millionaires, this year it was 63. Beresford admits it was the most inaccurate chart he had ever published – because in the weeks that had passed since the deadline for his research, rising share prices had made a lot of the contenders even wealthier. 'It was the first time I had been caught up in a hysteria,' Beresford told me. 'I was under siege – the world was changing every day.' High on the list was Dr Mike Lynch of the internet software company Autonomy, whose wealth was valued at £682 million – and that before the latest rise in his share price. 'His wealth doubled in a couple of weeks after the deadline,' Beresford told me, shaking his head in wonder. Terry Plummer and Wayne Lochner, founders of the website construction company Affinity Internet, had each seen their wealth rise from £4 million to £294 million on the back of a successful stock market flotation.

From the venture capital world Geoffrey Chamberlain of Durlacher was valued at £140 million, and at Amadeus Partners the wealth of Hermann Hauser was put at £100 million. Names that were totally obscure not only to the public but to most of the business community appeared to have built vast fortunes out of nothing. Charles Nasser, whose Internet service provider Claranet had been founded four years earlier and was still a small business, was said to be worth £300 million.

There was a separate list of young millionaires, which featured Tom

Hadfield, the teenage founder of Soccernet; his new venture Schoolsnet supposedly made him worth £7 million, even though it was not much more than an idea at that stage.

Publication of this treasure map came just as the lastminute.com IPO was creating two more multimillionaires in Martha Lane Fox and Brent Hoberman. And all sorts of most unlikely people were apparently reaping riches from the net. Celebrities were getting equity stakes for helping to promote dot.coms. Joanna Lumley was the face of Clickmango, Hugh Scully, the presenter of BBC TV's *Antiques Roadshow*, had a role advising users of the auction site QXL about antiques. His cash and shares package was reported to be worth £13 million. Charlie Dimmock, the television gardener, had sold the rights to her name to an internet company, and *The Times* confidently reported that she was on her way to becoming an internet multimillionaire – with no evidence to back up that claim.

Even politicians were getting in on the act. Alan Donnelly, leader of the Labour Group in the European Parliament, suddenly resigned his seat. In December 1999 he had invested £1250 in a Tyneside-based B2B company called just2clicks.com and by the end of February his stake was being valued at £1.5 million. It all seemed to confirm in the minds of the British public that the Internet was an easy way to make money.

The dot.com boom was a time of enormous enthusiasm about the new technology, and many were motivated to get involved by a sense that this was a once-in-a-lifetime event. For 1999 read 1789, and the spirit of an age where the old was being overthrown and a new class was storming the Bastilles of British business – although, as we have seen, many of the sans-culottes of this uprising were actually the sons and daughters of the *ancien régime*.

Amidst all this revolutionary zeal, one primeval urge cannot be discounted. It was the smell of money that propelled thousands of people out of their old jobs and into the new economy. As people perused the Rich Lists, open-mouthed at the kind of fortunes being accumulated by their contemporaries, our old friends greed and fear stalked the land. Greed because it seemed a simple matter to become fabulously rich. Fear because who wanted to be left in the office doing routine work on a boring safe salary when everyone else had gone to a job where stock options would obviously guarantee a property in Barbados and a Ferrari Testarossa a few months down the line?

A scene from my office at the BBC tells the story of those times. In October 1999 my colleagues and I clustered around a newspaper. The *Daily Telegraph* reported that former financial journalist Danny Bowers was celebrating a £6 million windfall after selling his personal finance website to a larger rival. The article quoted Mr Bowers ringing from a party in the pub: 'I spent my working life watching other people make money and I thought now was the time to have a go myself.' Some of us remembered Danny Bowers as the guy who read the financial report every fifteen minutes on the LBC radio station a few years back – not the most coveted job in our industry. There was a collective intake of breath followed by an outburst of envy. How could a hack just like us have made £6 million from a website? It just wasn't fair!

Journalists were peculiarly prone to dot.com envy, both because they were more likely to come across the young millionaires of e-commerce and because so many of their colleagues were jumping the fence and joining or starting internet ventures. The staff at the *Financial Times* had the example of Tim Jackson and Nick Denton to fuel their jealousy. Jackson's paper wealth from his stake in QXL had reached extraordinary proportions by the spring of 2000, making him worth £270 million. Denton's riches were less spectacular but he had a stake in First Tuesday – who knew how much that could be worth? – and a start-up company with offices in London and San Francisco.

Soon the editor of the *Financial Times* was finding that his journalists were queuing outside his office to tell him that they were quitting the *FT* to join the dot.com world. Some did go as far as leaving. Hugo Dixon, the editor of the Lex Column, a daily dissection of corporate performance that is feared and respected in many a boardroom, left to set up a rival online version. Breakingviews.com launched just as the dot.com bubble was bursting and, to the amusement of Dixon's former colleagues, supplemented its revenues by producing a column for the *Wall Street Journal*. An offline income was still handy while waiting for the late arrival of the online gravy train.

The *FT* managed to hold on to some of those who were threatening to jump ship by offering them promotion. The paper's parent company

Pearson even considered funding some of their dot.com ideas in-house. One member of staff, who had several meetings with Pearson's Chief Executive Marjorie Scardino about his plan, saw it all come to nothing after the Nasdaq started plunging. 'I have to say I'm rather relieved,' he told me a few months on. 'I'm still in a rather pleasant and comfortable job, not struggling outside in the dot.com wilderness.'

The *Financial Times* also poured many millions into FT.com, but failed to attract established journalists to the venture because there were no stock options on offer. Other newspapers pumped up their online operations, as the old media started to panic about the shock of the new. A slew of pure online ventures, such as thestreet.co.uk, Talkcast and the451.com crowded into British webspace, making enticing offers to journalists. Thestreet.co.uk, an offshoot of what was then seen as a very hot American online venture, attracted journalists from papers like the *Independent on Sunday* and *Sunday Business*. One reporter on a national daily turned down a salary of £67,000 plus £20,000-worth of stock options. Staff who did take the bait were talking excitedly by the spring of 2000 of what their options might be worth on flotation. At that time £500 million seemed a fair valuation on the company – and that would net them £200,000 each.

Not everyone was convinced that churning out material in bite-size chunks to be spooled through by impatient surfers was a great career move. Some were genuinely excited by the promise of a new kind of journalism, outside the control of the old media dinosaurs; but for many it was the prospect of the kind of wealth that they could never aspire to in their current jobs which was the main motivator.

Of course, at the BBC, service to the public rather than sordid financial gratification is what drives people. But as BBC Online grew ever larger, building a global reputation, an idle thought did begin to enter the minds of some staff. If Yahoo was worth $100 billion, surely BBC Online was worth a few billion pounds . . . and maybe one day soon it would be floated off as a private concern, and perhaps those who contributed to it would get options, and who knows, we might all be rich . . .

Aliza Blachman O'Keeffe, the headhunter who recruited many of the senior executives for dot.coms, saw the impact of the new money sweeping through British business. 'In the '80s everyone was going into investment banking –

in the late '90s it was dot.coms where it was "easy" to make millions.' At first, though, there was some caution. 'I remember one job which virtually guaranteed $10 million, with the possibility of $30 million later. But people were asking, "Why should I want to do something so different even if there is a lot of money?"' However, she was soon getting plenty of calls.

The American headhunter found that the British executive class, while more adventurous than their German and French counterparts, needed educating about the concepts of risk and reward. 'People were reading these rich lists and did not seem to realize that it was the founders who took the risks and made the big money.' Many of those who approached her agency seemed unfocused. 'We were getting waves of CVs from people who just wanted to join a dot.com – they had no vision of what it would do.'

In the United States stock options had become the obsessive topic of Silicon Valley café conversation. When would your options vest, what was the strike price – did you hear that so-and-so's options were now underwater? It was a whole new language and not one in which British executives were yet fluent. In early 1999 Aliza Blachman O'Keeffe was having to sit senior executives down and explain to them patiently how their options would work. By the end of the year everyone was picking up the basic vocabulary.

In Silicon Valley many were so eager to join internet companies that they were prepared to accept stock options in lieu of a proper salary – 'lieu losers' was to become the popular term for these people. In contrast, American internet companies arriving in Britain to recruit local executives found that over here, the candidates wanted it all. 'You had to pay more in the UK than in the US,' says Blachman O'Keeffe. 'Chief executives over here had to get at least £175,000 plus stock options, compared to £150,000 in the United States. Our clients were shocked – the British guys were playing hardball, demanding equity and cash.'

Later, a cartoon in the *Financial Times* summed up the attitude. A pin-striped gentleman sits in front of a surprised group of interviewers, saying, 'I want stock options in case the company becomes really big and a really big salary because I know it won't.'

Nonetheless, options did become increasingly attractive as stories spread of the huge sums they could generate. Rob Simon of the Raw Carrot recruitment agency remembers the phone calls he got on the day one of his clients, a software company, had its IPO. 'The shares had gone up 274 per cent on the first day. There were several guys who had turned down jobs at the firm who rang me up and asked, "How much did I lose today?"'

Option schemes were designed to motivate and retain staff in a very competitive job market – if you left before your options had vested, you were almost certainly kissing goodbye to some serious money. It was not just chief executives who stood to gain. Equity in the company was a means of attracting staff at all levels of a young dot.com, and it was also an attractive way of paying your suppliers – from accountants, to lawyers, to PR agencies. They had watched clients make millions in a hurry, now they wanted their share, even if it meant foregoing fees for a while. A magical currency had been created which could only appreciate in value.

Look at lastminute.com's IPO prospectus for evidence of how important a part equity played in the dot.com workforce. All of the full time staff were entitled to take part in an employee share scheme. A month before the trading in the shares began, around 200 staff had between them almost 15 million options at an average exercise price of 24p a share. That gave them the right to buy shares over a three-year period at the price at which their options had been granted, whatever the market value on that day. At the launch price of £3.80p the workforce was looking at a collective paper profit of £53 million – or about £250,000 each. So when that receptionist cried out 'We're all going to be rich!' at a meeting a few months before the IPO, she had a point. Of course, there was always a danger that the share price could fall before an employee's options vested and could be turned into real money – but that was surely very unlikely.

However, if options could bind a company together in a united quest for riches, they could also prove very divisive. One software engineer told me a cautionary tale. At first he was happy to see his name and his company published – later he decided that it could cause problems. So I shall just call him Jim. In the winter of 1999 he joined what was in his words 'a typical dot.com, founded with the aim of getting to IPO as quickly as possible and making everyone rich'. He was one of just eight staff – and soon there were tensions between the technical staff and four young executives with MBAs. 'We were doing masses of work and going down one particular route – then the MBAs would suddenly come in and tell us to do something else. Immediately we realized that some of these guys had no experience of the

Internet. They never used it, one of them didn't even know how to send an e-mail properly.'

But it was money that proved the source of the most serious quarrels. Everyone was told to expect a generous options package, although this could not be tied down until the firm got its second round of funding. 'The MBA guys were convinced that we would all be on a tropical island this time next year,' says Jim. 'We were going to IPO in May and we'd all be worth millions, we'd be as rich as the guys from Freeserve. You'd be watching the cars go by outside the office, and one of the MBA guys would say, "See that Porsche, next year that'll be mine."'

By the spring of 2000 it looked as though the company might run out of money before the funding arrived. Its staff looked on with envy as the last-minute.com IPO came to its deafening climax. 'I think everyone in dot.coms remembers that week,' recalls Jim, 'We all had jealous eyes for them.' The divisions between the rest of the company and the MBAs were growing. 'The people working in the front line of the operation could see that the sales figures were not going to meet expectations. Suddenly, the realization was that we were not automatically going to make it big, and worse, that we would possibly fail.' The technical and operations team blamed the business geniuses at the top. They still seemed oblivious to the impending doom. 'The atmosphere was further soured,' says Jim, 'because we didn't have second-round funding or stock options, which was why we were there in the first place.'

Then came an incident which showed just how dangerous a tool e-mail can be. A document drafted for the venture capitalists turned up in a public folder, containing details of everyone's pay and entitlement to stock options. 'That did more damage than any other thing, any dispute in the company,' says Jim. 'Everyone saw it and learnt that the people that had been there since the beginning didn't necessarily have the biggest share options.' One of those who had joined in the early days later left as a result, and others had their contracts renegotiated.

Shortly afterwards, everything worked out well for the company when it received substantial second-round funding from investors. Jim, who had been offered another job at a higher salary, was persuaded to stay on and got a generous options deal. But by the winter both he and his colleagues with the MBAs were realizing that their dreams of seven- or eight-figure sums were not about to come true. The IPO, which had originally been pencilled in for May 2000, was now impossible. The options were not going to change anyone's life until they could be traded.

In that brief heady period when a stake in a dot.com company appeared to be the key to a bank vault, how did the lucky few react? For many there was a degree of confusion and embarrassment. In dot.com offices you were as likely to find copies of the *Guardian* as the *Financial Times*, and there was a good dose of liberal guilt amongst those who realized that, in this game of capitalism in its purest form, their number had come up.

Late in 2000 I met a former internet executive, now safely ensconced in a job with a major broadcaster. In the early part of the year he had been sitting on what looked like a potential fortune. 'I had a friend who was an executive at Yahoo and we found ourselves constantly talking about just one thing – our options. How much they were worth, what day they would vest, how we felt about the money – which we hadn't really earned.' He describes a mixture of excitement and guilt. 'We actually worked out an equation featuring the value of the options, the amount of guilt, and the time it would take before we got the money. Of course, that all quickly became irrelevant as they sank under water.'

The *Guardian* newspaper, long a critic of the get-rich-quick, loadsa-money culture that had emerged under Thatcherism in the 1980s, was itself having to confront the issue of what motivated its own staff. The company was putting a good deal of money into its online ventures and was worrying about recruiting and retaining talented people. Because of the structure of Guardian Newspapers Limited, owned by the Scott Trust, it was impossible to offer options. The company set up a committee to consider whether it could create a 'shadow options' scheme, giving some reward based on the perceived market value of the online operations. Eventually the idea was dropped. 'Options aren't all they are cut out to be,' the paper's managing director told the *Financial Times*. 'If you can get a really good package and bonus, that can often be better than a dud options scheme.'

Over in Silicon Valley, billionaires who are asked why they still need to increase their pile of gold often come up with the same line – money is a way of keeping score. When Bill Gates's unimaginable wealth was briefly surpassed by that of his deadly rival Larry Ellison, you could sense the glee felt by the founder of Oracle. But while some of the new money in Britain was ringing up Philip Beresford and demanding to be counted, many of those in the dot.com rich lists retained a British reserve.

Geoffrey Chamberlain at Durlacher grimaced when I mentioned the *Sunday Times* list which had valued him at £140 million. 'You don't need that additional pressure. It is not helpful in terms of your family. I'm a reasonably private person – having your paper wealth flaunted is not helpful,' he told me. 'It's the tall poppy syndrome. They love to build you up and knock you down.' Chamberlain had earlier told me of his enthusiasm for the entrepreneurial culture of the United States, but he appeared less impressed by the sparring between billionaires like Bill Gates and Larry Ellison. 'They're behaving like silly boys. One of the nicer things about Britain is that we are more mature about money.'

Much of the publicity which Martha Lane Fox and Brent Hoberman attracted at lastminute.com was fuelled by the excitement surrounding their sudden wealth. Both of them were also extremely uncomfortable with questions about their money. Whenever they were asked about it they came over like modest pools winners, insisting that their lives had not been changed. Brent Hoberman still drove his K-reg Volkswagen Golf, Martha Lane Fox thought only of her company, not her bank account.

When I saw her in the autumn of 2000 she insisted that money had never been a big motivating factor: 'A year ago I was working for less salary than I had ever had in my life. It was phenomenally hard not seeing any of my friends. I didn't get out of bed in the morning because I wanted to make millions of pounds. One day my life could be changed – but it's not now.' Of course, both she and Hoberman had sold almost a million pounds worth of shares when lastminute floated. Enough money to change most people's lives. Still, they both did seem driven by more than cash, with an almost messianic belief in the power of their company to achieve great things.

Dan Thompson, chief executive of 365 Corporation, watched his net wealth soar at the end of 1999 as his company's shares took off following their debut on the stock market. 'There was a lot of knocking at the time,' he says, 'because people couldn't understand why these fortunate few were earning huge sums of money.' Of course, the reality was that he and others in the rich lists were only as wealthy as their share price that day. Chief executives of newly floated companies were also banned from selling shares for some months afterwards, and even when the moratorium ended, news of directors selling any of their holdings would be enough to send the share price tumbling. 'You are rich when you've got cash,' says Thompson. 'Not when you're management and you've got paper which you can't sell.'

If the 1980s was the age of conspicuous consumption, with City dealers blowing their bonuses on gallons of champagne and a Porsche, the dot.com bubble which marked the end of the century was, from a journalistic point of view, disappointingly free of excess. There was boo.com, of course, but most of the dot.commers seemed too busy and too driven to blow it all on fast cars and big houses.

And that was fortunate because it soon became clear just how quickly paper wealth could disappear. In the United States some young internet tycoons bought the boat, the house and the car – and then found that they could not pay for them because their wealth had evaporated as their share prices took the down elevator. Most of Britain's newly wealthy did not even have time to get their credit cards out before the crash came.

By the end of 2000 a series of sickening downhill lurches in their share prices had seen the value of some internet companies fall by as much as 98 per cent. Johnathan Bulkeley, the chairman of QXL, had been worth £141 million in March 2000 when the shares hit £7.44. By December, with the price hovering around 10p, his stake was worth not much more than £2 million. QXL's founder Tim Jackson had suffered almost as badly – but he had been canny enough to sell some shares at the beginning of the year, so some of his paper money had been turned into the real thing. Some in the high-tech sector pulled off even more spectacular losses. Dr Andrew Rickman of the fibre-optic firm Bookham Technology saw his stake in his company hit a value of £1.5 billion in the summer of 2000 as the stock market decided that the real value was not in these flaky dot.coms but in real companies which made the hardware behind the Internet. A few months later the market had decided that this too was an illusion, and more than a billion pounds had been wiped off Dr Rickman's wealth.

When I went to see Dan Thompson of 365 Corporation in December 2000 in his modest office just off Baker Street, he seemed pretty calm for a man who had lost many millions of pounds over the past nine months. In March he had been worth around £18 million; now his shares might just about fetch £2 million. 'The share price? It's miserable, it's no fun at all,' he told me. 'Nobody likes to lose huge amounts of money. But it's an amusing thing when you sit around on a Friday night with friends from outside the industry just to tell them how many millions you've lost in the past week.'

Further down the corporate ladder, wealth was also evaporating. By the end of 2000 staff at companies like lastminute.com and QXL were realizing that their options might just about pay for a night out at the pub rather than a villa in the South of France. Working in a dot.com did not seem so glamorous now. The hours were just as long but without the prospect of a huge windfall it was more difficult to persuade people to sign up to the dot.com revolution.

As Philip Beresford sat down to compile the next *Sunday Times* Rich List in the early months of 2001, he realized that the dot.com wealth mountain which had changed the landscape a year earlier had been wiped off the map. By the time his work was complete just 26 of the previous year's 63 internet millionaires were left on his list. In the United States the internet gold rush had been called the biggest legal creation of wealth in history. In Britain it was the briefest.

Nevertheless, there were a few people who did make some serious money out of the dot.com bubble. There were those pioneers who created and then sold the early dot.coms before the real gold rush was under way. People like Darryl Mattocks and Simon Murdoch who were looking foolish in the spring of 2000 but extremely prescient by Christmas. Then there were the company bosses who sold shares at the height of the boom. Amongst the smartest were David Potter, founder of Psion, whose shares were borne aloft on hopes that its software would power the mobile internet. Dr Potter made £65 million selling shares in the spring of 2000. A year later Psion's share price had fallen by more than 90 per cent. Dr Mike Lynch, creator of the Cambridge internet software firm Autonomy, sold £47 million worth of shares in the autumn of 2000. The following April those shares would have fetched less than £5 million.

But the man who comes out of it with the biggest smile on his face is Peter Wilkinson. After scribbling down the sums which made Freeserve possible, Wilkinson sold his Internet service provider Planet Online to Energis, netting £28 million for his stake in the firm. From early 1999 he then built up a new business called Sports Internet, which included the planetfootball.com websites and an offshore betting business. The company launched on the Alternative Investment Market and its shares were soon galloping ahead, but by January of 2000 the canny Yorkshireman was in a state of high anxiety. 'I was absolutely cacking myself to get rid of it,' is the elegant turn of phrase he uses to describe his business strategy at that time. 'I just felt we needed to get out before the bubble burst.' By March he was talking to BSkyB about a sale. The satellite broadcaster, like other parts of Rupert Murdoch's empire, was now embracing the Internet after some early scepticism on the part of its leader.

Wilkinson's anxiety level was increasing as the internet share market reached its peak. 'It was just going barmy. When you looked at the last-minute float you thought, "this is utter, utter lunacy".' As the air started leaking from the balloon in April and Nasdaq tumbled, the talks between Sports Internet and BSkyB continued, and Wilkinson's fingernails gradually disappeared. Finally the deal was signed in May.

Either Murdoch's lieutenants were not aware of the dot.com carnage all around them, or they thought it was a buying opportunity. They paid an extraordinary £301 million for Sports Internet, which was just fourteen months old. Wilkinson's 42 per cent stake in the company earned him £141 million. He described these events to me at the end of 2000. 'Never mind the deal of the year – that was the deal of the century,' he said. A light smile played over his lips as he rolled himself another cigarette. Roll-ups rather than Havanas were the Wilkinson style. The one downside of all this was inclusion in Philip Beresford's Rich List. 'Those lists cause me a lot of grief and it's bad for the kids,' he said. His four children went to school locally in Yorkshire and he did not want them to attract publicity.

Then his eyes lit up again. While his dealings with Energis and BSkyB were detailed in the company records, one source of wealth was far more difficult to trace. 'The only thing that Beresford can't pin down is the Freeserve payment,' he told me. By this time in early 2001 the shares he had received for his part in creating Freeserve were down by 80 per cent from their peak. But Wilkinson had also extracted real cash from his deal with the free Internet provider. For every minute users spent online, he got a tiny fraction of a penny. When Freeserve was launched there were modest expectations of how many might use it. By now there were over 2 million subscribers and the trickle of pennies had turned into a torrent. 'It's a humungous amount of money,' said Wilkinson, 'I'm like that guy who invented cats-eyes and collected a payment every time they put them on a road.' He told me roughly what he was now earning each week from Freeserve and swore me to secrecy.

If Wilkinson could afford to look smug, so could one set of people who had risked much less but still come away from the bubble with a sackload of loot. The bankers who had been so eager to shepherd dot.coms through the IPO process had profited hugely. The customary fee was 7 per cent of the proceeds of the share sale. Lastminute.com's accounts reveal that the costs associated with its IPO amounted to almost £12 million. The lion's share of that went to the bank which led the controversial issue, Morgan Stanley. By the end of 2000 the bankers were sitting idle as the market was unwilling to give a welcome to new companies. But they could still reflect on a fantastically lucrative year.

The headhunting firm TMP reported that pay packages in corporate finance were breaking all records. Its research showed that in what was by now known as the TMT sector – telecommunications, media and technology – the head of a team at one of the big firms like Morgan Stanley or Goldman Sachs could earn anything from £3 million to £6 million per annum. Even a young star in such a team, taking internet companies to the stock market, could be earning as much as £2.5 million for a year's work.

Flamboyant dot.com bosses might have made it into the rich lists, but it was their advisors who were quietly enriching themselves, with real deposits in the bank, not worthless pieces of paper. A good deal of that money was earned selling those pieces of paper to a whole new class of investors.

ELEVEN

Fill your boots

IN THE EARLY MONTHS of 2000 Britain was getting hooked on the Internet.
Freeserve had helped to turn the Net into a mass medium, and all over the
country people were logging on in the evening to spend half an hour sending
e-mails, reading their football club's website or maybe taking part in an
online game. At her home in Sussex, Maria Hodgson was in front of her
computer for rather longer than most. 'I was there all day, every day,' she
remembers. 'I couldn't leave it even to go out shopping, so I bought my
groceries online.' The reason for Mrs Hodgson's obsession was the need to
monitor a share portfolio which had grown from a few thousand pounds
worth of privatisation stocks to a collection of high-tech investments worth
a quarter of a million. She was constantly checking the performance of a
clutch of obscure companies that she believed were world-beaters and
talking to other online investors about where the market was going. 'I have
a whole new life out of it,' she told me. 'It's built up into a full-time job. It's
quite a sociable thing. I talk to a lot of people by e-mail and I've arranged
gatherings where investors can meet face to face.'

She had got interested in the stock market a few years earlier and had
then discovered the Internet. There she came across the strange world of the
bulletin board where thousands of people who never meet exchange views
on a myriad of subjects, from animal husbandry to Zen Buddhism, from

Anarchism to Zionism. What interested Mrs Hodgson, however, were the investment discussions. 'I read up a lot on the bulletin boards, and quickly learnt a huge amount. Then I started trading and it's become a full-time job.'

Maria Hodgson was one of a new breed of investors who, as the dot.com bubble inflated, became convinced that they could now take on the markets from a back bedroom and make a living – or even a fortune. Technology was what created this new breed. Some were long-term devotees of the Internet who were so starry-eyed about the technology that they were sure the companies behind it would soon be making extraordinary profits. Others were people who had a spark of interest in investment that was fanned by the arrival of the Internet in their lives. The Web made it easier for ordinary people, far from the dealing-rooms of the City, to get access to information about companies and then to buy and sell shares. It also provided a very noisy forum for investors to share their views, to praise or denigrate companies in the fruitiest of language, and to engage in shouting matches with each other.

In the first three months of 2000, Britain was playing the stock market as never before. Over 6 million shares were bought and sold by what the City refers to as retail investors, a 50 per cent increase on the previous quarter which had also broken all records. Angela Knight, a former Conservative Treasury minister who now ran the Association of Private Client Investment Managers, issued a jubilant press release: 'These figures tell the story of an amazing and exhausting three months,' she proclaimed. 'Investment in stocks and shares became a truly mainstream activity – more people traded shares this year than went to football matches.' And much of this activity was happening online.

After the explosion of internet share dealing in the United States, a host of American companies had set up shop in Britain, offering cut-price commission rates to attract new customers. The figures showed 930,000 online share deals in the first three months of the year, up from 371,000 in the previous quarter. Over £3 billion worth of shares was traded as the dot.com craze gripped small investors in the early months of 2000. The Thatcherite dream of a share-owning democracy was coming true in Blair's Britain – and it was the Internet that was making it happen.

In pubs and clubs across the country, shares – and particularly dot.com

173

shares – became almost as hot a topic of conversation as football or the soaps. The tabloid newspapers, always quick to spot a shift in the national mood, started giving space to investment issues. The *Mirror*, which a few years earlier had led the condemnation of business 'Fat Cats' like Cedric Brown of British Gas, started a daily column called City Slickers. In their brazen promotion of stocks that they already owned, and their confidence that share prices could only go one way, the column's authors seemed to capture the spirit of the age.

It was in September 1999 that one of the City's best-known faces began to realize that something was going on. Before he left Barclays Stockbrokers to start his own business, Justin Urquhart Stewart sometimes appeared to spend more time in a television or radio studio than in a dealing room. The broadcasters loved him because, in his trademark red braces, he conformed to their image of a stockbroker, but also because he could deliver information in the most accessible and colourful way. And beneath the showmanship, Urquhart Stewart was a hugely experienced and knowledgeable observer of the market.

That September he watched as the market in some shares, particularly those in internet and other hi-tech firms, began to lurch up and down – but mostly up. The rapid movement was being driven not by the big institutions but by the trades of thousands of small investors. A new breed, excited by the success of the Freeserve IPO, was invading the market. The chat board phenomenon had got underway – 'people who wore their shirts outside their trousers' as the dapper stockbroker puts it – and the swirl of rumour and disinformation, which had characterized the London stock market since it got under way in seventeenth-century coffee houses, had now moved into the virtual world.

Urquhart Stewart, who had watched the evolution of the private investor over the previous 25 years, christened this latest variant the 'Electric Henrys'. Before the privatisations of the Thatcher years, about 2 million people owned shares. 'Let's call them the Georges,' says Urquhart Stewart. 'They had a glass of sherry with their stockbroker once a year and let him get on with it.' Privatisation created the 'Sids' – the people who responded to the British Gas flotation campaign which entreated us all to tell Sid about the shares. 'After that you had the Super Sids – people who made sure that not only they but all their family signed up for the privatisation shares. They never sold any of their shares and they've probably got over £50,000 worth by now.'

Then there were the Henrys. 'Henry read the *Telegraph* city pages, sneaked a look at the wife's *Money Mail* and swapped share tips at the golf club. He started selling as well as buying, and traded about once a month. After him you got the Super Henry – retired, lives somewhere like Prestatyn or Ayr, follows half a dozen companies very closely and knows more about them than the brokers.' And so on to the final stage of development. 'The Electric Henry discovered the Internet, and he trades because he can – I can, therefore I will.' For people like this, there is more information than ever before and more means of acting upon it. But this is not necessarily beneficial. As Justin Urquhart Stewart puts it, 'The good news is they've never had so much information. The bad news is they've never had so much information.' The problem was that many of these people seemed to think that shares – and particularly dot.com shares – could only move in one direction.

In December 1999 I stood in the Birmingham call-centre of the American stockbroking firm Charles Schwab while my cameraman tried valiantly to make online investment into compelling television. The firm had made a big pitch for the business of Britain's small investors and was expanding its operation very quickly. While many of its customers were dealing on the phone, more and more were starting to use the Internet to trade.

So I asked the executive from Charles Schwab acting as my guide what kind of shares they were buying? He produced a list of the top ten most traded shares of that week. At the top I expected to find Marks and Spencer, Vodafone or Halifax – the kind of companies everyone had heard of. But instead the name at number one was 365 Corporation. The online sports and telecommunications company had just floated, and investors who had made a killing from other dot.coms were ready to feast on this one too.

We moved downstairs to complete our filming in a public area where Charles Schwab customers could come in to chat and check the latest state of the markets. I latched on to two Asian clients sitting in front of a screen. A smartly dressed young man was explaining to his rather bemused older friend just how this investment business worked. When I interviewed the younger man he pointed to the screen which displayed the value of his portfolio that day – around £250,000. 'I work for a management consultancy, but I'm making twice as much from share-trading as from my regular job,' he confided. At the same time he was keen to sound a note of caution for any viewers who thought there was easy money to be had. 'It can be very dangerous if you are not an expert on the markets,' he told me solemnly.

So who were the new investors attracted to the market by the dot.com bubble? Many fitted the stereotype – male, based in the South East of England and prosperous. But among those I came across were an actor, a 25-year-old market researcher, and a mature student doing a history doctorate.

The student was Sarah Green and, appropriately enough, her research was into the money markets of Regency England and the effect of the introduction of paper money. She had inherited a small portfolio of shares when her mother died and then after a while she had started using her computer to monitor their performance and to trade. She had sold her mother's dull old holdings in traditional blue chip companies and started buying what interested her – firms involved in communications and the Internet. Soon she was dealing more and more frequently, sometimes carrying out several trades in a day.

The work on her doctorate had given her some insights into the psychology of markets. 'It is completely addictive and it's completely infantile,' she said. When I spoke to her in 2000 she was taking a year out from her doctorate to devote all her time to the market. 'My aim is to pay off debt of £25,000 and buy a property abroad,' she told me. 'I'm now beginning to make more money than my husband – it makes him really mad.' She was also realizing that there were dangers in her new hobby. 'It is addictive – that is what worries me. If I'm out and away from market info, I'm nervous. I'm going to get a WAP phone so I can stay in touch.'

Crispin Redmond was an actor who, as he put it, 'has spent his life trying to find ways of making money that don't involve work'. He had bought his first computer in 1998 and when someone mentioned a company called Tadpole Technology he had looked it up on the Internet. 'Suddenly I realized that there was all this information out there. I stumbled across the Motley Fool website, downloaded its investment guide and gradually started educating myself, creating a mock portfolio.'

Soon he was investing for real. While reading the Interactive Investor International website, he had come across a mining company called Minmet. This obscure firm with hopes of discovering gold in Latin America was just the sort of business which online investors love. Difficult to assess, uncertain but potentially lucrative prospects, hugely volatile – it was like climbing aboard an unstable Russian rocket. Crispin Redmond took his seat and made some quick profits.

His first ambition was to make £7000 in a year – the maximum profit an individual could accumulate without paying capital gains tax. He achieved that in his first year, and went on to invest in companies like Freeserve, Scoot.com and Parthus. Soon the online discussions about shares were taking up much of his time. 'In the evening I would make any excuse to go down to my study and turn on the computer. My wife was complaining that she was an internet widow.'

By March 2000 things had worked out very well, 'I was massively in the money. It was all on paper – but it did great things for my morale.' However, when I met him in his London home just before Christmas that year, his ardour had cooled. For one thing, a new baby meant there was less time to be spent checking share prices, for another, much of his profit had been wiped out. Still, he was about 15 per cent up on his original investment. If you got in to the market at the end of 1998, it was easy to make money. Now it had become just as easy to lose it. 'But I'm not frightened of going back in again,' he told me, 'and it's given me something to talk about at work.' For once, Redmond had steady employment. Work was the set of a television mini-series that was currently proving much more lucrative than the stock market. In the long hours between takes, conversation would sometimes turn to shares. 'Money is usually the last topic actors want to talk about, but if you tell them a way of making it they're all over you.'

For Mickey Buccheri, the market was just a bit of fun, much like a visit to the races. He was a 25-year-old freelance researcher for opinion poll companies when he decided to get involved in October 1999. 'The American dot.com boom had been going on for so long and at last it was happening here in Britain' he says. He and a friend who was still at university both had some savings and decided it would be much more interesting to punt the money on the stock market rather than leave it gathering dust in the bank. 'It was all good fun because it was all happening so quickly,' he says. 'Shares were going up dramatically in the space of a few weeks. We knew none of our investments were long term, it was always a short-term thing.'

Their first investment was in a web software company called Merant. They had read on a website that big institutional investors were buying into the firm. So on a Friday in October they bought some shares. The following Monday the price started rising and by Christmas it had doubled. It all seemed so easy. 'You should really lose the first time,' says Buccheri, 'You're like the gambler who wins in his first game of blackjack. You can't stop.'

So they were soon buying more shares, often in the kind of obscure companies that were so popular with the new breed of investor – firms like Geo Interactive, a company developing video technology for websites, and Jasmin, which made smart cards for retailers. Over the next months they built up a portfolio packed with what were then believed to be the Microsofts of the future. 'I can't say we knew what we were doing,' he says. 'We were researching on the Internet. It was now easier for individuals to trade through websites, easier to get information, and it looked like it was easier to make money too.'

Early in 2000 Buccheri was between jobs and was not convinced that he needed to work at all. The £16,000 he and his friend had invested had quickly grown to £28,000. 'My girlfriend would say, "What happens if it all crashes?" and I'd say, "Don't be mad," and she'd say, "Why don't you get a job?" and I'd say, "I'm working all day, reading the business sections, and checking websites, trying to find out information – this is working."'

By the end of the year his girlfriend had proved more perceptive than him. The market had started crashing while he was away on holiday that spring. 'I was getting constant messages on my mobile phone about it, but there was nothing I could do.' Luckily, he and his friend had begun to diversify, investing in some old economy stock as well as the high-tech comets that were now burning up. Nevertheless, by the end of the year, most of that £12,000 profit had disappeared.

At one stage, when things were going well, Buccheri had contacted various friends and suggested they club together to put more money into the market. 'Thankfully, no one invested,' he says 'and I still have my friends.'

It was through share clubs that many thousands of new investors started dabbling in the stock market. ProShare, an organization dedicated to wider share ownership, had been toiling for years to get people interested. Suddenly in 1999 requests for its information pack giving advice on setting up a share club took off. Rakesh Mehta was among those who applied.

In 1998 he was posted to the United States for a few months by his employers, a telecommunications company. While he was there he spent a weekend with relatives who were doctors. 'They spent the whole weekend talking about shares. They'd invested in companies like Microsoft and Amazon, etc. and they were cleaning up. My wife got a bit bored but I took a great interest.'

He came home to Ilford in East London where he was part of a close-knit Indian community. Meeting in a pub with friends, who all worked for major banks and telecommunications firms, talk turned to the stock market. They were all fervent believers in the new technology and its power to change the world, and decided they would start a share club that would invest in the companies of the future. They called it the Innovative Indian Investors. 'February 1999 was a great time to start investing,' Rakesh Mehta remembers. Each of the dozen members put in £2,500 and they started buying stocks in companies like Freeserve, Scoot.com and Baltimore Technologies. Each month they would meet to review their portfolio and vote on whether to buy new shares, sell existing ones or just sit tight. With the market catching fire, there were few voices calling for a cautious approach. 'For a year we ate, drank and slept the share-club. It was all we wanted to talk about,' says Rakesh Mehta. 'Our wives got really fed up with it.'

I first came across the club in March 2000 when I was preparing a television report about the state of the dot.com market and wanted to gauge the mood of investors. We met in a pub just outside the City where the members gathered around a long table and the cameraman got some fine, smoky shots as the month's investment issues were discussed over a few pints. By this stage the portfolio had reached a value of £175,000. If all the shares had been sold right then, each of the original members who had put in £2,500 would have taken out £12,500.

It was the evening after the lastminute.com IPO and there was excitement around the table about the company. Rakesh Mehta was particularly enthusiastic, believing lastminute now had a valuable brand and could dominate an online travel market which should eventually be huge. The shares, which had headed above £5 when they started trading, had now sunk back towards £4. Rakesh argued forcefully that they were now a bargain and this was a great buying opportunity.

The next day the Innovative Indian Investors placed an order for £16,000 worth of lastminute.com shares at just over £4 apiece. By the following week the club had already lost quite a bit of money. The shares had fallen below their issue price of £3.80 and I persuaded the BBC's *Six O'Clock News* to run a report, suggesting that the air was now coming out of the dot.com bubble. We arranged to meet Rakesh at a café near his office and see what he thought of the club's investment now. A large, amiable man in his early thirties, he seemed relaxed enough. 'I'm not too worried – we're in for the long term and I see these shares doubling over the next year.'

The next time we spoke was in February 2001 when I was preparing a new report on the mood of small investors as the market in internet shares hit another all-time low. Lastminute.com now stood at 58p. Rakesh laughed when I reminded him of what he had said on national television almost a year earlier. 'That has come back to haunt me,' he said. 'Everyone saw that – it made me a bit of a celebrity. I was even invited to give a talk to another share club, advising them where to invest.' His own club had spent much of the year arguing about lastminute.com.

Things had immediately started going wrong after that March meeting. The club's members watched helplessly as the market lurched downward, wiping £100,000 off their portfolio in just a couple of months. 'It was as if we'd had the winning lottery ticket and then lost it,' said Rakesh. Some members of the club were also big investors in the market in their own right. One man in his late forties, who worked in the back offices of a bank, had been up by £200,000 at one stage. Having started investing before the boom got under way he was still £50,000 to the good, but he was full of regrets. 'I really wanted to make enough to change my life,' he told me. Dreams of early retirement had faded.

The biggest single contributor to the club's losses was lastminute.com. The club's monthly meeting moved from the pub to an office in Ilford, an indication that this was now a serious affair. They tried to limit each session to two hours – but found the first hour and a half was always spent discussing what to do with their stake in the online travel company. 'Each month there were some people who said we should sell, but we could never reach a majority. We just got sick of watching that stock – it would rally by 50p, then fall back again.' At last, in December 2000, they voted to sell lastminute.com. That meant swallowing a loss of more than £10,000.

When I came to film at the February meeting I interviewed Rakesh about that lastminute loss. I asked the classic question you are not supposed to ask, 'How did you feel?' Rakesh, sitting in front of the assembled members of the club, paused for a moment and said, 'Well, all in all, we were pretty pissed off!' There was another pause, and then a gale of laughter swept through the room. When I got the tape back to an edit suite, the programme editor felt that 'pissed off' was not really suitable for the *Ten O'Clock News*. But I think it summed up the mood of many of those who had climbed aboard the dot.com investment bandwagon.

The internet bulletin boards provided the stage where the new investors could experience all the drama of the markets, both as an audience and as players. Suddenly they realized they were not alone. They could share information, opinions and abuse with others who were equally obsessed with the fortunes of a collection of obscure companies.

Whole businesses were built on the back of this obsession. Interactive Investor International was a site that provided its visitors with share prices and the latest news about companies. However, the real attraction was its bulletin boards. Every company you have ever heard of and many more that were obscure to all but a few devotees had its own board. By March 2000 there were 65,000 discussion boards on Interactive Investor, although 90 per cent of them were completely inactive. That month investors were posting over 7000 messages a day. On the back of this success as a meeting place for those with an interest in investment, Interactive Investor held its own IPO, telling the world that a company which could attract subscribers in their millions could also act as a marketplace for all kinds of financial products. Its shares soared on flotation and the board devoted to the company itself became one of the busiest on the site.

To roam through the archives of old discussions still held on sites like Interactive Investor and Motley Fool is to be reminded of the passions which raged through the market from autumn to spring 2000. Some of the contributions are knowledgeable and well argued; many more are hysterical, abusive and ungrammatical. The biggest single source of hope, greed, shattered expectations and then rage was the IPO of lastminute.com. The shares came to the market in mid-March and by the end of the year 13,000 messages had been posted just on Interactive Investor's bulletin board alone.

As the boards got under way in the days running up to the IPO, many of those taking part had already made big profits from investing in the likes of Freeserve, 365 and QXL. To some, the most-hyped flotation so far seemed like a one-way bet. 'You can't buck the markets,' said 'Izulu' on the Motley Fool site. 'The markets are backing dot.coms because they are the new Industrial Revolution.' Izulu wasn't worried by the apparently crazy price placed on this young company. 'Don't look for justification of valuations etc – we just don't know where its leading. But there is no doubt it is leading to somewhere important and being in on the ground floor is the only place to be. Go with the market, not the Luddites.' Another message looked forward to a huge windfall: 'I've just booked my holiday in the sun on the strength of these shares. You never know, I might be able to laze the days away while I become a multi-millionaire just like our great mate Martha. COME ON PUNTERS. HOP ON. DON'T MISS OUT ON THIS. I CAN SEE SHARES HITTING 10POUND AFTER LAUNCH!! See you in the sun.'

Others urged caution. 'Lastminute.con [sic] may be well known amongst the Islington media luvvies as they're sipping their caffeine-free guacamole but as far as most of the world's concerned it's "who . . .?"' was the opinion of a poster by the name of 'Freesham'. He or she concluded: 'I'd just like to thank everyone concerned with this share offer for providing us with such an obvious signal that the market's gone completely mad.'

But investors who had profited from the madness of the market thus far were not put off and applied for the shares in their hundreds of thousands. So many wanted a slice of this sure-fire winner that the company was forced to ration them, handing out just 35 shares to each private investor. A wave of fury swept through the bulletin boards. By the day of the IPO new messages were appearing on the Interactive Investor board at the rate of two a minute. Their headlines tell the story – 'disgraceful', 'boycott last-minute.com', 'greed', 'this will backfire', 'we've been mugs'. The investors, who had to subscribe to lastminute.com before they could apply for shares, thought they had been exploited to help promote the company and then been given the scraps from the table while the big institutions had feasted on richer pickings.

Martha Lane Fox was roundly abused. 'The only people to have benefited from this pointless exercise is you and your institutions!! The loyal subscribers have been well and truly SHAFTED!!!!!,' read one message. 'If Martha what ever her name is thinks she can abstract any further money from me on her lousy website . . . she can think again,' read another. Many now said that lastminute.com was doomed and expressed the hope that its shares would rapidly head south. A few pointed out the lack of logic in the attitudes of those who complained about the share allocation and then derided the company's prospects. A Miss Christina Pagel wrote: 'If you want more shares then buy them now/next week and still make a profit! if you think the price is going to go down then be pleased you haven't got more of them.'

One bulletin board poster got a shock when he e-mailed Martha Lane Fox directly to complain. 'Disgraceful – that's the last time I will ever buy anything from lastminute as I may only receive 1% of my goods,' he wrote. 'I am embarrassed to be called a shareholder of the company.' A little while later he was to find in his Inbox a reply from lastminute's co-founder. She said she was sorry and went on to explain the thinking behind the allocation: 'We chose to give everyone something rather than a few people nothing. We have also set up a dealing facility for customers. It is not ideal and it has been a tough process to manage but we hope that our investors, like us, are in this for the long term and not a quick flip. Apologies again that you felt disappointed. Martha.'

The truth is that many of the investors were in it for 'a quick flip', and they were not mollified. 'We were very naive,' Martha Lane Fox told me a few months after the IPO. 'We didn't realize how much people wanted to make a quick buck and felt it was their right to make a quick buck. We thought it would be better to give everyone something. On reflection we should have done it differently. I don't think we got the right advice, I don't think we made the right decisions.'

And as the shares headed ever lower over the ensuing months, the level of abuse increased. One Interactive Investor subscriber suggested they should all sell together to drive the share price even lower: 'That will wipe off the smug grins from MLF and BH. I for one think that LMC are rubbish. Their business model is rubbish. Their management is rubbish.' Another subscriber fired back: 'I guess you went through the "brochure" with a toothpick before applying. Or can we assume your assessment was "Rubbish"?'

The tone of the lastminute discussions became more desperate, with contributors suggesting inventively obscene uses for their share certificates and aiming more and more colourful invective at the company's founders.

The bulletin boards were a playground not just for naive investors who wanted to learn more about the market but for more experienced players who wanted to manipulate it. There was ample opportunity for skulduggery because so many of the shares beloved of online investors were in tiny companies where just a few orders could move the stock sharply higher or lower.

Anonymity was a powerful weapon. In the early days of these discussion boards many of the messages were signed with what appeared to be real names. But soon they were sheltering behind nicknames – a quick glance at just one board reveals names like 'Shorters' Association', 'gotta pick a pocket or two', ' Take Profits', 'Techslayer', and 'Cosanostra'.

Such pseudonyms were often used to mount vicious attacks on other bulletin board posters or to make extraordinary claims about inside information that the poster claimed to possess. What, for instance, are we to make of one frequent contributor to the Interactive Investor discussions on the auction company QXL? In April 2000, as the firm was heading down the 98 per cent incline which would make it one of the biggest fallers amongst dot.com shares, someone called 'tricky 666' posted the following message: 'As the lead site architect at QXL, there is no better dot.com investment than QXL at the moment. The current and proposed technology is in place to make QXL the leaders at auctions now and in the foreseeable future, globally.'

Another contributor was soon pointing out the problems with this message: 'If you really work for the company in that capacity then you need to check both FSA rules and your own company's liabilities before expressing opinions.' The company confirmed to me that its policies forbade any employee from taking part in this kind of discussion. However, it was impossible to know whether or not 'tricky 666' really worked for QXL.

As the shares, which had peaked at over £8, headed south, their biggest fan kept on preaching the gospel: 'Are the MM's (market makers) deliberately keeping this share price down at a ridiculous level?' he or she cried on 19 April. 'WHAT is going on!?!? This share should be at least 400+ by now.' In July QXL fell below £1. 'This company will reach profitability sooner than the so called analyst predict,' was the prediction from 'tricky 666'. 'It may not be tomorrow or next week or next month, but when this stock moves it will rocket.' Any investors who took that as a signal to buy were still waiting for lift-off many months later. Early in 2001 the shares had fallen below 10p. 'Tricky 666' was now strangely absent from the bulletin boards.

The new breed of investors learnt the hard way that much of the information to be found on the bulletin boards was not so much from 'inside' as from outer space. In January 2000 a very unlikely company briefly became the hottest dot.com stock around. The Coburg Group was a tiny coffee-roasting business but a series of rumours on bulletin boards suggesting that it was about to transform itself into an internet firm helped its shares appreciate by 600 per cent over a couple of months. Eventually the firm was forced to issue a statement denying the rumours and warning that by all normal investment criteria its share price appeared to be 'seriously over-valued'.

Mind you, with its results for the previous year showing a loss of £1.6 million on a turnover of £3 million, you can see why investors might have thought it was a dot.com. Coburg was by no means the only company to see its share price go through violent gyrations after bulletin board rumours. Some saw the hands of skilful market manipulators behind such events.

Ric Evans and Tim Morris both had a ringside seat as the thrills and spills of the bulletin boards unfolded. Each of them started as habitués of the boards, and then, believing they could do it better, started their own investment websites. Ric Evans had been investing since the 1980s and by the time the dot.com bubble got underway it was pretty much his full-time occupation. He owned a boatyard on the Thames but with a serious heart condition he left that in his son's hands and got on with trading. He spent a lot of time on Interactive Investor and other sites, and started tipping shares. 'My tips had a 90 per cent hit rate and people were telling me to go for it, create my own board,' he told me. So in September 1999 he launched 'Fillyaboots.com.' It featured tips, advice for newcomers to the market and huge amounts of discussion about that old favourite Minmet.

The site attracted plenty of traffic and won an award from the *Sunday Times*. Ric Evans claimed that the *Mirror*'s City Slickers were among the visitors, and he often saw his tips a couple of days later in their column. But by the second half of 2000 it was the sellers, not the buyers, who were making the real waves. The dot.com boom had been perfect territory for the rampers, and the pumpers and dumpers – investors who were desperate to promote shares which they held, or whose aim was to pump up the price and then get rid of their holdings quickly before the rest of the market woke up. Now, as the market fell, it was a different type of investor who stood to profit.

'We're seeing plenty of de-rampers, particularly on the Minmet board,' Ric Evans told me. He mentioned one name that appeared frequently on his and other boards. 'He's a blackguard,' he growled. De-ramper is just one term for someone who is 'short' of a stock and wants to drive the price down. 'Shorting' is a technique which used to be familiar only to market professionals – but it was now spreading to the amateurs. In essence, it involves selling shares you do not yet own and promising to deliver them by a certain date, by which time the price will have fallen, generating a tidy profit. It is risky because if the price moves the wrong way you can lose all of your investment. It is also a more nerve-wracking game because the contracts involved last just a couple of weeks – so if the day of reckoning is approaching and the share price has risen, the pressure mounts by the minute.

Evans said all sorts of disreputable tactics had been used by the shorters. One had taken an official announcement with some bad news about one company, changed the name of the firm, and posted it on a board. The company had called in the Fraud Squad and someone had been arrested.

Tim Morris's journey had taken him in the opposite direction from most of those in the online investment world. He had started as a market professional, first as a broker then as a risk analyst with an American bank in the City. He then left to start a site called CityBull. Although it is aimed at the retail investor, he appears to have a cynical view of what anybody but the professional can achieve. 'On most occasion the retail investor just plays second fiddle,' he told me. 'There are a lot of sites out there claiming that they can give you the tools to compete with the market professionals, but it's all crap.'

Morris says he knows a few people who made serious money from watching the bulletin boards and then playing the market during the dot.com boom but they were all professionals, people he had worked with in the City. 'For instance, they'll watch a rumour emerge on a bulletin board – and they'll get onto their broker and execute a deal within minutes, knowing that about half an hour later all these online investors with their slower access to the market will be just getting their trades through. The next thing you know there's a new post on the bulletin board saying, "Wow, some professional trader has just bought £100,000 worth, it must be good." The price goes up further – and the professional gets out. It's the last people in who get burned.'

Morris believes that the problem with many of the investors was that they just got too attached to the companies in which they invested. 'People got too emotional – there was an inability to be clinical. I keep meeting retail investors at get-togethers and they've all lost all their gains because they haven't sold. You've got to know when to take a profit.' For the newcomers the period between the summer of 1999 and the autumn of 2000 provided a crash course in the behaviour of markets. They had arrived at a time when making money was easy. They had believed that if you were quick-witted, did some research and had a bit of nerve, there was a living to be made. When the crash came they found that losing money was just as simple. 'We've had boom and bust within eight months – usually that would take five years – so they've had a rare opportunity to learn,' Tim Morris told me. 'But most of those who have lost the lot have learnt nothing.'

Nonetheless, some have seen their lives changed by the bulletin board phenomenon. Maria Hodgson, the Sussex housewife who found her way into investment via the Internet, was soon treading the Interactive Investment boards. At first she had been naive. 'You make mistakes, you get hooked by bulletin board ramps and then you learn,' she told me. Gradually she became one of the players rather than an onlooker. As one of the most frequent contributors to the discussions, her name was known to thousands of other online investors. 'I'm a bit of a celebrity on the boards,' she told me. 'A lot of people listen to what I say.' She had helped introduce a lot of people to Geo Interactive, the Israeli firm that had become a cult amongst small investors. She had made a lot of money from that investment, then lost it after putting the proceeds into a company which turned out to have some rather questionable accounting methods.

By the end of 2000, however, her approach to the market had changed. Her broker had allowed her to open a 'bear' account so that she could do some short selling. She had even 'shorted' her beloved Geo Interactive. Her downbeat views of where the market was heading had led to clashes on the boards. 'Some people did not like what I was saying in October when I said the market still had further to fall. People had a go at me – it was a stupid row. So I went quiet for a while.' Part of the dispute centred on whether participants in these discussions should talk privately – 'off-board' as they put it – or whether everything should take place in public view.

When I spoke to Maria Hodgson again a few weeks later there had been a dramatic change in her life. She had left her husband and was now living with a man she had met through an Interactive Investor discussion. An 'off-board' encounter had led to this: 'He told me he was attracted by the intelligence of what I said on the board, and we started talking on the telephone.' Her new partner had helped to change the way she saw the market. 'He's a tax adviser and he's always been very sceptical about some of these valuations – he's looked at the fundamentals.' Now the two of them had moved in together and sat side by side, watching the markets, trading stocks and discussing their investments. As the markets continued to tumble they were both making money by shorting everything in sight.

It was 8.45 in the morning when I last called Maria and I sensed it was not the best time for a long conversation. The markets were feverish that morning, with high-tech shares suffering more big losses. She told me she had been up early to get her daughter off to school and had then started checking the overnight e-mails from fellow investors. She was kicking herself because she had not responded to a tip that Cable and Wireless was on the verge of announcing big job cuts. She had missed the chance to short a stock that had fallen by 20 per cent in one day after the news emerged.

Many of those who had been drawn into the investment world by the dot.com bubble had now retired to nurse their wounds, having decided that it was a mug's game. Not Maria. 'I'm still watching the markets as closely as I was a year ago,' she told me. 'It's just that then I was buying, and now I'm almost always selling.'

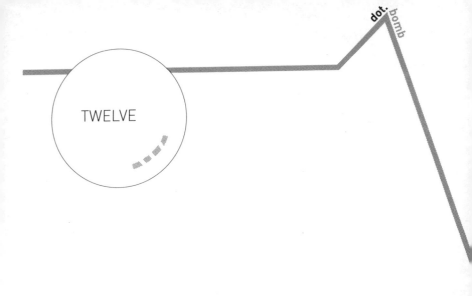

TWELVE

Pollyanna meets Cassandra

POINTING OUT THAT THE emperor is naked is never likely to win you many friends. And if everybody else is seeing fine garments stitched with gold, you can begin to question your own eyesight. Some of those who thought the dot.coms were walking around without a stitch had lost their employers a great deal of money by betting that the high-tech bubble was bound to burst in 1998, or at the latest in 1999. But by the middle of March 2000 the mutterings of those who had always thought that the potential of the Internet to transform business had been grossly exaggerated had grown into a roar. It was at this point that Dot.com Britain started to crumble.

The war between the Cassandras, who felt that the dot.coms and all who had climbed aboard were heading over a cliff, and the Pollyannas, who thought that things could only get better, carried on right through the dot.com bubble. Many of the Pollyannas were concentrated in the big investment banks. It made sense for equity analysts and corporate financiers to believe the hype – indeed to promote it – because they were growing very fat on the proceeds.

In March, however, simple mathematics began to make an impression even on those who were true believers in the alchemy of the new economy. In New York the Nasdaq index of high-tech shares climbed above 5000. This meant that share prices had risen by 140 per cent in just two years. And in London the FTSE 100, the league table that measures Britain's most valuable companies, appeared to be going through an identity crisis in which it had lost touch with reality.

At around 5.30 p.m. on 8 March I was on the equity dealing floor of one of London's major European banks, hoping that something would happen soon. FTSE International was due to make its quarterly announcement about arrivals and departures in the 100 share index. Promotion and relegation are determined by the market value of the leading companies on a set date. Normally this event would have as much chance of featuring on the BBC's *Six O'Clock News* as a minor earthquake with no injuries in Ulan Bator. What made this occasion different was the symbolic nature of the imminent changes. A clutch of 'old economy' shares was due to be swept aside by a collection of high-tech companies, most of which had been corporate minnows just a few months earlier.

When the announcement arrived – thankfully in time for me to do my live broadcast – it fulfilled all expectations. Nine companies were to enter the FTSE 100. While they were by no means all dot.coms or internet related, they had all been borne aloft by the wave of euphoria about the potential of new technology. In came companies like Freeserve, the electronic organizer firm Psion, the computer security business Baltimore Technologies, and the telecommunications company Thus. Out went dull old firms making dull old profits – businesses like the brewers Whitbread and Scottish and Newcastle, and the utilities Thames Water and Powergen.

The FTSE 100 was not just a statistical exercise. With increasing numbers of investment managers now simply tracking the performance of the index, promotion meant that your shares would have to be taken seriously by many of the most powerful institutions.

But when people started doing a few sums, more and more of them began to conclude that the numbers just did not add up. Take Freeserve, for example. It was entering the FTSE 100 at a position somewhere in the 40s with a market value of more than £7 billion. Yet the free Internet provider was just eighteen months old at the time and was a long way from making a profit. One place lower stood the Bank of Scotland, a sober yet ambitious institution, much admired for the way it handled its business. And that business had earned profits of over a billion pounds in 1999. The stock market, however, is always looking forward not back – and in March 2000 the assumption was that ancient businesses like the Bank of Scotland had seen their best years, while thrusting young firms like Freeserve were well placed to profit from the world's fastest growing industry. Even so, traders were assuming that in the not too distant future Freeserve too would be making a profit of a billion pounds.

Half a dozen places further down the table stood one of Britain's most successful retailers, Dixons. This desperately old-fashioned company with its rather naff devotion to profits – over £200 million the previous year – would have been a lot further down the list but for one thing. It still owned 80 per cent of Freeserve, the company it had started with the odd million pounds washing around in its accounts in 1998. At current prices that stake was worth £5.7 billion. As the market capitalisation of Dixons now stood at £5.9 billion, this put the value of a business with a chain of over 1100 stores at around £200 million. What it also implied was that a lot of people just did not believe in Freeserve's valuation – otherwise Dixons' shares would have climbed even higher.

Or what about Baltimore Technologies? It had shot into the FTSE at around 70 with a market capitalisation of just under £5 billion. This despite losses the previous year of £31 million at a company whose security software was widely admired but had yet to generate much revenue. Baltimore was now valued more than twice as high as Thames Water, the company which ran London's water supplies and had seen over £400 million in profit sloshing through the pipes the previous year. Just a few years earlier privatised water companies had been seen by the Left as the symbols of all that was worst about the 'get rich quick' mentality of Britain under the Conservatives. They were monopolies generating big profits for their shareholders and outrageous pay rises for their managers. Now, under a Labour government, they were tired old industrial relics, trampled underfoot by the internet hordes.

To the Cassandras who had been warning the dot.coms to prepare to meet their doom, these sums provided new ammunition.

Professor John Kay spent two years sticking pins into the dot.com bubble and then sat back and enjoyed its deflation. Professor Kay is one of Britain's most respected economists and has moved seamlessly between academia and the business world. The Institute of Fiscal Studies, the London Business

School and Oxford University are all on the academic section of his CV. On the business side there is London Economics, the consultancy he founded and which made him wealthy enough to allow him to do what interested him.

He is also independent to the point of prickliness. He resigned as the first director of Oxford's Said Business School after clashes over his plans, and proceeded to take his revenge with articles bemoaning the University's inability to behave like a modern institution.

He first decided that something very illogical was happening in the way the market valued the dot.coms when he asked some of his researchers to have a look at the numbers behind Amazon.com. Professor Kay was a keen customer of the online bookseller but was astounded to find out how much it was costing Amazon to win new customers like him and then send them books. 'When I looked at the numbers it was clear to me that this company was about selling shares, not selling books. Investors were paying for me to buy cheap books.'

It was Amazon that wrote the bible for all the other dot.coms in the United States and in Britain. The crucial thing was to understand the speed at which the Internet was developing and the need to move quickly to grab a dominant share of your market. There would only be a couple of winners in each area and they would be in a position to make huge profits. So staking out your claim to this virgin territory was the key – and it was worth spending whatever it took to win the customers. If that meant losing a lot of money while your business was built, so be it.

This argument was then taken by investment bankers and sold to investors. Shares in companies like Amazon rose to extraordinary heights on the basis of calculations of their future earnings. The new investors were taught to look at a different set of numbers from the old breed. Profits were not important – indeed, they were a sign of a company not ambitious enough in its spending to reach the Promised Land. The key was to show rising traffic and revenue. Every new customer – or in many cases every person who just happened to land on a website – increased the value of your company, whether or not they generated a profit for your business.

This was the creed against which John Kay blasphemed. 'I thought it was barmy,' he told me. In a series of articles in the *Financial Times* and elsewhere, he clinically dissected the methods used to value internet companies.

What really amazed him was that the cheerleaders of the new economy assumed that the rapid growth in revenues that characterized the early years of companies like Amazon and Freeserve would continue without mishap. The sums done to justify the valuation of Freeserve by one banker at JP Morgan assumed that Freeserve would eventually earn profits of £2 billion – as much as Sainsburys, Tesco and Marks and Spencer put together – on revenues of £2.5 billion. 'No established business earns margins of that size,' he wrote in the *FT*. Enthusiasts were assuming that nobody would spot this free money and come charging into the market to grab a slice.

It is worth a quick diversion at this point to consider the role that spreadsheet software played in the dot.com bubble. The spreadsheet was the 'Killer Application' which helped to persuade small businesses across the United States and then around the world that they needed a computer. The software made it possible to calculate and present accounts, sales forecasts and all the other numbers at the root of any business with a minimum of effort. When it came to writing a business plan, spreadsheets were an invaluable tool. Stick in a few numbers projecting your sales in four years time, and a few columns further down the spreadsheet generates a nice round number representing your profit.

'Anyone can build one,' says Professor Kay. 'It has made it possible to give a spurious rationale to your forecasts. But they are mindlessly mechanical.' In other words, if you put the right numbers in at one end, you get the right numbers out at the other. Garbage in, garbage out, as computer programmers have always put it. After the bubble had burst, the manager of one internet incubator told me about the spreadsheets attached to the dozens of business plans he had been receiving just a few months earlier. 'No matter what the sales numbers at the top of the column,' he explained, 'just about every business was forecasting that it would be making a profit of £25 million in 2004. That just seemed to be the number they had to arrive at.'

Unfortunately, John Kay found that his tactless comments on the emperor's goose pimples were not welcomed by his readers. 'When I wrote pieces in the *FT* I thought I might get some people saying, "Thank god someone is saying this" – but no, I just got e-mails telling me I was wrong. A lot said, "You just don't get it." There was a feeling that nobody over 25 could understand it. At that point I wanted to say, "Haven't you heard of 1929?" There were substantial parallels.'

Professor Kay told me that the pressure to conform had been almost irresistible. At that time academia – especially the major business schools – was just as bound up in the dot.com euphoria as everyone else. Many students on MBA courses were trying to set up their own dot.coms, and some were leaving before they had even finished their courses. Business schools have to pay their way by convincing companies and foreign governments that they are at the cutting edge, so anyone suggesting that much of e-commerce was built on sand could pose a threat to the bottom line.

'Academics were continually being told to make sure that e-commerce was featured in every course,' Professor Kay remembers. 'Luckily by that time I was not attached to any institution. If I'd still been at the Oxford Business School, it would have been a lot harder for me to speak out.' He draws a striking parallel with previous hysterias: 'It was like saying there are no witches in Salem, there are no Communists in the State Department.'

For others who swam against the tide, there was more at stake. Tony Dye was one of the best known fund managers in the City, with an enviable record for working out where the markets were heading and investing billions of pounds worth of pension funds to good effect. As the head of fund management at one of the City's most respected firms, Philips and Drew, his view was taken very seriously. Until, that is, the late 1990s. For some years Dye had been convinced that shares on both sides of the Atlantic were dangerously overvalued. Then, as the dot.com boom took off, his warnings about the coming crash became more and more urgent. As a result, his clients found themselves sitting on the sidelines as shares surged ever higher. Philips and Drew began to lose customers. Taking a contrarian view can sometimes be good for your career if you are an academic trying to make a name for yourself. Not so for a fund manager where your performance is totted up in big black numbers every few months and compared with that of your rivals.

While those rivals were bending with the wind, Tony Dye stuck to his guns, refusing to advise his clients to buy into any of the high-tech stars. 'Many of the people who bought these shares on behalf of their clients thought those clients were stupid,' he says. 'But their view was that if the market is mad, you too have to be a little bit mad.' Dye insists, however, that he did not feel particularly isolated: 'Sometimes in life, which is a pretty uncertain business, you feel that there is a certainty. This time I was certain.'

Once again, it was a mixture of mathematics and simple common sense that was behind that conviction. The arrival in London of the dot.com IPO, which saw young loss-making companies come to the stock market on huge valuations, left him aghast. 'Companies like Freeserve should not have been floated, because they were early stage speculative ventures, not businesses with a track record.'

Dye is scathing about the record of the investment analysts who provided the research which people like him were meant to use to judge a stock. 'One investment bank provided me with some of the numbers behind their valuation of one tech stock. As a bit of fun, I did some calculations and worked out that in a few years this company would account for 15 per cent of all profits made in the UK. I rang up the analyst's boss and told him not to send me research like that again – he should not be sending out rubbish like that.' Sadly, others were taking what the analysts said at face value.

Of all of those who took part in the great dot.com bubble it is the analysts at the major investment banks who emerge with their reputations most tarnished. It was they who taught investors the language and rules of the brave new dot.com world. They patiently explained that victory would go to the bold. Companies with 'new business models' that used their 'first mover advantage' would soon be able to 'monetise the eyeballs' of all those millions of internet users who were drawn to their sites because they had had the courage to spend huge sums on 'customer acquisition'. Profits did not matter at this stage – the analysts were valuing a company by the number of eyeballs.

It is the job of the analyst to carry out exhaustive research into each company they cover and then deliver an impartial view on its valuation and on whether the shares should be bought or sold. A well-regarded analyst can have a major impact on share prices. As the dot.com market took off, many of the American analysts – people like Mary Meeker at Morgan Stanley and Henry Blodgett at Merrill Lynch – attracted loyal followings amongst small investors as well as their corporate customers. They became stars, making frequent television appearances, and their salaries reached Hollywood proportions.

That never quite happened in Britain, simply because there was not enough time. It was not until the summer of 1999 that banks like Credit Suisse First Boston, Goldman Sachs and Merrill Lynch started appointing internet analysts in London. Just as those analysts were beginning to make a name for themselves, the market crashed.

Unfortunately, just like their peers in the United States the internet analysts often seemed more like fans cheering from the terraces rather than objective commentators. Simply look at the various reports on two of Britain's most prominent dot.coms, Freeserve and QXL.

In the first four months of 2000 only one broker, HSBC, had Freeserve down as a 'Sell'. The others that covered the stock were all advising investors either to hold on or to buy more. With the price heading all the way up from £1.50 at the IPO in the summer of 1999 to more than £9 at the peak in March 2000, the analysts could at least say they had helped those who had got in and out quickly to some speedy profits. Whether they had come up with a sensible valuation of the company is another matter.

What is more bizarre is that most of the analysts stuck with Freeserve all the way down. Throughout the summer and autumn, companies like ABN Amro, JP Morgan and Daiwa were telling investors to buy more of Freeserve. Anyone who followed their advice found their money melting away as the shares headed back below the £1.50 issue price. The most enthusiastic advocate was Credit Suisse First Boston. Throughout Freeserve's history as an independent company, one word stood out clearly at the top of CSFB's research notes: 'Buy'. But then this was the bank that had steered Freeserve through its IPO.

It followed up that flotation with QXL, and once again its analyst was an enthusiastic advocate of the stock. In March the shares which had floated the previous October at £1.95 briefly climbed above £21. They had slipped back a little by 27 March when Credit Suisse First Boston issued another 'Buy' note. Lehman Brothers and Goldman Sachs also described it as a 'market outperformer' at that time. With the price becoming unwieldy, the company carried out what is known as a 'three-for-one split' – in other words, every investor got three new shares for each existing one, so that a price of £21 would now be a more manageable £7.

Early in April came the single most extraordinary piece of misjudgement by any analyst during the dot.com boom. Not by CSFB but by a newcomer to the world of internet stock research. Thomas Bock had just joined the respected American stockbroking firm SG Cowen, now part of the French group Société Générale. He was about to move to London to take up his post as the firm's first European internet analyst, but before setting off he wrote his first research note. It was about QXL and it was immediately clear that Bock spoke fluent dot.com. He stated boldly, 'We believe the QXL story represents a unique combination of large market opportunity, defensibility, first-mover advantage and attractive business model.' What was truly extraordinary was the price that Bock put on the company.

By now QXL's shares had fallen below £3, and the decline in all of the high-tech stocks was well and truly underway. However, Bock forecast that by the end of 2002 the shares could have climbed to as much as £44. He had reached this conclusion by comparing QXL's valuation with that of Ebay, America's online auction giant. If Ebay was worth $25 billion why shouldn't QXL – its counterpart in what was bound to be a huge European market – be just as valuable? There were two problems with this piece of thinking. Firstly, it did not question whether there was anything fanciful about Ebay's valuation. Secondly, it ignored the fact that Ebay itself was already in Europe and was poised to steamroller the British upstart.

Immediately the research note was released, the price of QXL more than doubled and the bulletin boards lit up. 'Get in now before it's too late,' wrote one feverish investor on the Interactive Investor board. Another of the share's supporters agreed and said he had been vindicated by Bock's pronouncement: 'QXL are now in place to take on the world, its only now u will start to see the full value of all its investments. It seems that the analysts now agree with what ive know for some time. Get ready to retire in 24 months!!!!!!!!!!!!!'

But as it emerged that the analyst behind this frenzy of buying was a novice who had been fixing telephones and computers just a couple of years earlier, the mood changed. 'As an individual investor I heavily rely on analyst opinion when making an investment decision,' wrote one contributor in an open letter to SG Cowen published on the Motley Fool website. 'As a respected investment firm your company should be chastised for poor judgement allowing an inexperienced uneducated novice (in this arena) to make such a public blunder.'

Soon the shares were back on the downward path. Far from getting ready to retire in 24 months, those who had bought during the brief April spike in the price may have been contemplating using their share certificates to paper the bathroom. A year on from Thomas Bock's prediction, there was some work to be done to reach that £44 target. QXL's shares stood at 6p.

Mr Bock hung on to his job at SG Cowen for a while but there was a price to pay. Every time he asked his colleagues what he owed them for a cup of coffee or a round of drinks after work, they gave the same answer: £44. Quite apart from the joshing of his colleagues, there were more serious pressures. A fellow analyst says Bock received death threats from angry investors. Eventually he left the company.

Anyone can make a mistake, and at least SG Cowen's new internet analyst got his out of the way early. Nevertheless, the charge against some of the bigger investment banks is that they were so obsessed with the battle for lucrative IPO business that objective analysis went out the window. The Chinese walls that supposedly separate a bank's corporate financiers hunting new business from its investment analysts appeared to be paper-thin. The analysts were employed as marketing tools by the bank – look at how Mary Meeker was used to win the lastminute.com IPO for Morgan Stanley.

So how do the analysts defend themselves? Peter Bradshaw of Merrill Lynch was probably quoted more frequently than any other British analyst during the dot.com bubble. To his credit he is still prepared to step up to the plate and defend his record. 'The life of an analyst is one of perpetual humiliation,' he said with a grin as we sat down in his office just off the dealing floor at Merrill Lynch, the biggest player in the London stock market. As prices in internet companies hit new lows, predictions made a year earlier were not looking too good but, as Bradshaw pointed out, 'It's very easy with 20/20 vision to be wise after the event.'

When they deliver verdicts on shares, five ratings are available to the analysts at Merrill Lynch – buy, accumulate, neutral, reduce or sell. But in recent times what some have described as 'ratings inflation' has been introduced to the analytical trade: 'In the Merrill universe there are almost no sells,' Bradshaw explained. 'And neutral means do not touch this with a bargepole.' However, he insisted that investors understood the language perfectly, so there was no question of anyone being misled.

Bradshaw's defence of his trade is that while in the long-term many of the verdicts on companies now look fanciful, in the short-term they made a lot of money for investors. Take Freeserve, a company in which 40 per cent of all the share trades were carried out by Merrill Lynch. 'We started with a buy note when the shares were at £2.35. Then they went to £9 and we felt complete heroes.' Following this, Merrill Lynch had to refrain from any comment for a few months because it was advising a company connected to Freeserve. 'We came back in with another buy note when the shares were at £6. OK, we did not issue a "neutral" until £4.38 – but if you had bought on our original note, you would still have doubled your money.'

When I asked him about the conflict of interest for any analyst in a bank looking to be involved in IPOs, Bradshaw would only say that there was 'always one eye on banking'. But in some ways he was lucky. Merrill Lynch, to its chagrin at the time, did not win a major role in internet IPOs, so its analysts had a greater degree of freedom.

One analyst from another major investment bank, who would only speak off the record, had an intriguing defence for his string of 'buy' notes on dot.coms. His argument was that there were coded warnings even in research that appeared to recommend a purchase. 'You had to read way beyond the first line. In most of our reports from December 1999 onwards you would find a large section devoted to risks. Most of the big institutional investors who are our customers quickly decided that there were more risks than rewards in these companies and they wouldn't touch them with a bargepole.' In effect, he was putting 'buy' on the top of his notes to keep his colleagues in corporate finance sweet, while telling his clients to steer clear.

'But what about the small investors?' I asked. The analyst pointed out that he never appeared on television or gave quotes to the newspapers. 'No retail investor ever gets a chance to read my research and they never should. It is only designed for our customers.' He blamed the media, in particular the American financial news channel CNBC, for much of the hype around internet stocks, and he was scathing about 'egotistical' analysts who wanted to be on television.

One of those who was not shy about his views was Miles Saltiel of WestLB Panmure. But Saltiel's role on television and the newspapers was as a prophet of doom, warning against a misplaced faith in the prospects of the dot.coms. Saltiel was no teenage scribbler but a veteran of the technology sector. He had worked for Marconi and then joined a City firm in 1979.

After some years as an emerging markets analyst, he went back to his roots in 1998 when his employers asked him to become a technology analyst and look at the impact of the Internet. He might have been expected to be a true believer in the power of the new technology but from the start he approached it with some scepticism. 'There was an evangelical character about a lot of the talk about the Net and I'm not given to evangelism – I'm too old for all that.'

It was in the summer of 1999 that Saltiel made a name for himself by pouring cold water on the Freeserve IPO. He was deeply sceptical about the way the company was being valued and told his clients to avoid it. While his doubts were genuine and deeply held, when we met for a coffee next door to his offices in November 2000, he conceded that there was also another motive. 'I thought, "We're not well known, I think this IPO is bollocks, so let's not flinch from saying it." I admit I was keen to establish a reputation, to promote my own bank and to promote myself.' It worked. Any journalist wanting to inject a note of scepticism into a report on the Freeserve IPO turned to Miles Saltiel for a quote.

Saltiel said Freeserve behaved well in the circumstances. He was invited to a meeting with the Chief Executive John Pluthero and the Finance Director Nick Backhouse. 'They tried to talk me into seeing it their way – they winced a bit at what I said but at no point did they lose it. Both of them were good guys and will go on to do great things elsewhere.'

Despite this, his note on Freeserve did cause some tension within WestLB Panmure, which, like every other bank, was desperate to win business in the internet sector. 'When I wrote the note some of my bankers got nervous. They said, "You're going to trash our reputation with our clients."' Saltiel said the bank had not put pressure on him to change his mind. But over the next few months there was an intense debate at WestLB over how the dot.com industry should be handled. 'I was an enemy of the dot.com model. Every time people put up a dot.com deal I'd say, "don't do it". So we managed to avoid a lot of the crap.'

Freeserve may not have appealed to Saltiel, who had said in his note that a fair price was around 60p a share, but it appealed to plenty of investors who made money when the shares rose from £1.50 to more than £2 on the day of the IPO. By September they had fallen back but were still above the issue price. As the next internet IPO trundled onto the launch pad, Saltiel did not lose his nerve. His note on QXL, entitled 'Camden Lock Not Harvey Nicks', began like this: 'After making rude noises in church during the Freeserve flotation (which sits at 157-middle, as we look at the screen, uncomfortably close to the issue price but still breezily above our 60p target), we now tie ourselves to the track in the face of the locomotive from QXL.' He then proceeded to trash the thinking behind the valuation of the online auction firm, while conceding that recent history showed that investors who sold quickly were likely to come away with a profit.

By the following spring when lastminute.com was preparing for IPO take-off, QXL investors had seen their shares rise fivefold, but Miles Saltiel was not to be deterred. If he had been sniffy about Freeserve and dubious of QXL, he was appalled by lastminute.com. 'It seemed to me to be absolutely typical of all the worst excesses of the dot.com bubble,' he told me. He felt that the online travel company's whole purpose had been to promote the sale of its shares rather than build a sustainable business. He was also contemptuous of the idea that it constituted a valuable brand. 'You build a brand by actually doing stuff, not just by advertising.'

Unfortunately, Saltiel had one rather serious problem with lastminute.com. His employers had actually bid for a role in the IPO but had not been chosen. To the dot.com's executives this was evidence that the analyst's refusal to buy their story was motivated by sheer pique. Sources at WestLB Panmure see it differently. They say the attempt to win the IPO business had been opposed by Saltiel. He was present at a meeting with last-minute but the travel firm got the clear impression that he was not a believer. That cannot have helped win the business for WestLB. Losing out cost the firm valuable fees – but saved it from the ignominy now attached to anyone associated with the IPO.

Miles Saltiel's record as one of the few analysts to take a dim view of the dot.com bubble now looks very creditable. However, there is one blemish. As Freeserve's shares climbed ever higher, he suddenly changed his mind about the company. He issued a 'buy' note when the shares were trading at £6. Saltiel insists that this was a short-term response to the prevailing market conditions, and that he turned negative again around the time that Freeserve's shares peaked. But a rival analyst has a different interpretation. 'He got spooked and he puked,' is how Peter Bradshaw of Merrill Lynch puts it. 'If Miles had stuck to his guns he would have won a lot more respect. People would remember him as the man who got it right.'

The strangest aspect of the dot.com madness that gripped the financial world was that by the spring of 2000 just about everyone knew that it was mad. Even some of those running the dot.coms knew that there was something deeply wrong about the new economy gospel which said profits were irrelevant in the quest for growth.

Dan Thompson, Chief Executive of 365 Corporation, had seen his company storm the stock market in December 1999 when selling shares in internet companies was about as difficult as giving away £20 notes. As he toured the world promoting the share issue to institutional investors, he did not encounter the most rigorous of examinations: 'It had all gone mad. The only thing people were checking was that we didn't have two heads. The institutions just felt they could make so much money out of the stocks.'

In the next couple of months Thompson found himself dealing with the analysts – one of the less enjoyable parts of being the chief executive of a plc. What amazed him was their two main concerns: firstly, 365 described itself as a 'multi-channel' operation – in other words it wanted its sports and music content to be available not just on the Internet but on other media too. But many of the analysts told Thompson they would prefer it if the company was a 'pure play' – solely devoted to the Internet. 'Nowadays, of course, that's anathema,' Thompson told me with a wry smile when we talked in December 2000 at a time when companies were desperately dropping the '.com' from their names and pretending that the Internet was just a small part of their business. The other concern was just how much money 365 was spending on marketing. The analysts said it was not enough. Thompson felt there was a new orthodoxy in the investment banks that defied common sense. 'All that mattered was spending more on marketing, doing high profile deals even if they didn't bring you any money, and being a pure play. The analysts are bright people but they've never run a business. It was a funny old world.'

The ultimate expression of the lunacy of the new economics came in March 2000 when the Internet service providers appeared to decide that they could survive with virtually no revenue. One Friday afternoon a PR man called my office offering the BBC an exclusive story for the following

Monday. The UK operation of a big American search engine, AltaVista, was to offer free internet access. 'So what?' was our response. Freeserve and dozens of others already did that.

The PR man patiently explained that not only would the service be free – so would unlimited telephone calls, all for a one-off fee of between £30 and £50 and an annual charge of between £10 and £20. Now this did sound like a story. There had been mounting concern that the cost of being online was going to keep Britain lagging behind in the internet race. In the USA internet users could take advantage of the country's flat-rate telephone charges. Even the Labour government had weighed in, calling for flat-rate access to be made available. Nevertheless, we still found it difficult to work out quite how AltaVista would pay for the service. The PR man said the revenue would come from e-commerce and advertising as millions of new customers marched through AltaVista's portal.

That Friday the man who had pioneered free connection to the Internet in Britain was at an industry awards dinner. John Pluthero, the Chief Executive of Freeserve, ran into the man who wanted to take his business away, Andy Mitchell, the boss of AltaVista in the UK. 'He explained to me rather sheepishly what they were going to announce on the Monday, and said they wouldn't be competing with us,' Pluthero remarked. The man who had founded a business that was only viable because of its share of telecommunications revenue from its partner Energis could not believe what he was hearing. AltaVista's service would only work if another telecommunications firm was prepared to offer a flat-rate deal of extraordinary generosity. 'I said to him, "Andy, nobody gets a better deal from UK telcos than we do."' Eighteen months earlier Freeserve's initiative had been derided as unworkable by its rivals. Now its creator just could not see how AltaVista's sums added up. Even in the United States, internet users paid on average around £120 a year.

But on the Monday AltaVista's bold, nay suicidal, initiative won it the kind of media coverage most companies would kill for. Not only was it all over the BBC, it was the front-page lead in the *Sun*, with the headline, 'Free Internet'. Andy Mitchell was everywhere, proclaiming that this was the initiative which would bring a step-change in internet use in the UK and make e-commerce viable. The following day the cable company NTL upped the stakes by offering a totally free service – no signing on charge, no subscription. The announcement was timed to coincide with a speech by Tony Blair, who praised the NTL deal and pledged to make sure that the whole population got internet access within five years.

The internet industry, with government backing, was now telling the country that it could be wired up for nothing. So convinced was everybody that there was gold under the surface of the World Wide Web that they were prepared to spend unlimited amounts staking out their claim to the territory.

It was in March 2000 that one man who believed that this was all a fantasy decided that he had had enough. Tony Dye's steadfast refusal to believe in a stock market pushed ever higher by internet hysteria had left his fund management company Philips and Drew at the bottom of the league. He resigned.

There is an old Chinese saying that if you sit by the river for long enough, you will see the bodies of your enemies come floating by. Tony Dye did not have to wait for long. Within days the bubble was bursting. Within weeks the bodies of the dot.coms were making their way down the river.

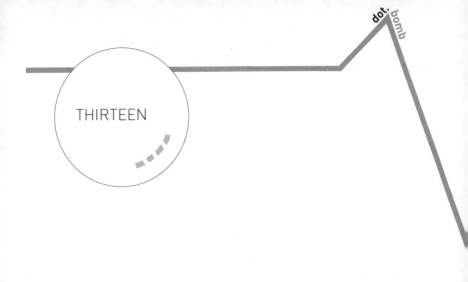

THIRTEEN

Boo to bust

IT IS A VERY long time since Carnaby Street was at the cutting edge of fashion but plenty of tourists still make their way there in the mistaken belief that they will find some remnant of Swinging London. Instead, they find the pedestrianized street fringed with chain store outlets, designer coffee shops and tacky souvenirs.

On the morning of 18 May 2000, however, the tourists were right. Something really was happening in Carnaby Street. Reporters and photographers were gathering outside a purple doorway, waiting to cover the first major collapse of a European dot.com. Boo, the online fashion retailer that had come to symbolize all that was most glamorous, ambitious and excessive about the internet boom, had called in the liquidators.

I stood outside its offices with a cameraman, hoping that there would be something to film. Luckily, someone in an office across the street from boo had stuck a notice in their window with the message, 'Don't jump!' But there was little chance of any of the boo crew taking a suicidal leap from the fourth floor. After all, the Carnaby Street office was now home to the company's technical team that had become increasingly disillusioned with the way the business was being run. Many of its occupants were freelance contractors, and they were already looking around for the next lucrative contract, suspecting that boo was not long for this world. Some had rushed back to the office late the previous evening to claim computer equipment after receiving a tip-off that the end had come.

The door opened and a stream of young people in the techie uniform of T-shirt and combat trousers set off on the short walk around the corner to boo's headquarters in Regent Street, where they had been invited to attend a meeting at 10 a.m. Few had ever been to Chesham House, home to what they regarded as the beautiful people in marketing and finance who had steered the company onto the rocks. Now, as we filmed the procession, one of them pushed a piece of paper into my hand.

It was an e-mail from the Chief Executive Ernst Malmsten to all of boo's staff. 'I wanted to write to you one last time as a group,' he wrote. 'I'm very proud to have worked with all of you to create this business. I'm sorry that in the end we couldn't turn things around and maybe that was my fault.' After telling them that the liquidators from the accountancy firm KPMG were now in charge, he promised that he was not just going to walk away. 'I will still be around to help anyone with anything I can, especially finding new jobs, and want to spend time with people individually. You'll be able to find me in the global café, Golden Square during the days and at various bars around Soho (to be advised) during the evenings at any time over the next few weeks.'

While 18 May was the day that boo died, there were many days over the previous few months when it could have breathed its last. Ernst Malmsten and his co-founder Kajsa Leander had battled constantly to persuade their backers to provide more cash as the company continued to burn up millions of dollars a month. As far back as January they had made a desperate appeal for more funds.

Of course, that was not how it had been painted. When Ernst Malmsten wrote to his shareholders on 26 January inviting them to contribute another $50 million, he presented it as the next logical stage in boo's journey. Glossing over the fact that this was a company in crisis, struggling to make its software work and close the huge gap between revenue and costs, he was still talking about floating boo on the stock market in a few months' time. The existing backers were being 'offered the opportunity to participate' in a new round of financing, which would 'fund the company through to the end of June 2000 allowing timing flexibility to execute the IPO during the second quarter'.

Despite the generosity of this offer, it was difficult to get any of the shareholders to bite. Some of them had already quietly written off their investment, convinced that boo was doomed. Eventually around $28 million was raised from four of the investors, with Lebanon's Hariri family now becoming the most generous backer. But by the time the money arrived, every last dollar was needed to meet the demands of creditors. The quest for new funds began immediately.

By the beginning of April the man some thought might be able to impose a bit of discipline on boo's chaotic finances and convince the backers that it was worth keeping the patient alive had gone. Dean Hawkins' tenure as Chief Financial Officer had lasted just two months before he decided that better opportunities lay at another internet company, Chello. One of the bankers close to boo says Hawkins left when it became clear that no more money was going to be available.

Charlotte Neser, who at 26 was now Vice-President for Europe after joining boo right at the beginning, had been a perpetual optimist about the company's prospects, but even she began to wonder how long they could survive. 'It was clear when Dean left that things were bad,' she says. 'There were rumours flying round that he had said the only option now was a trade sale. We knew we were going to run out of money in three weeks.' Somehow Ernst Malmsten managed to squeeze a little more cash out of Lebanon.

Neser and her marketing team were now like the last defenders of a doomed fortress, surrounded by the enemy but determined not to surrender: 'We had a very good team – it was highly motivated. They had decided to stay on and fight it out. People were saying to me, "I'll work for nothing, I love the brand."' By now the marketing budget had been frozen, which meant that Neser and her team had to be a lot more inventive in promoting boo. A fortune had been spent the previous summer, before boo was open for business, on putting the company's name on bus shelters across Scandinavia and making television commercials with an expensive director. Now when there were products to sell that money could have been put to better use.

Charlotte Neser insists that as the financial crisis came to a head, boo was at last getting everything else right. 'Between January and May we increased our subscribers to 300,000. There was a big dip in February but March, April and May were good.' In April sales topped $1 million, but that had

207

been achieved by dramatic discounting. Subscribers had received an e-mail offering them $20 off any purchase. However, one of Neser's colleagues is critical of the way she handled this promotion. 'The trouble was that Charlotte – this supposed marketing genius – had forgotten to set a limit. It meant you could get a $15 football for nothing. The figures came through at the top line – the cost of the promotion was buried.'

For the many true believers in the whole project, the ascending sales curve was proof that one day they would arrive on the broad, sunlit uplands. But with costs running at ten times revenues, this was still a distant dream. Meanwhile, the investors and the bankers at JP Morgan, who had shared in this dream of creating a global online retailer and thereby reaping huge rewards, were becoming ever more agitated.

Some were suggesting that there was a need for change at the top. 'It's typical for an entrepreneur to be good at starting a company but not so good at actually running it,' is the tactful way in which one person close to the situation expresses his view of Ernst Malmsten. When boo's Chief Executive approached one of London's top headhunters to seek advice on recruiting a chief operating officer, the company advised him that what was really needed was a new CEO. Despite this, the captain was to stay at the wheel as the ship headed remorselessly towards the rocks. Persuading him to step down was tricky when he and Kajsa Leander still controlled nearly 40 per cent of the company.

It was JP Morgan that had turned boo from the pipe dream of two twenty-something Swedes with little business experience into a huge concern backed by some of Europe's corporate giants. In persuading the likes of Bernard Arnault and the Benetton family to put their money behind Malmsten and Leander, the investment bank had put its own reputation on the line. Unfortunately, by this stage some of the company's original sponsors at JP Morgan had left and the new people in charge had less emotional commitment to the company.

In April boo, its bankers and its backers awoke from the dream that had united them. Written on the company's heart were the letters IPO. Greater than any ambitions to change the world of retailing or build a global online brand was the desire to take boo to the stock market and thereby turn the paper of their share certificates into cash. Just months earlier Patrik Hedelin, the third Swede behind boo, had been talking wildly of an IPO valuation of as much as $2 billion. But by now the Nasdaq index had begun its head-long journey back down the hill it had been climbing for eighteen months, shares in companies like lastminute.com had fallen below their issue price, and nobody was going to buy into another dot.com with big promises but bigger losses.

This was when JP Morgan decided to say goodbye to boo. There is some dispute about what caused the divorce. Sources at the bank say a point had been reached where it was not possible either to proceed to an IPO or to raise any additional funds, and therefore there was no role left for JP Morgan. Others say that the bank's lawyers had warned that it was in danger of being sued by the aggrieved shareholders it had helped to bring on board and now needed to distance itself from boo.

What is clear is that the bank was worried that some of the desperate plans being put forward to try to raise cash would have benefited some share-holders but not others. One such plan involved an American investment firm called Texas Pacific that had a reputation for taking on troubled businesses which nobody else would touch. The Texans had ridden into town in early March, offering to put together a package that would offer boo a lifeline.

However, when they eventually presented their details to the Board, the offer could hardly have been less palatable. Texas Pacific agreed to take on all the debts and provide the funds to restructure the business on a slimmed-down basis. In return they would pay the existing investors just $1 for their equity. There was the promise that if the company was turned around, and did manage to get to IPO, those shareholders would get some reward. The Board angrily dismissed the plan. 'Go to hell!' was the response of one investor.

Soon afterwards, Charlotte Neser was among a number of the senior executives who took part in a meeting to decide the next move: 'We got together one night and said, "Let's go back to the investors with our own restructuring plan." We wanted to use the infrastructure we had created and turn boo from a B2C firm into a B2B.' In other words, most of the grandiose plans to create an online fashion retailer that would appeal to the coolest shoppers around the globe would be dumped. Instead, boo's future would be as a provider of e-commerce services to other retailers. Boo still believed it had developed ground-breaking technology, even if it had not yet managed to turn that expertise into a sustainable business.

The new plan would involve the closure of most of the network of offices across Europe and the loss of many jobs. That would make the whole operation cheaper to run. Nonetheless, the shareholders would still need to put up more money to make the restructuring work. Time after time they had been asked to dip into their pockets. Now $20 million was required. As the drive began to convince them that it was worth going the extra mile to save their original investment, the two founders put on a brave face for the rest of their staff. 'We were told by Ernst and Kajsa that the investors had complete confidence,' says Charlotte Neser. 'And I thought that if the investors had put so much in, surely they weren't going to turn round and say "no more" when we could offer them a chance to save the company.' In the last couple of weeks of boo's life the constant refrain in the Regent Street offices was 'the money is coming'. Meeting followed meeting, late into the night. The problem was that while some of the shareholders, notably Bernard Arnault's europ@web fund and the Hariri family, were prepared to put up more cash, this offer was conditional on new investors coming in with more money. At the same time new investors were saying they would only come in if the existing shareholders put up more money.

By the beginning of May rumours had reached the press that the end was near. Swedish newspapers were reporting that Malmsten and Leander were going to be forced to resign. 'There's no truth in that whatsoever,' a spokeswoman for boo told one paper. 'We are in the process of closing a new round of financing, but it's not final yet.' In the second week in May, with contractors asking why they had not been paid and lawyers warning of the dangers of trading while insolvent, Ernst did what he always did in a crisis. He brought in another PR man.

David Bick was a financial spin doctor with a contacts book packed with the numbers of journalists and leading City figures. He had sat in on many a multibillion pound deal and had also been present at the burial of a good few companies. When he was called in to boo he quickly saw that the game was up. He attended a board meeting at which Ernst Malmsten and Kajsa Leander were the only directors present, with the others joining in by phone. One of the investors asked the PR man to put out a statement saying that the company was going ahead with its restructuring and would be closing down offices and cutting jobs. Bick refused: 'I said, "Not unless you've got the money to pay for the restructuring." The man went quiet. It had not crossed his mind that it would cost money to sack people.' There was still not enough money on the table even to make a smaller, humbler boo viable.

The following Sunday reports in some newspapers predicted that boo would not last the week. By Monday boo's press office had developed a new tactic for dealing with journalists. 'I wasn't answering the phone at this point,' remembers the Press Officer Alison Crombie. It was probably a sensible move, since she had been told virtually nothing about the ongoing negotiations. But during the morning an e-mail from Ernst Malmsten went round the company inviting everyone to come and have a drink at one of boo's favourite watering holes, the Midas Touch on Golden Square. The message seemed to be that the money was now on its way.

The technical team were not convinced. One programmer, Andy Genovese, who like many was a contractor rather than on the staff, had been asking for days whether the company could guarantee that he would be paid. He had not received a satisfactory answer. Nobody quite knew what to make of the session at the Midas Touch. Mark Deal, another of the software engineers, remembers it as an uneasy occasion: 'We all thought Ernst would be announcing his resignation. But he just wandered around saying nothing. We couldn't work out why we were there.' Alison Crombie, one of those who felt that working for boo was the best thing they had ever done, had seen the lunchtime drinks as confirmation that everything would work out. 'Then on the Monday night there was the sense that things were going wrong again.'

On the morning of Wednesday 17 May a document was faxed to all of boo's shareholders. One of them describes it wryly as 'the Stalingrad letter'. It was the last appeal to reason from Ernst Malmsten. 'Dear Shareholder,' he began. 'I am writing to inform you that boo.com Group is facing a serious financing crisis which, if not resolved within the next 12 hours, would force me to act in accordance with English law and to file for insolvency by midnight tonight.'

He urged them to examine closely a report on boo's recent sales performance and its cost-reduction plans. 'Once our proposed company split and cost-base reduction are complete, we will become a profitable business.' He went on: 'After many trials and tribulations and a rocky start, our pioneering company has quickly learned from its own mistakes and is now a proven business operating successfully and with little risk of new

211

surprises.' Unfortunately, shareholders who had seen so much in the way of 'surprises' viewed that promise with a degree of cynicism. Malmsten told them that some shareholders were willing to commit new funds, but were reluctant to do so unless their colleagues followed suit. He warned that unless he received a written commitment of further investment by 1800 GMT that evening, he would be forced to declare the company insolvent.

All day Malmsten, Leander and a couple of senior colleagues sat in the boardroom calling the shareholders and waiting for their response. When 6 p.m. came they were still $12 million short. A board meeting was called for 8 p.m. to conduct the last rites. It did not last long. Once again the investors who had poured in so much cash for no return took part by phone. Their record throughout boo's short history is not impressive. One shareholder had invested simply because he had read an article about the company in *Forbes* magazine. They had rushed in, greedy for quick returns, paid scant attention to the waste and mismanagement endemic in the company, and then departed without ceremony.

Charlotte Neser came into the boardroom a few minutes after the meeting started. 'It was very quiet. The people who did most of the talking were the lawyers.' It took less than fifteen minutes for the board to vote in the appointment of KPMG to liquidate the company. A few executives stayed on in the offices to call staff and let them know about boo's demise before the news became public.

Strangely, the mood the next morning as the crocodile of staff made its way from Carnaby Street to Regent Street for the final meeting was anything but funereal. With London's e-commerce industry still buzzing despite the stock market's loss of faith, nobody felt that they were being consigned to the scrapheap. As they stepped outside they encountered a pack of reporters and camera crews and a collection of sharp-suited characters holding clipboards.

Kris Raven of Computer Futures, a recruitment agency for the dot.com industry, had heard the news on breakfast TV. He had already suspected there were problems. His firm had talked to boo about a contract to recruit for them just a couple of months earlier: 'We credit checked them through Dun and Bradstreet, the credit ratings people, and they just looked too risky. We said we'd only work for them if they paid upfront but they weren't prepared to do that.'

Now he assembled a team and rushed down to Carnaby Street to offer his firm's services to the redundant staff. He knew other firms would already be on the same trail. Mr Raven followed the crocodile round to Chesham House. 'I even managed to blag my way inside,' he boasts. There he was confronted by Kajsa Leander who asked him to leave.

As staff gathered inside for the last time, most were sympathetic to Leander and Malmsten. Their chief executive climbed onto a table, tears in his eyes, and told them of his regret about what happened. Kajsa Leander stood beside him in an elegant black suit, looking pale and tired. Neither had had much sleep the night before. 'They just looked so sad,' remembers Alison Crombie. 'Ernst is a really undemonstrative guy – I used never to be able to work out what he was thinking – but he just seemed totally devastated.'

The unlikely couple who had taken more than 400 people on boo's helter-skelter ride to oblivion told them that they were heartbroken, they were disappointed, they were sorry that their fabulous staff might not get paid. And they were greeted with a round of applause.

There was one dissenting voice, though. Andy Genovese had been working for boo for nine months and was now owed five weeks' money. 'I wasn't impressed by the Swedes' teary speech,' says Genovese. 'I got up to demand the £6000 I was owed but everyone just shouted me down.' The people from the marketing and business divisions who had stuck it out right to the end were still intensely loyal to boo and to the vision of its founders: 'Andy Genovese had been charging a fortune. It was difficult to feel sorry for him,' says one of them. After the meeting the software engineer went straight out and registered the internet domain name ernstmalmsten.com. That enabled him to continue his feud with a website attacking Malmsten and all his works.

The rest of the staff of a company that had always known how to party were determined not to let a little thing like failure get them down. For most reporters, hanging around outside a company where the entire workforce has been sacked is a rather shaming experience, much akin to doorstepping mourners. As the workers stream out, most will remain tight-lipped, a couple will curse you and perhaps one will be persuaded to stop for a brief, 'We're all gutted.'

As a television reporter in Wales in the mid-1980s, I stood outside many a colliery or car plant threatened with closure and always found it a miserable assignment. Boo.com was different. As the smiling faces emerged after the funeral oration, I found myself muttering to my cameraman 'Can't they at least shout "Vultures" at us?' But they had reasons enough to be cheerful. After all, they were young, and they were now stars – or at least supporting actors – in a drama that had gripped the rest of the dot.com industry. What is more, they had instant evidence, in the form of the recruitment executives lining the pavement, that they were very marketable.

With the dot.com economy still humming, many of them received offers of new jobs that very day. Soon, two nearby bars were packed with the boys and girls from boo. The fun was fuelled by the arrival of two of the recruiters bearing credit cards and promising that the next round or ten was on them.

That evening, after filing reports for the *One* and *Six O'Clock News* on the demise of boo, I got a call from the firm's last spin doctor, David Bick. Kajsa Leander was available for interview. Later he told me what his advice to the two Swedes had been. 'I said, "You have two choices. Either you can jump on a plane and go back to Sweden or you can face the music and take your share of the blame." To their credit they chose to face the music.'

I arrived at Chesham House that evening to find the doors guarded by men who appeared to be former members of the Gurkha regiment. A security firm had been brought in to make sure that what remained of boo's assets were not spirited away into the night by any disgruntled employees. The huge open-plan offices that had been home to so many pierced noses, combat trousers and expensive haircuts, were now virtually empty. In one corner a couple of people who had been kept on to help the liquidators were going through some numbers on a computer screen. Boxes of designer trainers, with the familiar boo.com logo, were piled here and there.

We were shown into a featureless conference room and waited while whispered conversations took place outside. Eventually the door opened and in came Kajsa Leander with David Bick. She sat down and spoke in a low monotone about the death of her company. I asked her about the tales of profligacy that were now emerging. Why, for instance, were we sitting in huge offices in Regent Street rather than on a trading estate in Slough? She insisted that they were here because they had been given a very good deal by the landlords. She told me this was a grim day for the rest of the dot.com industry. 'A lot of people are going to go through a very hard time. If investors don't even believe in a company like this, it's going to be very hard for others.'

The clear implication was that the real failing was on the part of the investors who had lacked the courage to see the vision of Leander and Malmsten through to fruition. Now the rest of the industry would reap the whirlwind. For the backers who had watched their cash treated in so cavalier a fashion, this must have been a little hard to take.

Over the following days there was brave talk from the liquidators, KPMG, of realizing substantial sums from boo's assets. They demanded that anyone who even wanted to be considered as a buyer for the revolutionary software system developed over the past fifteen months put £1 million on the table as a mark of their goodwill. But when it was sold to another e-commerce company it raised just £250,000. Bright Station, the buyers, told the papers they had got themselves a bargain – after all, over £30 million had been spent on developing the system.

Mick McLoughlin, the KPMG liquidator, was like a visitor from another planet. The grey-suited, middle-aged accountant sitting in Ernst Malmsten's office amidst the debris of what had been the hippest company in the dot.com universe could not have been more different from the previous occupant. He was used to company failures – that was his job – but his usual beat was engineering firms which had slowly expired after years of struggle, rather than an internet start-up which had gone through its money like a pools winner in Las Vegas. Now he was dealing with the world's media who were keen to pick over the bones of this spectacular failure. 'It was a very interesting job,' McLoughlin told me a few months later. 'It was the first time I'd been on Swedish television. I managed to keep my clothes on.'

Just about everyone else ended up without their shirts. When the final sums were totted up, shareholders had lost all of the $130 million they had put in. Various creditors were owed another $50 million. All of the assets had raised just over £1 million. It seemed extraordinary that so much energy, so many eighteen-hours days and so much hype could have ended up producing so little. There was much talk during the dot.com era of 'virtual' companies. Boo seemed to have taken this theory to its logical extreme. The biggest losers were the Hariri family and other Middle Eastern investors who stayed loyal to the end and were persuaded to put up more money when others demurred. With rather atypical hyperbole, one banker described it to me as 'the biggest disaster to hit the Middle East since the Gulf War'.

So who was to blame? Many of boo's staff remain loyal to Ernst Malmsten and Kajsa Leander, like disciples of some discredited cult. They regard their time at boo as a golden age and never expect anything to be so absorbing again. They are of the 'one more heave' school of thought. Boo was just beginning to prove itself and if it had been given a few more months it would have fulfilled its promises. They accept that that there was too much chaos, too little adult supervision, but lay much of the blame at the investors' door.

Certainly, boo was a dysfunctional family, with the 'parents' in the form of Bernard Arnault, the Benettons, JP Morgan et al unable or unwilling to step in when the kids in Carnaby Street started scribbling on the walls and chucking dollar bills out of the window. One investor insists there were attempts to instil discipline. 'There was clear direction given by the Board, but they never delivered. The forecasts were always optimistic, budgets were never met.' Another blames the structure of a Board where the dominant players were the Swedish founders. 'We didn't have access to the management accounts, that was the problem,' he told me, shaking his head as if in disbelief. 'Usually, with the firms where I invest, I can just walk in and demand to see the figures.'

This man had at first advised his own firm – a company with a prestigious name – against getting involved, but had eventually conceded that it was worth a small gamble. 'I hate the fact that we were ever associated with boo. But I can now look back on it as a few million dollars worth of education in how not to run a company.'

So managerial incompetence is another view of why boo failed. The six-month delay in getting the site launched was certainly pretty disastrous. The huge marketing spend completely out of synch with that launch was another massive blunder. Then there was the failure to realize that online shoppers wanted a clean, simple, reassuring site which would enable them to find the product they wanted in a few minutes and buy it, rather than a magnificent firework display which many of them could not even see. The wrong people were hired – too many fresh faced consultants, too few wrinkled old retailers, and far too many warring factions. Ernst and Kajsa had energy and vision, they set the pulses of the bankers at JP Morgan racing, and they were obviously adored by those staff admitted to the clique around them. What they did not have was any idea of how to manage a hugely complex operation – or, more realistically, any ability to hire the people to do that job.

The profligate culture of the company was also a serious flaw. Not just because money was wasted – champagne and First Class travel did not push boo over the edge – but because of the signals it sent right through the organization. Because money was no object, and the status of the finance department was relatively low compared to the marketing clique, nobody seemed to remember what the prime duty of any company has to be. To make a profit.

But even amongst the obituarists who blamed boo's downfall on profligacy and incompetence, there were still plenty who believed that the original vision had been right. In May 2000, despite the tumbling prices of dot.com shares and the sudden reticence of the venture capitalists, there was still confidence in the inherent ability of the Internet to transform business. Boo might have failed – but others with greater discipline and more sober advisors would succeed.

In the coming months, with the climate for the internet industry growing ever harsher, this judgement, too, would seem wide of the mark. As other, less flamboyant companies also began to fail, it became clear that boo's problem was one of timing. Its vision of online retailing had won the support of investors, but neither the consumers nor the suppliers were yet ready to adopt it in significant numbers. When the investors lost faith in that vision, plenty of companies founded on the promise of the revolution were bound to fail. Boo simply got there first because it spent its money more quickly.

On the night of 18 May the Midas Touch and other bars around Carnaby Street were humming late into the evening. The credit cards put behind the bar by the recruitment agents keen to lure boo's staff to new jobs in e-commerce were taking a thorough pounding. It was a fitting end for boo – fashionable young people enjoying a drink at someone else's expense. But elsewhere the first high-profile collapse in an industry that had believed it could defy gravity was already having a sobering effect.

FOURTEEN

The dominoes fall

AFTER BOO, EVERYTHING WAS different. Until then it had been possible to believe that falling share prices were just a temporary loss of nerve. After all, the same thing had happened for a few weeks the previous autumn, only for the market to take off again. But even if many in the dot.com industry had been jealous, even contemptuous, of the fashion victims from Sweden, they had still been shocked by their spectacular downfall. It was like a teenager's first encounter with death – disturbing evidence of their own mortality.

On the very day that boo went into liquidation, the accountants PriceWaterhouseCooper produced a piece of research which seemed to underline the flimsy nature of so many of the dot.coms. Their report introduced the term 'burn-rate' to a wider public. The firm had looked at 28 internet companies floated in London and had found that one in four was in danger of running out of cash within the next six months. All but three of those examined were on course to use up their cash reserves by August 2001.

Dwindling cash piles had not seemed a problem until now. After all, in a climate where venture capitalists and investors were desperate to have a stake in any internet business, there was always more where that came from. Now, however, the climate was changing and the flow of cash was drying up. The PWC partner behind the report, John Soden, wagged his finger at the internet companies. 'Just because it's the new economy, it doesn't mean that the traditional rules of business can be suspended,' he said in a BBC interview.

After boo, everyone was waking up to that reality. Robert Norton of Clickmango was right in the middle of his company's battle for survival when boo went bust. Plunging stock markets were already making venture capitalists very uneasy but he believes the manner of the fashion retailer's downfall made things worse: 'The whole episode really hurt the whole reputation of the net in Europe. OK, Nasdaq crashed – but after that it was the *folie de grandeur* at boo which was really harmful.'

A few days after the departure of Kajsa Leander and Ernst Malmsten from London's dot.com scene, I went to thechemistry.com, the networking event that by then was taking over from First Tuesday as the hot date for dot.com entrepreneurs. It was held in the Imagination Centre, a high-class conference venue off Tottenham Court Road. There were bouncers on the door and the chilled white wine was flowing freely inside.

The curious thing was that everyone inside was talking about boo – but nobody seemed to see in its demise a lesson for them. 'It's very healthy, some of the froth is coming off the top of the bubble,' was how many put it. 'This will sort out the strong companies from the rest,' was another theme. Funnily enough, everyone seemed convinced that their companies were the strong ones. Yet there was one interesting pointer to the changing mood. One of the guest speakers at the event was Mark Bernstein, a comparative veteran of the internet world, who ran an online games company called gameplay.com. A few months earlier BSkyB had bought a stake in gameplay and the shares had peaked at over £10. But Mr Bernstein announced to the gathering that he was dropping the '.com' from the company's name – it no longer reflected the multi-faceted nature of the company.

Gameplay was just the first of many to decide that it was no longer fashionable to be a dot.com. But the problem was that such companies had only been propelled to extraordinary valuations because they carried the magical suffix. Getting rid of it fooled nobody. A year later, Gameplay's shares were trading below 20p and it was desperately looking for a buyer.

Through the summer and autumn of 2000 the dot.com corpses began to pile up. Clickmango was among the first casualties, although, as we have seen, it was careful to make its departure a more dignified and low-key affair than boo's spectacular crash. But the online health and beauty products retailer faced the same problems, albeit on a much more modest scale. It had raised money on the hope of spectacular growth. Then, as its cash reserves ran low, its founders had come back to the venture capitalists to raise their next round of funding. This was all in the rules of the game, as invented in the summer of 1999. But by the spring of 2000 those rules had changed. The markets had foundered, closing the exit door for VC investors, and boo had shown the perils of throwing good money after bad. Exit Clickmango and a string of other start-ups that had briefly blazed their names across the dot.com firmament.

Within months, some of the bigger, more established dot.coms on the other side of the Atlantic were hitting the rocks. American enthusiasm over new economy companies had turned to cynicism. A raft of websites chronicling the downfall of the dot.coms suddenly appeared. The most scabrous was fuckedcompany.com, which awarded points to visitors who correctly predicted the next casualties. Here was how the site saw the death of boo.com. 'Can you possibly think of anything that is a more eloquent testimony to having your head three feet up your Calvin-Klein-covered ass than to spend tens of million dollars on a dot.com start up AND NOT HAVE THE WEBSITE WORK?!'

Back in the spring, the word had been that, while B2C firms were toast, B2B still had a good future. Forget those pesky consumers who spend hours clicking from page to page without ever managing to buy something. Place yourself instead in the middle of the marketplace where companies do business with each other and where the Internet could help to cut their costs. Even PriceWaterhouseCooper in its damning report on dot.com burn rates had said business-to-business firms were much more likely to get new funding. However, in September Efdex, which had set itself up as an online marketplace for the food and drinks industry – 'the best thing to happen to food since sliced bread' – became the first major B2B casualty. Another piece of received wisdom was consigned to the dustbin, which was where plenty of other B2B firms ended up.

By the autumn Tom Teichman, the first backer of lastminute.com and a number of other start-ups, was in despair over the new climate. 'Sentiment could not be more negative,' he told a newspaper. 'Cash is everything to these companies, but the taps have been turned off almost completely. Many investors are not even looking at business models and could be missing some gems.' The pain was making its way along the food chain so that internet incubators like Teichman's New Media Spark were suffering. During the bubble they had got in at the ground floor, providing seed funding and then seeing the value of their stake rise as other investors climbed onboard at higher valuations. Now nobody wanted to get into an elevator that was crashing towards the basement. The following spring Tom Teichman resigned his post as a non-executive director of lastminute.com to spend more time with his ailing incubator.

If you had managed to get to the stock market by March 2000, you at least stood a chance of surviving. The likes of lastminute.com, QXL and 365 were all on their way to joining what was to be called the '90% club' of shares that had fallen precipitately from their peak. At least they had managed to extract a decent amount of cash from the investors who had rushed in when they floated. That March others who had been waiting in the queue for their IPO bonanza watched in dismay as the market's doors closed behind lastminute.com.

Lastminute's IPO and its aftermath were the source of much bitterness in the rest of the dot.com community. A couple of months after the float, I listened in amazement at a dinner organized by an internet PR firm as the guests expressed their disdain for the company which had been seen as one of Britain's brightest. The site was derided, the personalities of Brent Hoberman and Martha Lane Fox were taken apart, but the real venom was reserved for the handling of the much-hyped IPO. 'Lastminute killed the IPO market stone dead,' said one of the guests. 'OK, they raised their money – but it was a heist, they got away with it like the Brinks Mat robbers.'

Elsewhere I encountered much pious talk from venture capitalists and analysts of how regrettable the 'get rich quick' attitudes of so many firms had been. But a few months earlier those same people had been trampling each other in the rush to cash in.

Among those left stranded by that stone dead IPO market was Boxman, the European online CD retailer that had merged with one of Britain's internet pioneers IMVS in 1999. In the autumn of 1999 the company had been told by its investment bank Morgan Stanley that it would come on to the IPO runway immediately after lastminute.com. David Windsor Clive, the IMVS founder, had stayed on with Boxman as head of investor relations. It might have seemed a minor role, but if the company was going to float, it would assume ever greater importance. Windsor Clive was unhappy that lastminute.com was being given precedence. 'We felt that it was not a real business and we were.'

By the spring of 2000 Boxman was being hailed as one of Europe's internet success stories. It was operating in eight countries, had sales of £12 million pounds in 1999, and its chief executive was the music industry veteran Tony Salter. Of course, it was still making big losses, but with sales growing rapidly, nobody was focusing on that. Morgan Stanley was preparing to float the company at a valuation of around £300 million. The company also had a touch of showbusiness about it – among its share-holders were the Madness lead singer Suggs and the Swedish band Ace of Base.

But after lastminute.com everything changed. As the online travel firm's shares headed down below their issue price and the market turned against the rest of the dot.coms, it became clear that Boxman could not float. 'After that it was always going to be difficult,' Windsor Clive admits. 'We had built a model that required either an IPO or a take-over. But everything turned at once – private punters disappeared, the investment banks went away, and corporate investors went negative.'

Through the summer Boxman touted itself around the record industry looking for a buyer. Suddenly the revolutionaries who had promised to over-turn the old order were looking for a refuge in its arms. Unsurprisingly, having woken up to the fact that glamorous e-commerce start-ups were basi-cally small companies making big losses, nobody wanted to do a deal. Earlier, all an old economy had to do was team up with a dot.com and watch its share price soar. That was no longer the case. 'When e-tail became retail again, the scales fell from everybody's eyes,' is how Windsor Clive puts it.

Still, in July 2000 the *Sunday Times* put Boxman at number two in its E-100, a list of Europe's leading internet ventures. It had established a 'leading pan-European brand' and was becoming a 'powerful force in online retailing'. The term 'brand', once reserved for names like Coca-Cola and Rolls-Royce, was used with reckless abandon in e-commerce circles, but it was quickly becoming clear that internet brands could disappear as quickly as they had arrived.

Even amongst its e-commerce peers, Boxman was looking fragile. There was now strong competition in the online CD market from both Amazon and the German media giant Bertelsmann. This meant Boxman had stopped delivering the rapid growth expected of internet companies. In the first six months of the year its turnover was £5.8 million but its losses topped £24 million.

By October Boxman's search for new funds or a new owner had failed. The company went into liquidation, the most high profile failure in Europe since boo.com. Its 120 staff were out of a job and its investors had lost £50 million. Among them was Bernard Arnault's europ@web fund, which was not looking too clever having already lost a sizeable sum in boo.

The day after the company had been wound up I talked to David Windsor. The Old Harrovian had founded one of Britain's first internet firms, sold it to Boxman in return for shares, become a paper millionaire and then lost it all. He was philosophical about the way five years' work had just gone up in smoke. 'At least I had private money to invest,' he said, 'I wasn't risking my house.'

As 2000 drew to a close, the carnage continued. Thestreet.co.uk became the first major casualty amongst the online publishers. The financial news service closed after its ailing American parent pulled the plug in an attempt to stem its losses. Huge amounts of newspaper coverage were generated by the demise of this tiny business. Partly because journalists are obsessed with their own industry, but also because there was a degree of *schadenfreude* as colleagues who had departed to become millionaires on the dot.com scene began returning to the grubby world of newsprint, sadder and wiser.

Just a few days later came a dot.com collapse that had everything: two posh founders, a splash of nudity and a new term in the lexicon of business failure – 'hibernation'. Ready2shop had been started by the fashion-writing duo Trinny Woodall and Susannah Constantine, who wrote a column in the *Daily Telegraph* and were always popping up on television commenting on Ascot hats or Fergie's dress sense. Now they announced that it was going into hibernation – not closing down, you understand, just ceasing operations and laying off its staff. The founders promised that it would be back once the market had improved.

Ready2shop appeared to be the very model of an internet business – no products, no revenues, and some brilliant marketing. The idea was that the website would trade on the expertise of the fashion duo, offering advice to female surfers facing a fashion crisis. Visitors would enter their measurements and then be presented with suggestions of what to buy and where. To promote the site Trinny and Susannah posed naked except for strategically placed melons and fried eggs in pictures which made it to page three of the *Sun*. 'One of the most exciting partnerships to hit the Internet in years,' was the gushing description of the duo in Heroes.com, a coffee table book about the stars of e-commerce in Britain. 'Ready2Shop is indeed a colossal business,' the chapter on the company continued breathlessly. 'A visit to the site is akin to having a glass of wine with a switched-on friend prior to an afternoon's shopping.' WAP phones and interactive television were said to be the next exciting avenues for Ready2shop to explore.

What was not clear was just how the company planned to make any money. It refused to take advertising on the grounds that its aim was to give impartial advice to shoppers. It did receive £600,000 in sponsorship from Cable and Wireless but the business plan envisaged the real payback coming after Ready2shop had built up a huge database of its customers likes and dislikes. The theory was that this information could then be sold to retailers and manufacturers, enabling them to spot trends and to serve their customers better.

'Information is currency' was one of those internet clichés taken a little too seriously by the venture capital industry at the height of the boom. In September 1999 Ready2shop had been backed to the tune of £5 million by venture funds, led by Atlas, which was putting money into Clickmango at the same time. A year on, with £80,000 a month burning up, the firm was looking for another £7 million to 'take it through to profitability in 2002'. That path to profit was now being mapped out for VCs by a host of desperate dot.coms, aware that soaring subscriber numbers were no longer the way to a financier's heart.

But by now Atlas had woken from its dream. Ready2shop had yet to sign a contract with anyone who might want to buy its information. Trinny and Susannah could not persuade them or any other venture capital fund that now was a good time to put more money into the vague promise of future e-commerce profits. Trinny Woodall was scathing about the new-found caution of the VCs: 'They preferred not to make a decision they could be fired for, rather than taking a risk.' But having taken that risk on a host of sketchy dot.com ideas the previous autumn, the venture capitalists were right to be worried about their jobs.

At its height the company employed more than 30 people who worked in light, airy offices in Notting Hill – now home not just to Hugh Grant and a hit British comedy, but Ernst Malmsten, Brent Hoberman and many others among the dot.com aristocracy. By November the Ready2shop offices were empty apart from a couple of people kept on to run Trinny and Susannah's 'offline' activities in newspaper and television. For a while they had promised to become two of Britain's most colourful internet business leaders. Now Trinny and Susannah were returning to the dull old world of newsprint and television studios.

That month I was preparing a television news report on the dot.com death toll. I interviewed Brent Hoberman and Martha Lane Fox about their collapsing share price and I filmed at a First Tuesday event where entrepreneurs were still touting ideas but venture capitalists were thin on the ground. Both lastminute.com and First Tuesday employed Gnash Communications as their PR consultants. Gnash, based in Notting Hill, had virtually cornered the dot.com market, but now many of its clients were struggling. Clickmango and Ready2shop were among those it had skilfully propelled into dozens of articles. Now, on the day my report was to be broadcast, I got an anxious call from Gnash. I must not, under any circumstances, list Ready2shop as one of the dot.com casualties. That would be a complete travesty of the truth. The business was in hibernation, it had not collapsed. Not dead, just resting, like Monty Python's parrot, it seemed to me.

A couple of weeks later I called Gnash about something else to find that the telephones no longer worked. Eventually I found the company on a new number. 'Oh yes, we've moved,' the receptionist told me. 'We've got new offices – they used to belong to Ready2shop.' It sounded as if the hibernation was pretty permanent.

However, the real symbol of the death of Britain's dot.com dream was not the demise of a host of small firms with hazy ideas of how to make money, but the sale of the company which had promised to be the country's internet flagship to new French owners. In December 2000 Freeserve, which had seen its valuation rise to £10 billion back in the spring, was sold to Wanadoo, an Internet service provider owned by France Telecom, for just

£1.6 billion. And that was in Wanadoo shares, which promptly started heading lower, decreasing the value of the deal.

Under John Pluthero's leadership Freeserve had continued to enjoy spectacular growth, both in its subscriber numbers and its share price. While it was still making losses, it was delivering just what it had promised in terms of revenue. In March 2000 it entered the FTSE 100, an extraordinary achievement for a firm founded less than two years earlier. At 36 Pluthero was now one of the youngest chief executives ever to have run a company in the premier division of British business. Sadly, relegation was to beckon very quickly.

Freeserve's elevation had coincided with the arrival on the scene of AltaVista and a clutch of other Internet service providers promising unmetered access to the Net for a one-off fee. Suddenly the business model on which Freeserve had been founded in 1998 appeared to be broken. The company depended for its revenue on a share of the call charges which its users incurred every minute they spent online. John Pluthero says he had never seen the telecommunications revenue as the company's route to profit. That income was just to tide the company over until the big money from e-commerce and advertising started rolling in.

Nevertheless, Freeserve's share price started falling as worries mounted about its vulnerability in the face of new competition. Pluthero had always been sceptical about the stock market hysteria and its effect on his staff who could see their wealth increasing every day. 'Back at Christmas, when it hit £4, we said to people, "Stop looking at the share price – you're counting your money while you're still at the table."' He wanted everyone to concentrate on growing the business, but the poker game now being played out in the markets had a real effect on companies like his, intent on rapid expansion. Shares were used as a currency for take-overs, and now that currency was being debased.

By late summer AltaVista's plan to put millions of people on the Net for virtually nothing had come to grief. The company had signed up nearly 300,000 people for the service, but had never launched it. John Pluthero's scepticism about AltaVista's ability to do a deal with a telecommunications network at a price that would make it viable had been proved accurate. Somehow the company had unveiled its product without signing up a network provider. AltaVista's UK boss resigned in August, and a number of other Internet service providers were also forced to admit that flat-rate access was going to take longer and prove more expensive than they had promised.

But by then Freeserve was up for sale. Dixons, which still owned 80 per cent of the business, had decided that it was just not big enough to thrive on its own in a world where the likes of Yahoo and America Online were flexing their muscles. Its investment bank Goldman Sachs was asked to scout the market out for a potential buyer. John Pluthero says he had no quarrel with that strategy. 'Yahoo had 600 people working on new tools like instant messaging. We just could not compete with that. We had to grow. That meant either raising money from the stock market – and that was not possible after March – or getting into bed with someone bigger.'

The first potential partner was T-Online, Germany's Internet provider and a subsidiary of Deutsche Telekom. But by June the talks collapsed, with the Germans apparently deciding the price was too high. There were rumours that T-Online had come close to paying as much as £6 per share for Freeserve. In the aftermath it was suggested that John Pluthero had been reluctant to join up with the Germans and had proved a stumbling block to a deal which would have seen Freeserve's shareholders emerge with four times what many had paid for their stake the previous July.

He says that this is a long way from the truth. 'There was never a deal on the table with T-Online,' he told me a few weeks after the Wanadoo take-over had been completed. In part, he blames the way the banks conducted the negotiations. 'The banks decided the way to do it was to conduct the talks through the press. Goldman Sachs briefed journalists that we were talking to lots of people. T-Online's bank briefed that they would not pay more than £5 a share. It was not very impressive.' But the eventual collapse may have had more to do with mounting chaos at T-Online. The German firm was in constant disagreement with its owners at the former state monopoly Deutsche Telekom, and eventually there was a shakeout at the top.

As the year progressed, Freeserve continued to sign up more customers, announcing in September that it now had more than 2 million subscribers, cementing its position as the number one Internet provider in Britain. Six months earlier that would have been enough to send its shares further into the stratosphere. Now investors concentrated on the mounting losses and wondered when the e-commerce revenues that Freeserve had promised would arrive. The share price continued to fall.

By December Freeserve had lost its place in the FTSE 100 and its shares had fallen below the issue price. So when Wanadoo came along with an offer there was not really much choice. The question was why a French company that had been one of the many across Europe to follow Freeserve's lead would end up as the senior partner? Mainly because it had the deep pockets and long-term ambitions of France Telecom behind it.

Freeserve's parent Dixons had decided, perhaps wisely, that it was better off sticking to its core business of selling televisions and computers in high street stores rather than trying to change the world. Its online adventure had lasted two and a half years, with its initial investment of a few million pounds now producing a payback of £1.25 billion, albeit in French shares. Small investors were less happy. Freeserve had been their first dot.com experience. They had seen their shares rise from the issue price of £1.50 to more than £9 in the spring of 2000. Now those who had failed to get out found themselves being offered less than they had originally paid. There was plenty of bile flowing through the discussion boards, much of it aimed at Dixons. Investors were discovering that they had little say when 80 per cent of their company was still owned by its parent.

The deal also looked like a downbeat end to John Pluthero's time in the spotlight. The high-flying but anonymous young executive had blasted his way out of Dixons' Hemel Hempstead offices to become a standard bearer for the dot.com industry, with more newspaper profiles and television appearances than many corporate titans had notched up in decades at the top. Now he was going to play second fiddle to his new French bosses. Pluthero insists that this did not worry him. 'When I talked to John Clare [Dixons' Chief Executive] about the Wanadoo deal, he said, "You can still be the dog's bollocks of the UK Internet." I said I did not care about that. I've never found the PR bit a pleasant or good part of the job.' Andrew Cornthwaite, the banker who shepherded Freeserve through its IPO, confessed to Pluthero that he had once described him as an industrialist rather than an entrepreneur. 'I said I wasn't offended – he had got me right.'

Yet some felt that Freeserve had needed just a little more entrepreneurial vision. Peter Wilkinson, whose sums scrawled on a napkin had been the inspiration behind the company, had not been involved since the launch except to collect an ever-larger cheque each week from his licensing deal. But when I spoke to him soon after Freeserve had been sold, he was disappointed that it had not achieved more. 'The company had 2 million subscribers and 20,000 businesses on board, yet it never worked out how to make a profit from them. John Pluthero is a great guy, a good operations man – but what they needed was a visionary.' Wilkinson felt that Freeserve should have used the inflated currency of its shares to buy a big profitable business, just as in the United States AOL had taken over Time Warner in the deal which seemed to symbolize the triumph of the new economy.

Freeserve's arrival on the stock market in July 1999 had shown that Britain was at last ready to join in the dot.com boom that had been raging for nearly four years in the United States. It encouraged others to believe that they too could create billion-pound companies in a matter of months. Now its departure appeared to signal the end of those ambitions.

The year 2000 had opened with fireworks across Britain, the non-appearance of the millennium bug which was supposed to destroy the world's computer networks, and boundless optimism about the potential of the Internet to create businesses which would keep the economy booming for years to come. As it ended, the Millennium Dome was closing as quietly as possible after proving a costly disaster and the other great white hope, the dot.com bubble, had expired with an enormous bang. So had it left anything behind?

FIFTEEN

After the fall

ON BILLBOARDS ACROSS BRITAIN in the early months of 2001 the car company Hyundai was running a campaign for a speedy new model. 'Disappears faster than a dot.com company' was the slogan. Just as the rise of the dot.coms had invaded every corner of the culture, so their collapse was now becoming part of the scenery.

A year on from that day when Martha Lane Fox had posed for the cameras as her company arrived on the stock market, trailing clouds of glory, everything had changed. The dot.com landscape, which had been verdant and flourishing, now resembled a desert littered with the bones of the dead, with just a few emaciated creatures struggling on.

Lastminute.com had seen its share price fall so far that it was valued at less than the cash it had in the bank. The company had brought in some retail expertise in the form of Allan Leighton, the former Chief Executive of the Asda supermarket chain, but his appointment as chairman had only provided a short-lived boost to shares. Disgruntled shareholders were suggesting that it would be best if the company shut up shop and handed the money back to them. Other dot.coms that had made it to the stock market were in a similar position. The shares of companies like QXL, 365 Corporation and Interactive Investor International were now worth so little that they had almost disappeared off the radar. Every day through the early months of 2001 more companies were closing down or selling up.

The venture capitalists appeared to have gone into hiding. The big, well-funded firms were sitting on their money, letting the business plans pile up in their in-trays, unwilling to invest until the stock market gloom had lifted and they could see their way to the exit again. The smaller firms – the incubators, accelerators and other creatures of the internet age – were looking at the value of their investments and wondering whether it was either feasible or attractive to stay in business.

Tony Dye, the fund manager who had dug in his heels and refused to climb aboard the dot.com bandwagon, was now looking like one of the few in London's financial community to get it right. A year after he had left Philips and Drew, which had stuck by his policy of putting money into 'value' stocks rather than high-tech companies, the fund management business had moved from the bottom of the performance table to the top. Dye himself had started the Contra Fund, a hedge fund that was able to short stocks he thought were heading lower, as well as buying those he favoured. Despite the big falls in internet and technology shares, he was still preaching more doom. 'The problem for the market really is that it is still on new era valuations,' he told one newspaper. 'And I'm pretty sure the belief in the new era, if it's not already died, will be dying quite rapidly.'

In just a couple of days in April 2001 I noted a series of events which seemed to capture the mood. First came the resignation of Dan Thompson, the Chief Executive of 365 Corporation, after reports of a disagreement over strategy with the rest of his Board. Shares in 365, one of the first dot.coms to float, were now priced at 20p after reaching a high of 303.5p. On the same day, Gameplay.com – or rather Gameplay since it had dropped the '.com' the previous May – was reported to be looking for a buyer. It had already cut 275 jobs two months earlier and its cash reserves were thought to be less than £20 million.

The next day I glanced at the online edition of the *Industry Standard Europe*, an offshoot of the American publication widely regarded as the best source of news about e-commerce. One headline read 'Baltimore warns on Sales' above a report that the internet security software company based in Ireland had seen its shares fall by 20 per cent after warning that sales would be lower than forecast. 'Lastminute denies European Claim', was the next headline, on a report that Brent Hoberman had denied the firm was pulling out of Italy and Spain because of disappointing sales. But that very day came news that the *Industry Standard* itself had been submerged by the waves of dot.com gloom.

Its European edition, launched with a laser show and a swanky party at a smart London restaurant the previous autumn, was closing with the loss of 60 jobs. 'The market we swim in today is far different than the one we anticipated when we first began planning this magazine one year ago,' the magazine's editor explained. 'Some of our most likely advertisers have gone out of business; others have cut back dramatically on advertising.' The magazine had employed good journalists at high salaries and had produced some excellent work. In the end, however, it was no more able to defy economic logic than the dot.coms whose demise it had reported in minute detail.

While pure internet companies, started with the aim of overturning the lumbering giants of the old economy, were withering away, it seemed for a few months that the internet future lay with the old firms who were learning new tricks. 'Clicks and mortar' became the new mantra as big established retailers combined a high street presence with an online operation. In September 2000 Jungle.com, an online electronics retailer, was bought by Great Universal Stores (owners of the Argos store chain) for £37 million. A few months earlier its owner Steve Bennett had been hoping to float Jungle at a valuation of anything up to £750 million. The sale was reported as something of a humiliation for Mr Bennett, who made about £7 million, but it looked very shrewd a few months later when valuations had shrunk even further. It was one of a number of deals that saw ailing dot.coms snapped up by old economy companies.

Back in the spring of 2000 I had begun to notice that the suits were arriving in force in the dot.com world. The glitzy launch of oneswoop.com, an online car buying site, was held in the Oxo Tower restaurant with a splendid view over London. There was hardly a T-shirt or a pair of chinos to be seen. Instead, there was a sea of grey pinstripes, as executives from Arthur Andersen and Marks and Spencer, backers of the venture, sipped champagne and snaffled the canapés. The minister for e-commerce had even turned up to stress how excited the government was by online commerce – a sure sign that things were about to go pear-shaped.

As I listened to a series of mundane speeches describing how this new service would revolutionize the way the British motorist bought a car, I was struck by the contrast with the 'two geeks in a garret' model which, until recently, had been typical of dot.com start-ups. The grown-ups had arrived, the Internet was becoming a respectable place for respectable companies, and the dull old business establishment was taking over. E-commerce would continue to grow but it would be much less fun to cover.

Later on even this conclusion seemed wide of the mark. By the spring of 2001 many of the companies which had paid fancy prices to acquire internet businesses or invested heavily to develop their own online interests were beginning to retrench. Rupert Murdoch, who at first had been wary about the promise of the Net, and had then jumped in with some vigour, now ordered his lieutenants to retreat again. BSkyB, having paid over £300 million for Peter Wilkinson's Sports Internet in May 2000, wrote that investment down to £60 million the following spring. Disney, which had paid a fancy price for Soccernet, the company started in his bedroom by twelve-year-old Tom Hadfield, was looking to offload the business for much less eighteen months later.

Newspaper groups were next to execute a U-turn. They had been warned that the Internet would destroy their businesses and had spent heavily to develop an online presence. The *Financial Times*, seeing many of its brightest and best depart for the dot.com world, was keener than most to prove that it could be big on the Net. The newspaper invested more than £100 million in its online activities. It was providing vast amounts of content, both from its regular journalists and from new staff, nearly all free of charge.

Like everyone else in the dot.com world, the media companies were far more focused on grabbing a share of the territory than on working out exactly where their revenues were going to come from. Advertising was the main hope. All of the big agencies were touting the Internet as the first place where you could actually measure the effectiveness of a campaign. You could follow the surfer's progress from clicking on a banner advert right through to buying the product.

There was an explosion in online advertising in 2000 with £154 million spent in Britain, overtaking cinema advertising. But at least the cinemas were charging for admission. That £154 million was the principal source of revenue for an industry that had spent billions building websites and employing staff. And much of the money was going round in circles – the banner ads on many web pages were selling the merits of other sites.

By 2001 the very efficiency of the Internet in measuring the value of advertising was putting its effectiveness in to question. Advertisers were discovering just how few surfers actually clicked on their messages rather than swerving past them. The explosion in online spending failed to materialise and without it much of the online industry looked like vanity publishing. The media companies started cutting back. The *Financial Times* shed 40 online posts, *Trinity Mirror* closed many of its websites. Journalists who had migrated online in the hope of big salaries and lucrative share options found themselves out of a job.

In 1999 all kinds of unfashionable old economy companies had found that merely announcing a move into an internet venture would put a spring into their share price. By 2001 this form of corporate Viagra no longer worked. With no kudos to be gained from the Internet, they were no longer prepared to subsidise loss-making operations. Businesses that had been told by consultants to get an e-strategy or face obsolescence were disappointed with the results of following that advice.

In a report entitled 'E-Business 2001', a team of Birmingham-based academics found that half of the companies they surveyed reported no increase in their sales as a result of e-commerce investments, and two-thirds had not reached new markets via the Internet. 'Much of the currently available hard evidence seems to belie the rosy picture many practitioners hold,' the report concluded. 'The hype should be rejected in favour of reasoned analysis of costs and benefits.'

So what does reasoned analysis tell us about what remained of Dot.com Britain once all the hype had faded? At first sight it is a depressing picture. With Freeserve just part of a French business, there was no major player to act as standard bearer for Britain's internet economy. While American dot.coms had gone out of business in droves, the likes of Yahoo, Amazon and Ebay were building global businesses, despite mounting worries about a lack of profit.

Some British businesses were still finding the Internet a happy hunting ground, although for many it was just a small part of their business. The world's biggest online grocer was Tesco, which was taking 70,000 orders a week worth £6 million by the spring of 2001. The service was even making a profit, but it was still very much a niche operation for a company that had just reported a £1 billion profit made from conventional retailing. The idea that there was a lot of money to be made from charging a customer £5 for an operation which involved employing staff to take the groceries from the shelves, put them through the checkout and then drive them round to their house, seemed fanciful. After all, shoppers had been perfectly prepared to do all that work themselves for nothing. Businesses were finding to their cost that the Internet was a tool that shifted the balance of power in favour of the consumer.

More intangible services were proving better bets. The budget airline easyJet had quickly found that its customers were keen to buy tickets online. More than 90 per cent of passengers were booking over the Internet by 2001. The Internet was also transforming the betting industry. New companies had set up offshore to enable punters to avoid British betting duty. Sportingbet.com, based on Alderney in the Channel Islands, was one such pioneer. But, as in other industries, the old players soon woke up to the threat to their businesses and started developing internet operations offshore. So effective was this move that the Chancellor of the Exchequer was forced to act. In his budget in March 2001 Gordon Brown abolished betting duty after cutting a deal with the big betting companies in which they agreed to end their offshore operations.

Finance was supposed to be the great internet industry. New online banks, without all those tiresome and expensive branches, would be able to take business away from the big high street players. New operators did appear, the most successful being Egg, the bank set up by the Prudential insurance company. Mike Harris, the company's Chief Executive, explained to me in 1999 that simple economics would make companies like his triumph – every transaction cost ten times as much for a bricks-and-mortar bank to administer as an online operator.

Egg grew rapidly – but only by offering unsustainably high interest rates on its savings account. The lesson seemed to be that if you tell customers that free £10 notes are on offer, they will arrive in droves. Others that came along offering similar give-away deals flowered briefly then faded. By 2001 it appeared that Egg might be one case where first mover advantage did apply. It had begun to achieve what every internet firm talked about – it was 'monetising its eyeballs'. Customers who joined because of the attractive interest rates were now acquiring credit cards and other financial products. True, the company had still managed to make a loss of £37.9 million in the first three months of the year, but there was rash talk of breaking even by the end of 2001.

The giant high street players, however, had not been forced into retreat. On the contrary, they seemed even more powerful than ever. All had offered their customers the opportunity to service their accounts online. For now, the sobriety of a brand name like Lloyds TSB or Barclays, with just a sprinkling of new technology, seemed more attractive to most of the public than a flashy newcomer with a wacky name like If or First-E. For consumers this was the golden age of the Internet. Every newspaper was offering all of its contents online and much more for nothing, the supermarkets were promising to take the drudgery out of shopping for a nominal fee, and new banks were giving money away.

There was one company which should have made a big contribution to Britain's internet economy but somehow failed. BT was the dog that did not bark. Across Europe the big former state-owned telephone companies like Deutsche Telekom and France Telecom were throwing their weight around in the internet world. Their internet providers, T-Online in Germany and France's Wanadoo, had become numbers one and two in Europe by 2001.

It seems extraordinary that BT should have stood by and let Freeserve become the market leader in internet provision in the UK – and then fall into French hands – but that is what happened. Freeserve's John Pluthero was himself bemused. 'Why are BT so rubbish?' he pondered, 'that's what you should be asking when you look at e-commerce in Britain.'

To be fair, BT was hemmed in by its regulator Oftel, and it was under constant attack from the likes of Freeserve every time it proposed a new deal for internet users. Nevertheless, the lumbering giant should have made a bigger impact. At every stage its management seemed to be too slow to react to a fast-changing industry – either by offering its customers better deals or by buying fledgling internet companies.

Nevertheless, as the tide went out, there were some impressive new companies left standing amidst the dot.com flotsam and jetsam. Mostly these were businesses that had developed groundbreaking technology. They included Autonomy and Orchestream, two internet software businesses, and

Bookham Technology, which made optical components to speed up the Internet. All three had seen their share prices savaged as the gloom about anything connected to the Internet spread ever wider; but it still appeared that something had been built which would endure beyond the dot.com dreams. The cluster of high-tech firms around Cambridge, including Autonomy and the chip designer ARM, had at last reached critical mass. That provided hope that when communications technology came back into fashion, Britain would have businesses able to play a role.

And the curious thing was that while the dot.coms went from boom to bust, the Internet just kept on growing. By March 2001 the Office of National Statistics was reporting that 51 per cent of the UK's population had used the Internet, with 35 per cent of households now connected. The new technology was infiltrating every aspect of life – schools were being wired up, old age pensioners were learning how to use e-mail, and small businesses were rushing to get online. Britain was neck and neck with the United States in terms of the number of businesses trading online. Huge changes, many of them invisible to the outside world, were taking place deep within the fabric of major organizations as they began to use the Internet to control the way money and information flowed through their systems.

The Internet, meanwhile, was changing. The race was on to provide a much more satisfying experience through faster connections. Technologies like ADSL were enabling home users to download information ten times faster than before, making services such as video and music much more attractive – although once again BT was acting as a drag on the internet economy, rolling out the new technology at a feeble pace.

The next stage was to deliver online services on the move. Third generation mobile phone networks promised to deliver the Internet anywhere. There was the prospect of watching video clips on the train home, shopping and banking from your phone while sitting in the park, or having information beamed to your car by local businesses as you drove past them.

For a few months in the summer and autumn of 2000 the promise of the mobile internet set off a new investment hysteria. The mobile phone companies paid £22.5 billion for licences to operate the new networks in the UK. The venture capitalists suddenly found a new craze – wireless services promising to profit from the mobile internet were shoving aside the B2C and B2B firms in the fight for funding. First Tuesday even started a Wireless

Wednesday event. Then, as investors started to ask whether anyone really wanted to watch videos on a mobile phone, this bubble burst too.

While the technology continued to advance at a measured pace, the investment cycle went through wild gyrations that proved damaging. In the boom all sorts of companies that should never have been funded walked away with millions. After the bust, it seemed that no dot.com idea, however well constructed, could be entertained.

It was not the predictions of the Internet's growth that had proved so wrong-headed, but the forecasts of how it would be used and what that would mean for the companies seeking to benefit from the new technology. Companies like Freeserve and lastminute.com had been valued as if they would very quickly grow into industrial giants. The road ahead was seen as smooth and straight, not pot-holed and full of twists and turns.

There are extraordinary parallels between the dot.com bubble and two previous instances of investment hysteria surrounding the arrival of new technologies: the railways and electrification. In his history of financial speculation, *The Devil Take the Hindmost*, Edward Chancellor compares the language used in nineteenth-century Britain to describe the importance of the Railway Age with that used by the more messianic exponents of the Information Age at the end of the twentieth century. One Victorian newspaper proclaimed that railways would 'eventually render all men as brethren . . . and will, there is no possible doubt, above all spread knowledge and diffuse intelligence over towns and cities, and finally tend to universal good'. In his 1995 book *The Way Ahead*, Bill Gates wrote, 'the Information highway will transform our culture as dramatically as Gutenberg's press did the Middle Ages'.

Investors with scant knowledge of the new technology listened to the Microsoft founder and his fellow visionaries and poured their money into dot.com shares, just as, in Victorian times, the public became intoxicated by the potential of railway shares. The railway boom of the 1840s ended, like the dot.com bubble of the 1990s, with companies collapsing and investors losing their shirts. Even those companies that survived and prospered were badly hit. The best time to buy shares in Great Western Railway was before the trains actually started running.

When electrification arrived at the end of the nineteenth century it promised to transform the way industry worked. It was responsible for the arrival of the production line and it led to the emergence of new indus-tries. But this did not mean that investing in electricity was the road to riches. The share prices of the power companies in the United States took off in the period from 1890 to 1900 – then underperformed for the next twenty years. The railways and electricity did bring about profound changes, both in business and in society. However, this did not guarantee that indi-vidual companies or their investors would benefit from those changes.

Likewise, the Internet will change all our lives but its effects may take longer to work their way through industries and social structures than the digerati predicted in the mid-1990s, and they may be very different from what was first imagined. Consumers have a habit of catching companies unawares in their adoption of new technology. They took to text messaging, offered as an incidental extra by the mobile phone companies, with enor-mous enthusiasm, but were completely underwhelmed by WAP phones, the first manifestation of the mobile internet.

Early in 2001 I was talking to an investment analyst about the outlook for various internet companies. 'It's a marathon, not a sprint,' he pronounced solemnly. A year earlier the same man had been banging the drum for first mover advantage and rapid IPOs. Now there was a new orthodoxy. The revolution had been postponed.

On the surface, the fabric of British business emerged from the dot.com bubble relatively unchanged. The tidal wave on the horizon threatening to sweep away old economy companies had turned out to be a mere ripple. What of the changes the internet boom had promised in the way business was perceived and in our attitudes to work?

During the bubble, coverage of the business scene in the mainstream media had been transformed. Journalists had been delighted to find that the new companies were run by people who did not fit the template of corpo-rate Britain. The likes of John Pluthero, Martha Lane Fox and Tom Hadfield were held up as examples of the way the Internet was allowing a new breed to make an impact in business.

In the broadsheets, business fought its way out of the ghetto at the back of the paper onto the front pages, as these new personalities became aston-ishingly rich. The tabloids were not to be left out. They were quick to spot that many of their readers were taking an intense interest in shares as dot.coms arrived on the stock market, and they began to cover business far more extensively, often with the same kind of vigour and raucousness with which they approached football.

More surprisingly, the *Guardian* launched a daily page on e-business. The newspaper had long been the spiritual home of readers who thought that business was not only tedious but wicked. Now it was devoting thousands of words to the activities of people whose ambitions were often very simply to get rich as soon as possible. The paper stuck with its extended coverage of e-commerce long after others had scaled theirs down. In part, this reflected the fact that the young, creative types who worked in new media were more likely to read the *Guardian* than the *Telegraph*.

Yet as the dot.coms tumbled, the heroes who had graced a thousand magazine covers quickly became villains. Many of the commentators who had watched uneasily as this cast of unknowns had built fortunes in months now turned on them with delight. The tone of much of the coverage seemed to suggest that the dot.com entrepreneurs had not only been stupid to think that they could defy the rules of economics, they had been wicked. There was general satisfaction as the paper fortunes disappeared and the ambitions were frustrated. The return of colleagues who had left in search of dot.com riches added to the *schadenfreude*.

In September 2000 Britain was in the grip of a crisis that seemed to underline how foolish the country had been to believe the Internet would change everything. Disgruntled farmers and lorry drivers demonstrated outside fuel refineries in protest against the high price of petrol. Fishermen joined the protests. With the tanker drivers refusing to work, the petrol pumps quickly dried up. Food ran short in the supermarkets, industry started laying off workers and essential services were threatened. So much for a world where every kind of service would be delivered online and smoky old industries would be eclipsed by the knowledge economy. A few days without fuel and we were retreating to the dark ages. A government that had tried to paint Britain as a high-tech pioneer was being rocked by some very low-tech forces.

At the height of the crisis a *Guardian* reader in Devon wrote to the paper. 'Farmers and fishermen . . . do dangerous, dirty work to provide basic necessities for us,' the letter began. 'They have seen their income falling while at the same time dot.com companies make millions providing frivolous "services" that no one really needs. People recognise that this society has its priorities wrong, that hard work and essential services are neither valued nor rewarded.' Not only were the dot.com pioneers now seeing those millions melt away, they were earning the contempt of *Guardian* readers.

In the following months there were major job losses at car plants and in the steel industry. Once again, they were greeted with coverage that suggested that if Britain could no longer make cars or forge steel then its virility was also in question. When a telecommunications company suggested that it might be able to retrain the redundant steelworkers as engineers in an industry of the future, some of their union officials suggested that these were not proper jobs.

One evening I was sitting in a BBC video editing suite looking at pictures of the offices of a small internet company where everyone was under 30 and the boss was in his mid-twenties. I told the producer sitting next to me that this young dot.com entrepreneur had been a paper millionaire a year earlier but was now struggling to keep his business afloat. 'Good,' said the producer, who was in his thirties. 'What a tosser, serves him right.' His attitude appalled me but it was not unusual. Much of the excitement, glamour and optimism of that period between the IPOs of Freeserve and last-minute.com had receded as the tide went out. The great British traditions of scepticism and derision, the 'I told you so' mentality, were fighting back.

There were still reasons to be cheerful, however. Even if many of those who had rushed to start companies had ended up failing, they had been given a glimpse of the possibilities of entrepreneurship. A survey carried out by the London Business School at the end of 2000 found 40 per cent of British business people questioned saying it was a good time to start a business, twice as many as the previous year. There was a big change too in the perception of entrepreneurs, with 80 per cent of adults saying they admired friends and colleagues who started companies – again a doubling compared to 1999.

Those who had climbed off the corporate conveyor belt to launch a dot.com or join a start-up had often found the experience exhilarating. Even if they had failed, many were unwilling to return to the security of a big company. Silicon Valley had always prided itself on removing some of the stigma of failure. After all, plenty had seen businesses melt away in previous downturns and had managed to start again. Now there were some signs that a similar mentality was arriving in Britain.

Even those who left their dot.coms and returned to more traditional companies found that working life had changed in their absence. The dress-down culture was spreading through far more of the major British firms, and there were attempts to break down the hierarchies. Heidi Fitzpatrick found she no longer needed her suits when she returned to the City from boo.com, and my friend the management consultant eventually left his post with the B2B construction industry exchange to return to his old firm. He had been promised that it had been transformed in his absence – decisions would be taken quickly and young talent would be given its head. How long such attitudes will last as the threat from the dot.coms disappears is open to question. But bright young people have now become accustomed to changing jobs as often as they change their mobile phones. Companies that do not respond to their ambitions will not be able to keep them

Perhaps an outsider is best placed to judge whether Britain has been changed. Eva Pascoe, who arrived from Poland in the 1980s, set up the Cyberia internet cafés in the mid-1990s and went on to run a major e-commerce business, is optimistic about the lasting impact of the dot.com bubble. 'It gave people a lot of empowerment,' she told me. 'I remember when I finished my doctorate in computer psychology you just couldn't get a job. Now people in that situation just immediately think about starting their own company.'

Pascoe felt that the internet boom had also helped to break down what remained of a class-ridden financial system. 'When I arrived in Britain I was appalled by the class system. It was so wrong for the end of the century. In the City it was difficult to raise money and what was available was going to people's mates. It's much more meritocratic today. The venture capitalists don't care who you are as long as you've got some management expertise.'

The defining characteristic of the dot.com bubble was its speed. Internet time was one of those new economy clichés that had some substance. Companies were funded in record time and then grew at a phenomenal rate. Fortunes were accumulated in weeks and disappeared just as quickly. New acronyms – B2C, B2B, P2P – sprang up every few months and were gathering dust on the shelves a few weeks later. And perceptions changed just as quickly. From 'What the hell is the Internet?'

to 'The Internet changes everything' to 'The Internet is soooo last year'. Even during the six months it took to write this book, the landscape appeared to change every day.

Everything appears to be slowing down now. The Internet is there in the background, gradually infiltrating more aspects of the way consumers and corporations behave. But just like personal jetpacks and holidays on Mars, the future is further away than we first thought. In the words of the Chinese leader asked about the lessons of the French revolution, it is too early to tell what the impact of the dot.com bubble will be.

What we can say is that few of those who took a risk and climbed aboard the dot.com bandwagon now regret it. In the spring of 2001 I spoke again to Michael Smith, the young entrepreneur who had started Firebox.com. His short business career had taken him on a journey from a back bedroom in South Wales to a multimillion pound paper fortune within eighteen months. Now he was just battling to keep his firm afloat in much harder times. 'For my first experience of business to have been in the dot.com years has been extraordinary,' he said. 'A year ago people were ringing us up and pestering us to take their money. Now they don't want to know.'

The year before he had appeared in a television documentary, he had been invited to all the glitziest dot.com events and must have been the envy of all of his friends. Now, as we sat in his firm's cluttered and distinctly unglamorous offices in South London, I reflected that he was just another small businessman. But Michael Smith was not depressed. 'It's been a fascinating, invigorating experience and I've learnt a lot,' he said.

And what of Martha Lane Fox and Brent Hoberman, the duo who for a few months had become symbolic of the youth and energy of dot.com Britain? They seemed bemused by the abrupt change of mood that had seen them transformed in the public mind from heroes to has-beens. When I went to their offices just before Christmas 2000, Martha was brandishing a newspaper with yet another article about the rise and fall of lastminute.com. It was full of inaccuracies and she was striding around the open-plan offices, expostulating about the unfairness of it all and asking colleagues whether she should ring the journalist up and complain. 'Martha, Martha, it's just not worth the bother,' sighed Brent Hoberman, wearily.

But despite the abuse that had been heaped upon them ever since the hubris of their IPO, lastminute's founders kept a brave smile fixed to their lips. 'We've just had a fantastic Easter,' Brent Hoberman told me the last time we spoke. While profits were still some way away, in the minds of Hoberman and Lane Fox everything was proceeding according to plan. They had always predicted that most of the dot.coms would fail, but they still believed that their company would succeed. The sad thing was that hardly anybody was listening any more.

For a few, brief months Brent Hoberman, Martha Lane Fox, Michael Smith, Kajsa Leander, John Pluthero and many others had believed that they could defy gravity. Their ascent into the stratosphere was enormous fun to watch, their return to earth equally spectacular. Britain is a duller place now that the dot.com revolution appears to be over. But be sure of this – in a back bedroom somewhere, a teenager with a computer is plotting to start it all over again.

GLOSSARY

B2C: Business-to-consumer website like lastminute.com. Later, 'back to consulting'.

B2B: B2C is dead. Let's try business-to-business – there's got to be some money in that. Later, 'back to banking'.

First mover advantage: Nobody else is selling wigs online – we'll be global in two years before they've woken up.

Marketing: Putting our name on the side of every bus in London in the vain hope that someone will buy something.

Customer Acquisition Cost: It's costing us £1500 in marketing to win each new customer. Unfortunately, they each buy one CD and never come back.

Viral Marketing: We've spent the entire advertising budget – let's tell our customers to e-mail their friends about how great we are.

Disintermediation: Let's cut out the middleman. Give people a chance to advertise their houses on the Net and the estate agents will be toast.

Demand Aggregation: You want a cheap deal on that TV, I want a cheap deal on that TV – if we all get together on the Net, we'll force the price down.

Pure Play: We're a totally internet-based company – everything about us is online and that saves us lots of money.

Clicks and Mortar: Maybe we should get a few shops so people can actually touch the goods and speak to a real person.

VCs: Rapacious ignorant bastards who demand half of the company you have just thought about in the pub with two friends in return for a measly few million pounds in funding.

Business Plan: A few numbers scribbled on an envelope which, when entered in an Excel spreadsheet, magically produce a £25 million profit in year four.

Diverse Revenue Stream: We're not entirely sure how we're going to earn anything from this site.

Burn-rate: With £2 million a month going up in smoke the money runs out at Christmas – but we'll have made it to IPO by then.

IPO: Initial Public Offering. Nirvana for dot.coms – stock market debut guaranteeing instant billions.

Exit Strategy: The VCs say they've got to be able to sell out to some other mug within a year – otherwise they're not interested.

ACKNOWLEDGEMENTS

This book would not have happened if Graham Coster of Aurum Press had not rung me in the summer of 2000 and asked me whether I fancied writing something about the dot.com bubble. Many is the time, hunched over my keyboard in the small hours after returning from my day job, that I have cursed him for that call. But he has been the perfect editor, adept at nursing me through the difficult stretches, astute at pointing out where I was heading off course, and always immensely encouraging.

My researcher Sam Rich dug out many of the stories of the people of his generation who leapt on to the dot.com bandwagon. He was an excellent interviewer, teasing out the excitement, greed and sheer fun of this frenzied period from his subjects.

I am also grateful to the many people throughout the dot.com industry who spared me so much of their time to try to work out how it happened and what it all meant. The people behind companies like Freeserve, lastminute.com and Clickmango were very willing to talk, even when their stories ended in disaster rather than triumph.

In general, the entrepreneurs have been more candid than those who financed them. While some amongst the venture capitalists, investment bankers and analysts have been very co-operative, others have been strangely reticent. The PR boss of one investment bank told me he thought it would be a very bad idea for his colleagues who had been involved in one very high profile dot.com to talk to me. 'I just find that journalists have so little understanding of the capital markets,' he sighed languidly down the phone.

Thanks also to Lindsey Fraser and Richard Evans, who both read parts of the manuscript and offered helpful comments.

My two sons have also been a big influence on the book. At ten, Adam is an apprentice geek who has patiently explained just what has gone wrong when the computer crashes. Two-year-old Rufus has arrived at opportune moments to bang the keys when my back is turned and cause general mayhem and amusement.

But none of it would have been possible without my wife, Diane Coyle. She wrote her first book, *The Weightless World*, in what seemed an effortless couple of months, just slipping quietly off to her study to polish off another chapter, and then completed two more books with equally little fuss. She has been monumentally patient during my noisier creative process and her economist's mind has also contributed greatly to my understanding of the rise and fall of Dot.com Britain.

INDEX